William Rathbone Greg

Political Problems

For our Age and Country

William Rathbone Greg

Political Problems
For our Age and Country

ISBN/EAN: 9783337069506

Printed in Europe, USA, Canada, Australia, Japan

Cover: Foto ©Suzi / pixelio.de

More available books at **www.hansebooks.com**

POLITICAL PROBLEMS

FOR

OUR AGE AND COUNTRY.

BY

W. R. GREG.

LONDON:

TRÜBNER & CO., 60 PATERNOSTER ROW.

1870.

POLITICAL PROBLEMS

FOR

OUR AGE AND COUNTRY.

———◆———

I.

CONSTITUTIONAL AND AUTOCRATIC
STATESMANSHIP.

IT has long been a common complaint that STATESMANSHIP is at a low ebb in England. What we have is of a poor kind, and there is very little of it. Among our public men there is abundance of political ability, of clever parliamentary strategy, of practical knowledge, of debating skill and eloquence, and a fair amount of administrative capacity. But the views and action of our public men, even the best of them, lack width, steadiness, and persistent harmony;—and it is the union of these three characteristics in an adequate degree that gives to politics the quality and dignity of statesmanship. We miss men gifted with the faculty of taking a wide survey of the present or the future, a true perception of the enduring elements of a nation's greatness, a clear comprehension and an unswerving pursuit of those measures by which

A

CONTENTS.

the objects thus distinctly seen can be as certainly attained. In place of such men we have two distinct classes, who rather caricature true statesmanship than imitate or approach it. There are some who have wonderful skill in gaining *party* victories— that is, in adapting immediate means to immediate ends ;—and there are others who are fanatically devoted to one object or one principle, and who pursue it as persistently as any statesman of any country ; but they are *doctrinaires*, not statesmen. They are irrational devotees. They are not so much thinkers, as men possessed with an idea. We have two admirable illustrations of this in our recent history, in the case of two men, of whom it is as impossible to speak without respect and gratitude as without regret and censure. Lord John Russell became eminent and powerful by identifying him- self with the cause of parliamentary reform at a time when reform was, of all measures, perhaps the one most essential to the well-being and progress of the country. He adhered to his object through long, disastrous, and disheartening years ; and when the tide turned and the victory was at last won, he rode into power with the flowing wave of popular strength, and as a just and appropriate reward became the prominent idol of the hour. His name was for ever associated with his cause, not only in the minds of the people, but, unfortunately, in his own too. The question became in a manner his possession, his hobby, his fixed idea. It haunted him, so to speak. He grew to feel that he owed it the homage of constant attention—perpetual, fidgety, fussy *petits soins.* From being the aim of a sound mind, it grew to be the crotchet of an infirm one. He seemed to be startled from his sounder condition by the clamour which greeted some unfortunate remarks which he once made about " finality." He took an opportunity not long afterwards of astonishing the soberer portion of the nation by announcing that he had been an advocate of parliamentary reform when he entered public life, that he was its advocate still, and that he trusted he should always remain so ;—in fact, that at one time before dinner he had felt very hungry, which was natural enough ; that he had had a plentiful dinner, of his own ordering, and that now he felt more hungry than before,—which did not sound very natural or healthy; and that he trusted his appetite would always continue as robust·and insatiable as ever, which sounded hardly like good sense or sound morality. Since that memorable declaration he kept on pertinaciously waving the old banner, and crying the old watchword, without perceiving that his face was set in a precisely opposite direction, and that he was confronting an entirely different set of antagonists from those whom he routed in his youth ; and has, in fact, steadily endeavoured to undo his own work, under the delusion that he was completing it. At first he toiled to transfer political preponderance from the aristocratic to the middle classes—*i.e.*, from a *fraction* of the propertied and educated classes to the whole of them. Subsequently he laboured, only too successfully, to transfer political preponderance from the middle classes to the ignorant and the working classes,—and he called the two opposite proceedings by the same name of " Parliamentary Reform."

Our other persistent politician was Mr Cobden.
His consistency was far more real than Earl
Russell's, and his errors and deficiencies were of a
different order. It was given to him to gain a
victory, perhaps even greater than that of parliamentary reform, and against a phalanx of foes even
more formidable to begin with. He stood upon a
simple truth, he fought for a distinct and definable
purpose, he conquered by the pure force of demon-
stration. He was truly grand when he was fighting
that battle; he never was truly grand afterwards.
He saw that peace, the wealth and prosperity of the
country, and the physical welfare of the masses,
depended on liberating trade and industry from the
shackles with which selfish aims and unwise fondness had bound them. He succeeded. The commercial, financial, and industrial results of the free
commercial policy which he persuaded the country
to adopt, have not only justified, but far surpassed,
not only his, but all other anticipations. No wonder
that he should have felt that it was impossible to
exaggerate the value of the principle he had pro-
claimed. His error lay in seeing it alone, or in
looking at it so exclusively and so intently as to see
it out of its due proportions; in deeming that free
trade would inevitably entail all other political blessings; in judging men and sovereigns according to
their faith in his own creed. His intellect was a
clear and powerful, but not a wide or philosophic
one. He saw one side of human nature so vividly,
that he forgot it was only one side. He would
have sacrificed, or risked sacrificing, every other
public aim to freedom of commerce, believing, we

doubt not, in his heart, that all other things would inevitably follow in its train. In his exclusive devotion to one object he endangered many blessings and outraged many cherished sentiments. He was blinded by the very concentration of his vision. He forgot, too, sometimes, that there are national objects nobler and dearer than peace, richer and more prolific than commercial wealth, more essential even at times than cheap food or light taxation for the poor. Hence, though about the most acute, vigorous, and honest intellect among the public men of our day, he was perhaps the least statesmanlike of them all ; because width and mellowness of mind, as well as consistency and force, are needed to constitute a statesman.

The fact is undeniable : whether we look to other countries or to other times, whether we compare France with England, ancient with modern days, the reign of Victoria with the reign of Elizabeth, the race of statesmen seems to have died out among us, and we have seldom been more painfully reminded of it than of late. " There were giants in those days ; " there are none now. Not only can we find no Pericles in this age ; not only do we see no one like Ximenes or Alberoni, who governed Spain so long, or like Richelieu or Sully who ruled France for half a life time, and through her ruled Europe, or like Barnevelt or De Witt, who for years contrived to govern and make great even their turbulent republic ; but we see no analogies to Cecil and Walsingham, who held power through a whole reign, under a most capricious and unworthy mistress. Our modern history can offer no rivals to such men as Napoleon I.

or Frederick the Great, scarcely even to such men
as Metternich or Nesselrode, or Cavour, or Napoleon
III. The only ministers who could pretend to the
name of statesmen in recent days in England, were
Walpole, Pitt, and Canning, and the last died upwards of a generation since.

Granted, however, the fact, two questions at once
suggest themselves for consideration :—*why* we have
now no such statesmen as those of other countries
and of former days ; and how far their absence is to
be deplored.

Now, in reference to the first point, a little reflection will serve to show that the current ideas on the
subject are of a nature to render us habitually, though
unconsciously, unjust to the public men of England :
not that we under-estimate their *actual* capacity and
merits, but that, in mentally measuring them with the
Richelieus, Cecils, De Witts, and Napoleons, we are
trying them by a standard which it is simply impossible they should ever reach. We complain, and
with perfect truth, that their political ability never
attains, and seldom approaches, to the height of
statesmanship, without pausing to inquire whether,
under a parliamentary system of government, there is
any scope or field for the development of statesmanship, properly so called. In comparing the ministers
and politicians of constitutional England with those
of despotic France, Austria, and Russia—as in comparing the ministers and politicians of the England
of Queen Victoria with those of the England of
Queen Elizabeth—we lose sight of the consideration
that the conditions, and therefore the possibilities, of
the several ages and countries are altogether dis-

similar. We lament over the fancied dwarfing and degeneracy of our statesmen :—the fact being, not perhaps that the dwarfing and degeneracy alleged are not in a measure true, but that they are the natural growth, the inevitable outcome, of that constitutional *régime*, of the reality of that self-government, of that increase of the popular ingredient in our complicated system for which we have been constantly contending, and on which we especially felicitate and pride ourselves. It is true, and may readily be conceded, that we no longer produce statesmen like those feared and venerated names we have enumerated a page or two since ; but it is because we should not know what to do with them if we had them, because they would find no fitting place among us, because they would disturb our polity, and we should hamper their action and paralyse their genius.

The position of a statesman in a free country is altogether different from that which he occupies in a despotic one ; the conditions of his tenure and the character of his functions are not the same ; the ability required from him is of a different order ; the power which he wields is different, the means he must make use of for gaining his influence and obtaining his ends are different. Under a despot he has to govern the nation ; he has sometimes to govern the despot : he may sometimes *be* the despot. He has to think and act for a whole people ; he is therefore under an awful obligation to think and act soundly ; and we all know how rapidly and enormously such responsibility ripens and strengthens an intellect which it does not paralyse. He can do what he wishes ; he is invested with real power ; he

may often retain that power for a whole generation
or for half a lifetime. It is worth his while to lay
deep and self-consistent plans, for he may feel confident that he will be suffered to work them out.
It is worth his while to trust to the future and to
prepare for the future, for he is not necessarily the
mere transient creature of an hour. It is worth his
while to sow slow-growing seeds of good and
grandeur, for it is not irrational to hope, certainly,
that they will be allowed to ripen, and possibly that
he may himself last long enough to reap the harvest.
He has only to consider two things : *first*, whether
his views of policy are feasible, beneficent, and wise ;
secondly, whether he can induce his sovereign to
adopt them and to confide in him.

In a free state, with parliamentary institutions,
where the *people*, or a section and selection of the
people, really guide and govern the political machine
—as in England, Italy, America, Switzerland, Belgium, Holland, France occasionally, and some other
lands—the case is widely different. Here, a minister may have great *influence*, but he can scarcely
flatter himself that he has any *power*. He can do
much in diffusing correct information, in dissemi-
nating sound views, in upholding great principles and
fertile maxims of wise policy—in appointing right
men, in exercising a sound strategic instinct as to
when to fight and when to yield, in resigning his
post when needful rather than surrender too much
or compromise too far,—but he can do little more.
It is seldom worth his while to be at the labour of
elaborating any grand or consistent scheme of
national action ; for he may be quite certain that he

will not be allowed to carry it out in its integrity, and he must be very doubtful whether he will remain long enough in office to carry it out at all. In fact, it is not for him to say what shall or shall not be done, what principles shall prevail, what objects shall be perseveringly followed up. It is for the aggregate mind of the nation, for the popular voice, for the slowly maturing and often vacillating public opinion of the country, and not for him or for his sovereign, to decide what the policy of the state shall be both at home and abroad. He can never direct or *command.* He can only *persuade;* and he has to persuade an assembly singularly complex in its structure, often varying in its composition, deplorably incapable of rising to the height of a great principle, and rootedly intolerant of philosophical and far-reaching views. He has to persuade, moreover, or to indoctrinate a people peculiarly fitful in its action, now waywardly torpid, now waywardly emotional, often instinctively sagacious, usually correct in feeling, but incurably illogical to the very core, and ignorantly suspicious of everything that bears the appearance of scientific consistency or system. On all occasions he has to feel the pulse of the country; and he must not only be sure that he interprets its beating aright, but that he can form a sagacious guess as to what its beatings will be a few months ahead. He can only be tolerably certain of two conclusions :—*first,* that in order to pass any measure, however great, however essential, however salutary, he will have to consent to let it be so cobbled, emasculated and adulterated, that all its grandeur and much of its value are sure to have

evaporated in the process. *Secondly*, that even if
he can induce the country to commit itself to some
important and characteristic line of action abroad,
the time must come when his antagonist will succeed
to office, and will induce the country to neutralise,
or to paralyse, his inaugurated policy. Everything
with us is in truth—everything in a parliamentary
nation must be—*compromise;* and compromise is
not a soil in which the higher qualities of statesmanship can take root, or flourish.

It was not always so. It was not so in Pitt's
days; it was not so to anything like the same
extent even in the days of Wellington and Canning,
or in the earlier days of Peel. Before the great
year of change, 1832, so long as a minister was a
favourite with his sovereign, moderately popular
with the nation at large, and the recognised leader
of his party, he really did possess a considerable
amount of positive power, and that power could
fairly count upon a reasonable term of duration.
The sovereign might to a certain extent be capricious and unreliable; but princely instability and per-
fidy are political dangers to be guarded against in
despotic as well as in limited monarchies. The
party would, of course, have in some measure to be
managed and consulted, and its wishes and suscepti-
bilities to be humoured; but a minister who really
belonged to it, and represented its views, was certain
of zealous, unswerving, and almost unquestioning
and blind support. Popular feeling, if very passionate and strong, needed then, as now, to be
watched and guided, and if resolute and pertinacious, to be yielded to for a time; but this is more

or less the case in all polities, and in the early part of this century the electing power was centred in so few hands, and those hands were subjected to such potent influences, that the mere popular voice had little weight except in periods of rare and exceptional excitement. The Tories had so large and steady a majority in both Houses; the preponderance of all political and social influences lay so clearly with them, that Pitt or Liverpool or Peel, unless they had attempted something desperately unwise, or unpopular, or premature, or had mortally offended their habitual supporters, were pretty sure of carrying any measures on which they were resolutely bent. They had to defeat the adversaries in their front; but they could always do this with ease and certainty in a pitched battle; and, this done, they had no reserve of enemies to encounter, no ulterior opposition to overcome.

But it is since the first Reform Act that the combination of political conditions which renders statesmanship so hopeless, has arisen, or at least has attained its complete development. In fact it belongs to, and springs from, and ripens with, the growing preponderance of the popular or democratic element in the State. The degree in which a minister can hope to carry out his own measures, to lay down and adhere to a special, distinct, and consistent line of policy—the degree, that is, in which he can approximate to statesmanship—depends on three conditions :—the balance of parties, the degree to which the question interests the masses, and the line taken by the press. Before the Reform Act there may be said to have been only two political parties, and from 1790 till 1825, or perhaps later, one of them was so unquestionably predominant in both Houses of Parliament, and in the support and sympathy of the Crown, that it was under no necessity of making any great concessions to its opponents, nor had it much reason to cower before the possible action of the people or the press. Since the Reform Act, not only have the relative weight and numbers of the two great parties in the State been far more equally balanced than of yore, so that only on rare occasions could either hope to *force* a measure down the throats of its antagonists, if their opposition were sufficiently desperate and determined ; but a third party has arisen and attained a distinct and most formidable position, numerous and energetic enough in most cases to turn the scale of victory between the two great rivals, and independent enough to make it impossible to count upon their assistance either confidently, steadily, or long beforehand. This third party, moreover, is not a compact and unvarying body, having a common interest, and a common policy, and a calculable line of tactics ; it comprises several sections who agree only in belonging to neither of the principal armies, and in impartially and alternately embarrassing and paralysing both. They all sit below the gangway, though they sit on both sides of the House, and are alike erratic and unaccountable. But whether they be Irish members who require to be kept in the ranks by jobs at home or by concessions to ultramontane predilections, or advanced Liberals who have their own special aims and creeds to which they will never be unfaithful, and which they will

never compromise or postpone, their existence in
their actual strength is alike fatal to the growth of
all persistent or forecasting statesmanship. Nay,
more ; they are, in a manner, false and hostile to
one of their own recognised doctrines. They hold
that the majority ought to govern, or at least that
the will of the majority should prevail ; but by their
singularly *arthritic* position, and the singularly skilful, and sometimes unscrupulous use they make of
it, they are, day after day, practically enabling a
minority, and sometimes a small one, to have its
way, by taking advantage of the emergencies and
bargaining with the necessities of the mightier contending factions.

The periodical press was always a great power ;
but in recent years it has grown to be incomparably
greater than of yore, as well as far prompter in its
operation. It is, in fact, the organ through which
the more highly educated classes—who are strong
neither in property nor rank, and who are often too
indolent to take much part in ordinary party and
electioneering struggles—assert their right to political influence, and make that influence felt. It is
also the organ through which that public opinion
which speaks by general elections once in every four
or five years, contrives to speak from day to day.
It is a power which no minister, however strong or
self-reliant, can afford to ignore or to pass by with
conscientious or supercilious indifference. It is, moreover, a power in the face of which it is especially
difficult for any minister to lay far-sighted plans, to
sow seeds for distant harvests, to adopt a line of
policy of which the cost and the drawbacks are

obvious and immediate, and the advantages below the surface and remote—of which the price must be paid down at once, and the return must be claimed (however certainly) hereafter. For it insists upon estimating every measure or course of action in its inchoate and imperfect stage, in sitting in judgment on it from day to day, when perhaps only a little of it can be seen, and when that little is far the least prepossessing portion. It insists, too, upon "the reason why," with an imperious wilfulness particularly embarrassing and disadvantageous to the authors of political schemes—to which the strongest motives, of which the most invaluable consequences, for which the most convincing arguments, are often precisely those which cannot be alleged in public without risking the success or the achievement aimed at. The statesman, in fact, has both to concoct and to defend his plans in the face of an audience which is too half-trained to think profoundly, which is too impatient to wait long, which is too shallow to look deep or far—which, as a rule, to use the phrase of Dr Johnson, is not sufficiently "raised in the dignity of thinking beings to allow the past, the distant, or the future to predominate over the present." The extent to which the press puts an extinguisher upon everything like wide-eyed statesmanship, is fully known to those only who have ventured on faint and timid efforts after that great gift, and have been cruelly maltreated for the venture.

The masses—the great body of the English people—again, take far more interest than formerly in political questions, and they take an interest in a greater number and a different class of questions.

A generation or two since, they were for the most part content to leave all matters in the hands of the representatives whom they had chosen, the aristocracy whom they worshipped, and the ministers whom these combined to install. They did not even care for or discuss the majority of subjects. They snatched at the reins, or put their fingers in the pie, only on those rare occasions when their personal, or class, or material concerns were directly involved, or when that honest and strange religious fanaticism, which lies so close to the core of most English natures, was roused by something which looked like Papal encroachments on the one side or liberal theology on the other. On reform, on corn-laws, on Catholic emancipation, they would wake up and speak out and threaten intervention. But in most home, and in nearly all external, matters they were content to be passive. We all know till how very recently our foreign policy was left, almost unchecked and unwatched, to our Foreign Secretary. A few senators criticised and assailed him ; but the public without listened in apathy or did not listen at all, and used to avow their ignorance and indifference with almost a chuckle of satisfaction. Now, especially since nation after nation has risen up to assert or to strive for its native liberties and rights, our populace have often felt more interest in foreign than in domestic questions. Sometimes, as in a late deplorable example, the people are so clear and decided in their views as completely to override the Cabinet, and compel it to alter its course and its language in a manner and at a moment which expose it to bitter and not wholly undeserved reproaches.

It is accordingly in foreign affairs that we see most clearly the disadvantages under which a British minister—especially one who has ever dreamed of becoming a British statesman—must ever labour. His free action is hampered at every turn.   He can scarcely venture to engage with other states for any particular line of conduct, for he can rarely feel confident to what extent his countrymen will endorse his policy, or to what extent his successors and rivals may reverse it.   One party in the State sympathises with "liberty" abroad; the other party sympathises with "order."   One set of politicians are enthusiastic for Italian freedom and consolidation; another set " stand upon the old way," and are, above all things, anxious to preserve the Austrian empire and the Austrian alliance.   One section is for upholding the " due and beneficent influence" of England in all questions and in every part of the world ; another is all for peace, economy, and non-intervention.   No party can have *all* its own way, or can have it always. Each party gets something of its own way, and gets it sometimes.   As one set of ministers succeed their rivals, they do not indeed act in a wholly different fashion—for there is always some decorum observed in the *volto-subito*—but they are languid, lukewarm, or dilatory where their predecessors were zealous, active, and peremptory ; and this is enough virtually to produce the effect of a change of policy, more or less complete.   Under these circumstances, it is not easy to see how a statesman *could* grow up.   If he were passionately in earnest, his heart would be broken in a session.   If he be a man of real genius, he becomes dwarfed or bent to the calibre of a

tactician, a strategist, a manager, an intriguer. A
minister, who is and must be, by the necessity of his
position, the servant of an untrained, varying,
meddling, many-headed master, may be an admirable administrator or a sound political thinker for
the hour, but he can never be a Richelieu, and could
not easily now become a Pitt.

The mention of this last name reminds us of
another reason why we must not hope, in our age
and country, to breed real statesmen, or at least to
see such raised to power.* Under our present parlia-

* When we wonder at the indomitable resolution and the inflexible self-reliance which Mr Pitt through life displayed, we may
lessen our wonder by remembering that he never endured the
bitter ignominy of youth ; that his self-confidence was never dis-
heartened by being " an unknown man ;" that he early received
from fortune the inestimable permission *to be himself.* . . . Years
of acquiescing in proposals as to which he has not been consulted,
of voting for measures which he did not frame, and in the wisdom
of which he often did not believe, of arguing for proposals from
half of which he dissents,—usually de-intellectualise a parliamentary statesman before he comes to half his power. From all this
Pitt was exempt. He came to great power with a fresh mind.
And not only so : he came into power with the cultivated
thought of a new generation. Too many of us scarcely remember
how young a man he was. He was born in 1759, and might have
well been in the vigour of life in 1830. Lord Sidmouth, his
contemporary, did not die till after 1840 ; he was younger than
his cousin, Mr Thomas Grenville, who long represented in London
society the traditions of the past, and who died in 1846. He
governed men of the generation before him. Alone among
English statesmen, while yet a youth he was governing middle-
agèd men. He had the power of applying the eager thought of
five-and-twenty, of making it rule over the petty knowledge and
trained acquiescence of five-and-fifty. Alone as yet, and alone
perhaps for ever in our Parliamentary history, while his own mind
was still original, while his own spirit was still unbroken, he was

B

mentary system—a system which, in this respect at least, is scarcely likely to alter for the better—no man can become Premier, or can even obtain high office and an influential position, scarcely even expect a seat in the Cabinet, till he has reached middle life. If he belong to the class of habitual politicians, and come of that rank out of which ministers are made, he will have been long subjected to all the influences of a public and senatorial career; he will have had to work his way up through subordinate offices, during which he will have been under the necessity of carrying out and defending, and therefore almost unavoidably *imbibing*, the views of his principals, and of suppressing or modifying his own—if he had any individual ones—as impediments to his advancement and success ; so that by the time he reaches a position where originality and energy would show and tell, originality will have been effectually crushed out of him, and whatever commanding and penetrating energy he may have started with, will have been exchanged for that flexibility and skill in navigation which goes further and lasts longer with us than resolute and imperious volition. If, on the contrary, he comes into public life from the outside, by force of genius or eloquence or popular sympathy, like Mr Bright and Mr Cobden for example, he must equally be a man of mature years ; and although in this case he escapes the ice-house and the flattening-iron of subordinate office and adminstrative routine, he has gone through the other narrowing processes with which professional

able to impose an absolute yoke on acquiescent spirits whom the world had broken for him.—*National Review*, xxv.

and mercantile life alike abound ; and unless he be a man exceptionally fortunate, both in social position and intellectual gifts, he is certain to be more or less limited and one-sided in his culture or his views ;— the more certain, because in England such an "out-side" man, who does not belong to the class who are politicians by profession and by birth, can scarcely have become the idol or the tribune of the people sufficiently to be forced into power by their strength and as their champion and spokesman, except he has either made himself mighty by being the eloquent and amended embodiment of their views (which, often right in the main, err always from incomplete-ness, exclusiveness, or excess), or has mounted on the pinnacle and been borne forward on the wave of some *one* great dogma, embraced at the ·critical moment and fought for with that concentrated deter-mination whose very concentration excludes large and mellow comprehensive wisdom. An English minister *may*, by a rare miracle or a happy accident, be a great statesman at twenty-five : only by a far rarer chance can he either be, or become, one at fifty. His case is even more hopeless than that of a clergyman ; for if he has signed the sad articles of English political faith at every step he has taken up-ward since he first entered the service of that un-philosophic and dogmatising Church, he must have bartered away every *individual* conviction or concep-tion long before he enters on its loftiest functions.

It is obvious, therefore, if we dispassionately weigh all the above considerations, that it is both idle to whine over the absence among us of that sort of statesmanship which our habits and institutions

effectually preclude, and unfair to contrast the statesmanlike views and capacities of British ministers and
politicians with those manifested by men placed
under altogether different circumstances.   The
Emperor of Russia or of France can, to a very considerable extent, lay his plans, mature and consolidate
them at leisure, and then carry them out as he conceived them.   Statesmen of that order can do pretty
much what they please, if only they have sagacious
heads and strong wills.   Statesmen in the position
of Palmerston and Russell, Gladstone and Derby, or
even Peel and Canning, can only do what the people
whom they represent and serve will allow them to
do.   It has usually been the same to a great degree
with our generals.   It was so with William III.; it
was so with Marlborough; it was so with Wellington.
Napoleon the Great not only commanded his own
armies, but was himself the despotic government
which provided them and sent them forth, and defined
their objects, and dictated their campaigns.   He had
no timid, or incapable, or envious, or antagonising
masters at home to fetter his arms and paralyse his
genius.   The duke, on the other hand, fought in
chains.   He was perpetually hampered and incapaci-
tated by orders from England, issued by men who
did not possess his information, and who could not
rise for a moment to the height of his conceptions.
His wisest and grandest schemes were often crippled
or rendered abortive by official neglect, or careless-
ness, or wilful inertia at home, which he could neither
punish nor prevent.   During a great portion of his
career he had to fight three antagonists at once,—
the French generals in front, the Portuguese and

Spaniards by his side, and the English ministers in his rear. It is only from a study of the ability and the temper with which he sustained this harassing and heart-breaking combination of contests, that we can draw an adequate conception of his real greatness.

If we would do justice to the real ability and strength of character that lie latent in British states-men, if we wish to estimate aright what we may term the *potential* statesmanship of our public men, we must first compare them with others fettered and conditioned like themselves, and then we must see what they can do and be when unfettered and favourably placed. We, as our readers know, have never been inclined to class in any very high rank our ministers in recent times, either the living or the dead, with two or perhaps three exceptions; but we may fairly ask, Do they in truth show so ill when weighed in the scale with the leaders of politics in other constitutional states, who have to do somewhat the same work, and to do it under similar conditions?—with Guizot or Thiers, for example, with Villêle or Polignac—with Webster or Seward, or Sumner, or Marcy, or Clay—with O'Donnel or Azeglio—with any *parliamentary* statesman, in fact, except Cavour? And what men in any land have shown grander capacities, intellectual and moral, for the noble task of government on the most magnifi-cent scale, and of the most autocratic sort, than many of our Indian Viceroys (who have in truth the only field offered to Englishmen for the display of such qualifications)—than Clive or Warren Hast-ings or Lord Wellesley; than Lord Dalhousie (though perhaps often wrong), than Lord Canning (so much assailed and so tardily done justice to), than Sir John Lawrence in the Punjaub, or even than Sir Stamford Raffles and Rajah Brooke? Compare for a moment, in idea, the Governors-General of India—nominally the subordinates—with the Secretaries of State for India and the Presidents of the Board of Control—nominally their chiefs—and the full scope and bearing of the distinction we have been drawing will become startlingly apparent. Very second-rate parliamentary celebrities are found, or are deemed strong enough for the latter post; for the former we need, *and we find,* men who can "administer government and war with more than the capacity of Richelieu;" men who are either great by nature, but whose greatness would never have been developed or made manifest at home, or who become great by the mere weight and grandeur of the work which is given them to do. And this same signal superiority of governing ability is found, and has been shown whenever the emergency has called for it, in the officials who have ruled minor Indian provinces, as well and as richly, perhaps, as in those who were appointed to rule the entire vast dependency. The work has made the men, probably, but then they must have had in them the material out of which such commanding statesmen *could* be made. Of the long list of men who have governed our Indian empire—all selected from the same class of politicians as our disappointing ministers at home—we cannot recall the names of more than two whom any one could designate as having shown themselves signally unequal to or unfit for the position. As a rule, they have proved what

English statesmanship may become under favouring
conditions, and have been men of whom any country
might be proud.

Whether the absence of forecasting and commanding statesmanship in Great Britain —an absence
which has been admitted and explained—is a matter
to be deplored, may perhaps admit of discussion.
But we are not going to discuss it now. We shall
content ourselves here with two remarks on the
subject. It may probably be said of statesmanship,
as of administration, that unless it is of a very high
order indeed, unless it is sound in its principles, and
comprehensive in its wisdom to a rare degree, the
less it forecasts and commands the better. We have
had more than one memorable warning in recent
history of the mischief and futility of looking far
beforehand where the vision is feeble and confused,
of that fussy and overshadowing sense of important
functions to be discharged, and an imposing station
to be adequately filled, which is not sustained by
any inherent dignity or any corresponding powers.
In political matters, especially in foreign politics, it
is rarely well to take too anxious thought for the
morrow; many of the knottiest problems, if left
alone, will solve themselves; many of the most perplexing will suggest and even dictate their own solution when the time for necessary action shall arrive.

But though, no doubt, possible enough, in home
as in foreign politics, to look too far ahead, yet thus
much of philosophy and forecast we have surely a
right to desire and demand of those who aspire to
take a lead in public life,—that they shall determine
distinctly *in what direction* it is wise and beneficent

that all legislative changes and all administrative
action shall tend ; and that they shall then take
heed that their whole conduct shall work to guide
the vessel of the State in that direction and to that
end ; that they shall form to themselves some
rational and feasible ideal of England's future, and
shall work with steady and converging purpose, as
far as in them lies, towards the realisation of that
ideal. At this point of our national history, for
example, every one fit to lead, every one called upon
either by position or by temper to speak, to write,
to act, to vote, in political concerns, is bound, we
think, to have some clear convictions, and some
resolute intentions, on the two following points.

First.—Is Great Britain henceforth to assert and
to maintain her old position as a first-rate influential
European power, who must have a voice, and use
it, in every European question, difficulty, and dispute—must, as of yore, never be silent, and never
speak without enforcing respect for what she says ?
Or is she to admit frankly, and without recalcitra-
tion or regret, and without having the admission
driven in upon her from without, that recent changes
in naval and military art, and other political events,
have altered her relative position, and with it her
social duties, and that she is by no means inclined
to deplore or resist the change ; that she does not
choose, after duly considering her obligations, her
vulnerability, and the progress which certain modern
ideas and doctrines have made among her people,
any longer to keep up such a military force as alone
would enable her to impose her will upon reluctant
peoples, or to take an active and supererogatory

part in continental quarrels; that she holds it inconsistent with her dignity to meddle in them by
counsel and homily alone; and that therefore she
is determined henceforward to look after her own
concerns more, and after those of other nations less,
than heretofore—satisfied that she is, and will
always be, able to suffice for her own defence and
her own guidance, but that she will do well to
abandon the pretension or the wish to defend all
the feeble or to guide all the foolish?

Secondly.—Is that tendency which has un-
doubtedly set in, and which to many seems so
desirable, and to many more so irresistible—the
tendency, namely, to extend more and more the
popular element in our system, to hand over more
and more political power and political preponderance to the numerical majority, that is, the less
educated portion, of the people—to be guided in
our policy by the mere *statistics* of opinion, to consider solely or mainly what a half trained and informed people ask, not what they need—is this
tendency one to be cherished, though moderated
and guided in its rate of action, or one to be
dreaded, checked, and counter-worked? The *means*
by which this tendency is to be forwarded or
resisted, is a question of measures, of strategy, of
feasibilities, about which those who think and
wish alike may well differ and split asunder into
sections. The *feelings* with which the tendency is
to be regarded—the estimate of the consequences
which will ultimately flow from it, should it prove
permanent and successful—involve principles which
lie at the very root of statesmanship, and separate

earnest men, not into sections, but into parties—not into disagreeing workmen, but into hostile ranks.

The above are questions of *directions* and of ends ; and without clear convictions regarding them, a man can scarcely make a single step in public life without much disgraceful vacillation and many miry falls.

II

ENGLAND'S FUTURE ATTITUDE AND MISSION.

A T the close of the preceding chapter, the doctrine was laid down, from which probably no one will dissent, that it is incumbent upon all who, either by action or advice, aspire to take a leading share in public life, to determine clearly and definitely in their own minds what ought to be the future course and goal of Great Britain in relation, *first*, to her domestic institutions, and, *secondly*, to her external policy ;—that, having once settled this question as to the *direction* in which the vessel of the State should steer, all their efforts, legislative and administrative, should tend to make her course as steady, consistent, and direct as shifting winds, disturbing currents, and intervening obstacles will allow ;—that all politicians are bound to have a rational and feasible ideal in their minds of what they would wish England's future to be, and to work with unfaltering and converging purpose towards the realisation of that ideal.

More especially was it urged—putting aside for the moment all internal and home questions of policy —that it was incumbent upon all public men to form a clear conviction and a resolute intention on this cardinal point :—Is Great Britain henceforth, as heretofore, to assert her old position as a first-rate influential European power, who must have a voice,

and use it, in every European controversy ; must, as
of yore, never be silent, and never speak without
enforcing respect for what she says ? Or is she to
admit frankly, spontaneously, and unrepiningly, that
recent changes in naval and military art, recent political events, and gradual modifications in her national
conceptions of what is wise and obligatory, have
materially altered her relative position and its incumbent claims, and that she is by no means disposed
either to deplore or to resist the change ;—that she
has duties and demands elsewhere, as well as new
ideas at home, which disincline, if they do not incapacitate, her from keeping up such a military force
as alone would enable her to take a constant and
supererogatory part in continental quarrels ;—that,
holding it inconsistent with her dignity to meddle in
them by counsel and homily alone, she is resolved
henceforth to abandon both the pretension and the
wish to restrain all the wicked, to defend all the
feeble, or to guide all the foolish ; satisfied that by
such a course she will most surely secure peace for
herself, and perhaps also be best able in great emergencies to prevent the perpetration of great wrongs ?

That this grave question should be decided by
each man for himself, and by the nation for itself, is
obviously not only important, but of the most imperious necessity ; but if we said that the decision was
an easy one, or the case a clear one, we should show
a very inadequate conception of the various material
interests and moral considerations immediately or
indirectly involved. A more difficult problem, and
at the same time a more urgent one, has seldom
pressed upon a statesman's mind. It admits of

neither delay nor dogmatism : the first may be dangerous—for events hurry on and questions press for answers, while we are digging for a principle and groping for a formula ;—the second would misbecome even the most experienced statesman and the profoundest thinker ; for the questions at stake arise precisely out of those altered aspects of affairs which bewilder and defy experience, and involve considerations rather of probable consequences and necessary compromises than of positive rights or indisputable obligations.   But the determination of the principle on which our future policy is to be based, though difficult, is all the more imperative.   It concerns our dignity, as well as our peace, that we should bring our *attitude* into harmony with our *action ;* that we should speak strongly only where we mean to act decidedly ; that we should encourage only where we are prepared to aid ; that we should lecture and dictate and direct only where we have made up our mind to act the patron as well as the pedagogue. In recent years, as regards our Foreign Office, the ideas and traditions of the past have been singularly at variance with the notions and powers of the present.   We have sometimes blended in most confusing ·inconsistency the sentiments and language which were suitable and becoming, and which were in a manner forced upon us, when we stood forth as the liberators of Europe, the conquerors of the great Emperor and Captain of the age, the encouragers and subsidisers of all other states through their crises of despondency and destitution,—with the utterly conflicting doctrines and feelings of a generation to whom all these things are become history, and a history to which we do not look back with unmingled reverence or pride. We still retain too much the inveterate habits of remonstrance, of warning, of uninvited teaching, of almost impertinent criticism, which sat not unbecomingly upon a nation that was always ready to go to war and seldom went to war in vain, when we have grown to be a nation hating war as an evil only second to spoliation or dishonour, and dreading it as a monstrous extravagance, a probable folly, and an incalculable risk—a nation coveting no territory, shrinking from all aggression, and anxious only for honest leisure and repose. No doubt this is a case of national rather than of individual inconsistency; it belongs to a people whose political ideas are in a state of transition and imperfect fusion; it arises partly from the fact that old men reign at the Foreign Office while young men sway the popular feeling,—that men of one generation and of one up-bringing sit at the helm and direct the details of navigation, while the men of another generation, and a widely different training, constitute the crew and the younger officers, and determine the port which the vessel is to make. It is not easy to steer a steady and persistent course, or one which shall be intelligible to foreign powers, when despatches, full, it may be, of menace, of promise, of encouragement, or even of positive engagements, are written in the silence and secrecy of Downing Street by Earl Russell, or Lord Clarendon, or Lord Derby, or Lord Malmesbury, and not till six months afterwards, perhaps, are laid before a House of Commons in which Mr Bright and the metropolitan members and representatives of

Lancashire and Yorkshire have a weighty and sometimes a preponderating voice,—and before a public over which that school of politicians hold a still more indisputable sway.   The Cabinet determines what shall be said : Parliament and the Press determine what shall be done ; and not until the NATION has distinctly and finally resolved upon the foundations of its policy, will such a harmony be re-established between the several elements of our complex government, that the Ministers, knowing precisely what the country will sanction, will know themselves precisely what it will be safe and wise to say.   But, however clear and natural may be to ourselves the explanation of our inconsistency and vacillations, the mischief done and the impression made abroad are equally unfortunate :—all parties are perplexed ; the strong are irritated ; the weak are disappointed and disgusted.   There have been occasion when we have almost been despised ; we were never much loved ; and now we are assuredly less feared and less trusted than we were : we have lost much respect in the eyes of others, and some also in our own ; and though the result is explainable enough, we can scarcely complain of it as unjust. It is clear that we must come to an understanding with ourselves, and know in future what we are prepared to say and do.

Now, we well understand what it is to abdicate a high position,—how much of noble and honourable pride, and how much of human weakness also, must be mortified thereby.   For a long period we had paramount influence in Europe, and on the whole we used that influence conscientiously and beneficently :

—at least we intended so to use it. England was a protector to be appealed to by the weak, a power to be deprecated and dreaded by the strong,—a sworn foe to all high-handed oppression and wrong-doing, —except such as she herself might perpetrate under some effectual disguise which hid its nature even from her own sight. She almost always threw her influence, and sometimes her sword, into the scale of people who were struggling for political and civil freedom; by example, by representations, by advice, by remonstrance, she laboured to multiply the number of constitutionally-governed states in Europe; and partly owing to her aid and partly to the general progress of enlightenment and popular power, there is now not a single state in Europe (except Russia and Turkey) without a parliament exercising greater or less control over the government. In her proceedings in reference to this head, England may often have been pedantic and *doctrinaire*, and sometimes far from judicious; but on the whole her mission was a great one; she believed in it, and she pursued it with zeal and disinterestedness. Sometimes, as in the case of Greece, we may some of us think she did too much; sometimes, as in the case of Italy and Hungary, we may some of us think she did too little. In the case of Denmark, we may perhaps be of opinion that she did both too little and too much. But in the main, so far as she did act, she was honest and consistent. Unfortunately, however, this mission of encouraging and multiplying free states, was not the only European one she deemed herself called upon to follow. She thought it incumbent upon her to look after the Balance of Power, to adjust the relative influence of other states, to provide for future contingencies and accidents of succession, and to enter into alliances and engagements with other European potentates for these indefinite questionable purposes. And herein we now see, reading the past by our present light, that she was unwise ; her influence was by no means always good, and was sometimes ineffectual ; the gain was rarely equal to the cost ; the complications that ensued were often exceedingly embarrassing ; and, on the whole, the game was one which required profounder statesmanship than she could bring to it—probably more prophetic vision than is given to any statesman—to play with profit. In retiring from the post of especial or joint European arbitress, therefore, perhaps she will do well and wisely ; because one of her functions was an undesirable one, and the other is well-nigh performed,—and for yet another reason in the background.

First. Our special work in Europe—that, as to the wisdom, the beneficence, and the duty of which (whatever may be our private opinion) it is idle to argue with Englishmen—is nearly done,—*quite*, perhaps, so far as we could act in it with efficacy. As we just now observed, nearly every nation in Europe now has a parliament and a constitution—and one of its own choosing ; not always equally influential or efficient, but still such as suits itself; such, at least, as itself accepts and endures, and such assuredly as we should never be guilty of the impertinence of presuming to attempt to change. Every nation has, in a manner, after our example, taken its affairs into its own hands. Italy has a parliament as free, as omnipotent, and almost as sensible as our own. Switzerland has a constitution only too preposterously popular. Spain and Portugal, under decided constitutional forms, are gradually working their own way to really free and popular governments. Austria has at last a Reichsrath that appears likely, and fit, to re-organise the empire on an entirely new and substantially free system : at all events, she has got her tools, and must now use them for herself. Prussia has chambers, turbulent enough in all conscience, and may be constitutionally free, if she wishes and deserves it. Holland and Belgium are as popularly and legitimately governed as Great Britain. France has universal suffrage, and uses it after a fashion of her own—startling enough sometimes. Russia is still a despotism, and most assuredly it is not for us to make her otherwise; but there are indications, just visible above the horizon, that even Russia will some day follow in the wake of other European states. And as for Turkey, even England would be scarcely insane or *doctrinaire* enough to give *her* a constitution such as that with which thirty years ago we cursed and saddled Greece.

As to our other understood, though rarely acknowledged, mission in the Past—that of encouraging and assisting peoples to arise and conquer freedom from oppressive rulers—this we have long since abandoned and loudly disavowed. We still occasionally remonstrate with the stupider and feebler despots, as with the Pope now, and with Bomba and others a few years ago ; and warn them that their silly oppressions and barbarities must end in popular risings, and that then we shall afford them neither help nor sympathy. But beyond this we now never go. Non-intervention in the internal affairs of other nations is now our published and enshrined, and, we apprehend, our irrevocable policy,—a policy to which we have more than once signalised our rigid adherence, in defiance of the strongest inducements that could be held out both to our higher and meaner nature. Having seen Hungary crushed without aid and without remonstrance,—and crushed, not by her own, but by a foreign despot ; having done nothing but withdraw our ambassador from Naples ; having protested against Garibaldi's Sicilian expedition, and only encouraged the interposition of Piedmont at the eleventh hour at Gaeta ; having, as a government, though not as a people, thrown cold water on the cherished popular scheme of Italian unity ; and lastly, having distinctly refused to interfere on behalf of Poland, and discouraged, if we did not actually prevent, the interference of France, and submitted with the best grace we could to the snub which the tone and language of our Foreign Secretary drew upon us :—having thus acted and thus abstained, we may be fairly said to have given hostages for our principle, and to have won our spurs in this new battle-field of masterly inaction.

Our third fancied mission—our mission of "long ago"—the purpose for which, according to Lord Russell, when he was in power five years ago, we ought still to *coquette* with intervention in the affairs of continental Europe—may still be under an obligation to interfere, at all events, with protocols and words—*viz.*, the protection of the weak against the

aggressions of the strong, we may be considered to
have finally surrendered in the case of Denmark.
It would be useless, therefore, to discuss whether, as
a rule and as a principle, we ought still to adhere to
this last and noblest fragment of our European obligation.   It is not likely that a stronger call for protective interference will ever again arise.   There
was, no doubt, some ground for the original action of
the two great German powers ; there was none for
the ultimate invasion and annexation.   It was an
instance of as high-handed and vulgar a spoliation
as any of Napoleon's ; and as such our Government
regarded and represented it.   The pretext, though
not wholly unjust, was utterly inadequate to the conclusions it was made to cover.   The State attacked
was small, feeble, and inoffensive.   The attacking
Powers were overwhelmingly superior in wealth, in
numbers, and in force.   The territory was greatly
coveted by one of the Powers, and a strong pressure
of national passion and ambition was brought to
bear upon the other.   The invasion and annexation
were in direct and insolent defiance of a recent
treaty inaugurated by Great Britain.   We all but
promised material assistance to the Danes in distinct
terms.   We certainly led them to believe that such
assistance would be granted.   At one period, there
is not the slightest doubt that our Government intended and desired to afford it.   We by no means
wish to argue that we ought to have gone to war in
aid of Denmark.   We think that, on the whole, the
country was right in refusing to take an active part
in a controversy of such singular complication and
such doubtful issue.   But assuredly we ought to

have taken an active part, or none at all. And assuredly, also, having shrunk from armed intervention in this case, it will be difficult, on the score of our alleged protectorate of weaker states, to intervene on any subsequent occasion.* The only grounds on which we can be supposed to be under an *obligation* to interfere in European quarrels and complications, where our own direct interests are not concerned, may then be held to be swept away, partly because our functions have been successfully completed and discharged, and partly because they have been deliberately abdicated, and can scarcely be resumed at our caprice.

It may be questioned, therefore, whether our interposition in Continental affairs is any longer needed. It may be questioned, also, whether, if needed, it could be rendered with effect. The Continental Powers may usually be trusted to keep each other in order. If not, we cannot do the work for them. There are four great European Military Powers ; and Italy promises one day to be a fifth. They are not ill-matched : France, no doubt, predominates ; but it may be assumed that any two united would be an overmatch for any single one. They are all jealous of each other, and have special and conflicting interests, or think they have. If one of them resolves to oppress and despoil any of the smaller states, and the others do not say her nay, she will do it, whether we object or not. If the others desire to prevent her, they will be able to do so without our active aid. Denmark was a

* Our inaction during the absorption of Hanover and other German States by Prussia, strongly corroborates the conclusion.

case in point.   Military interference was necessary
to save her, and we could not interfere militarily
without the assistance of a Continental Power.   If
France would have joined us, Denmark would have
been saved.   But if France had been disposed to
act, she might have saved Denmark herself.   We
did not interpose to create Italy : it may be assumed,
probably, that we should not interpose to save her,
if Austria were to assail and overpower her.   But
France, probably, would throw her ægis over, and
that ægis would be effectual and ample.   If France
did not interpose, we *could* not.   Take two other
possible cases.   Suppose Russia coveted and seized
Sweden : probably France and Prussia would both
forbid her.   If they did, the prohibition would be
decisive : if not, our prohibition would be of small
avail and of infinite cost.   Suppose France were to
attempt the annexation of Belgium or Holland ;
would not Russia and Prussia at once negative the
spoliatory scheme ?   If they stood by inactive,
drugged by bribes or terrified by menaces, neither
of which is very probable, what could we alone do ?
It is certain that we are almost powerless for
direct European action without the aid of one, at
least, of the great Military Powers of the Continent :
this may be considered a political axiom henceforward ; and cannot these Military Powers do their
own work without us ?

   These arguments appear of great, even of preponderating, weight ; but we must not lose sight of
two obvious considerations which may be urged on
the other side.   The first is, that though, *single-
handed*, we can do little or nothing to avert spoliation

and wrong-doing on the Continent, or the undue
and formidable aggrandisement of any of the great
Powers, yet, in alliance with others, we may do
much ; and that it may often happen that the
question of resistance to, or acquiescence in, such
wrongs and perils, will be decided by the prospect
of aid from England. Russia might allow France
to absorb Belgium, and France allow Russia to take
Sweden, because a costly and a doubtful war would
be necessary to prevent it if Great Britain were
inactive ; whereas, if Great Britain were known to
be ready to interpose, the project would be abandoned, as too dangerous and expensive. France
—especially under another ruler—might be willing
enough to do an ill turn to Italy, or to let Austria
do so, while both powers would be restrained by
the knowledge that England was prepared to stand
by the menaced kingdom with all her strength. In
a word, English intervention, or the prospect of it,
might be a make-weight, and often a deciding one,
on the side of right and independence ; and the
mere chance of it, though we believe it to be more
and more unlikely every year, may check the perpetration of much wrong. The argument, we admit
at once, deserves the gravest consideration ; such
cases as those hinted at may arise ; but can they
prove more than this—that though non-intervention
be our strict rule, it may, in rare and singular emergencies, be liable to exceptions ?

The second plea to which reference has been
made is this :—" How shall we fare," it is asked,
" in our day of trouble and of danger, if by our
selfish isolation we have forfeited all claim to amity

or aid ?   If we have refused to aid a just struggle,
or to oppose the consummation of a heinous wrong,
who will sympathise with us when injured, or come
to our rescue when assailed ?"   There are three
answers to this, none of them, perhaps, couched in
any strain of noble sentiment, but all of them sensible and weighty.   The first is : Have we not, as a
fact, incurred far more enmity than gratitude by our
interventions ? and shall we not always do so as a
certainty ?   With the exception, perhaps, of Portugal and Belgium, and possibly of Turkey, is there a
single nation on the Continent that does not dislike
us, and resent our action, so far as they have any
positive feeling in regard to us at all ?   The despotic
powers hate us for our known hostility to their
high-handed and barbarous proceedings : oppressed
nationalities are resentful against us, because, while
avowing sympathy, we have withheld assistance.   It
is hard to say whether, after the war of the Duchies,
we were in worse odour with Prussia or with Denmark.   Hungary has never forgiven our inaction in
the crisis of her patriotic struggle, and Austria has
never forgiven us for wishing that Hungary and
Venice could throw off her yoke.   The Emperor of
the French was deeply irritated because we crossed
him in the matter of the Congress, and the Emperor
of Russia, because, while we discouraged France
from interfering to save Poland, we lectured him on
his Polish atrocities.   Assuredly, hitherto no isolation or inaction from European controversies could
well have earned for us such general and such
bitter animosity as our unlucky and unceasing,
though well-intentioned, meddling.

But, again, are nations ever assisted in their dangers purely out of gratitude, or from recollection of bygone obligations? Are debts of that sort often repaid in kind? In our hour of peril we shall have aid from neighbours and allies, because, and only in as far as, it is not desirable for them that we should succumb or be too far enfeebled. They will help us, *if* they help, because they need us, not because they love us. It may well happen, indeed —and the reflection is worth deep consideration— that it will be worth while for Europe to stand by Great Britain, and preserve her independence and position, if she be an active and efficient member of their Areopagus, when it might not be so if she had become a mere indifferent and outside spectator, as insular in her sympathies as in her situation. In the one case they might be anxious to keep her as an auxiliary : in the other they might have no interest except to share her spoils. But are these calculations that need enter into a practical consideration of our coming policy?

Thirdly, however, wise men will probably be of opinion that we shall better secure our safety, in case we should ever have to struggle for existence or for empire, by *reserving* our strength, rather than by wasting it, in anticipation, in maintaining an influence which is costly, embarrassing, and exhausting, and in securing allies who may fail us in the time of need. The millions and the men that we have squandered, and may yet squander, by meddling in purely Continental controversies, and what is called "asserting our position" as a first-class European Power, if properly hoarded and properly applied, would have gone far to render us invulnerable. If we did not scent danger so far ahead, and take such elaborate, and costly, and often clumsy, precautions to forestal it, we should often be far more strong and ready to meet it when it comes.

But after all, perhaps the strongest plea in favour of withdrawing from our old habit of active and systematic interference in European complications, is to be found in the consideration that we are never sure of doing good. The only thing certain about these interventions is their cost and their bloodshed —their exhausting operations and their residual animosities : the success and the benefit are, and have been, nearly always problematic. If we look back, with the tranquil sentiments and the reflected light which belong to history, upon the earlier portion of the last seventy years, he must be a bold man who will pronounce with confidence that the world would have been worse off now had we let matters alone —that more wrong would have been done and more misery endured—that progress would have been more retarded or civilisation further advanced. And if we could estimate recent events with the same knowledge and impartiality, our verdict as to the interventions of the last thirty years would probably be 'much the same. Our interference in the affairs of France in 1793, the commencement of twenty-two years of desolating warfare, and accumulated debt, is now generally recognised to have been a mistake. We did not, as we fancied we easily and speedily should do, put down the insurgent nation : we only developed and concentrated its revolutionary energy. We did not, as we hoped,

protect England, by that war, from the contagion
of democratic theory and passion: the scenes and
deeds of 1794 and 1795 would have done that for
us had we left their example to operate alone; but,
by the line we took, we created in the heart of our
own Parliament and people a party, almost anti-
national, who, in their detestation of the minister
who had involved us in the war, were goaded to
espouse the cause, to endorse the doctrines, and to
defend the excesses of the enemy. But for that
fatal error of Mr Pitt, and the passions it aroused,
we might have had Parliamentary Reform, and all
its issues, forty years at least before we had. By
that war, then, we neither did good nor gained glory;
but we shed much blood, we squandered much treasure, we laid up many heavy burdens for the future,
How was it with regard to the Napoleonic wars?
Latterly, no doubt, it became almost a struggle for
existence, when the emperor had grown to hate us
as his one irreconcilable and unvanquishable enemy;
but suppose that we had accepted him, as the French
accepted him in 1799, as the legitimate, because the
chosen, sovereign of a great nation, and had confined
ourselves strictly and avowedly to a policy of self-
defence.   Napoleon would scarcely then have
attacked us voluntarily; for we should not have
thwarted his military ambition, and he would have
been too wise to bring upon himself an unnecessary
foe. Supposing, then, our opposition to have been
withdrawn, would his career have been more triumphant, more iniquitous, more desolating than it was?
Is it at all certain that it would even have been
shorter? In spite of us, he subjugated nearly the

entire Continent. In spite of us he defeated Russia, conquered Italy, absorbed a great part of Germany, annexed Belgium, twice utterly routed and prostrated both Austria and Prussia, placed members of his own family on the thrones of Holland, Naples, Westphalia, and Spain,—in a word, appropriated about half Europe, and made France incomparably more powerful and formidable than she had ever been before. Why did he fall at last ? Not because English troops beat his generals in the fields of the Peninsula ; not because English gold subsidised his enemies ; but because his maddened, insatiable ambition, which he had striven to keep within bounds, at last overleapt the limits of sanity, and involved him in a struggle with the might of nature ; because his incessant wars had exhausted both the life and the endurance of his country ; and because his oppressions and his outrages had aroused, in all the lands he had trodden down, that inextinguishable hatred which only waited for the turning-point of fickle fortune to pay back the long debt of treasured vengeance. It was the Russian campaign, and not the Spanish war, that decided Napoleon's fate. Had he never attempted that frantic enterprise, he would not have been forced to meet the combined forces of the three military Continental Powers—if at all—with young and untrained recruits. The veteran army that perished in the snows of 1812, would probably have continued, as before, more than a match for any troops that could be brought against them ; the allies of 1813 would not have dared to rise against their conqueror ; and Napoleon would have been able to turn his whole strength, and his personal genius and *presence*, to meet Wellington in Spain. Who can say with confidence that our army, with its miserable allies, would not then have been utterly overmatched, and that a dragging war, or a compromising peace, would not have left the emperor as secure as ever on his throne? What we contributed to his downfall—a contribution which cost us nearly half our present debt—was that, by our subsidies, we helped the Continental Powers to continue and renew, from time to time, a contest which must have been exhausting, and that at a critical period we detained some of his best generals and most veteran troops at a distance from the scene where the life-and-death struggle was carried on. No doubt the battle of Leipsic might have had a different issue had the armies of Soult and Massena been on the field. But, after the retreat from Russia, whatever had been the immediate course of events, Napoleon was either doomed or crippled; and, but for that disaster, it is very questionable if the utmost efforts of England could have done much to control or to dethrone him.

Since the fall of Napoleon our Continental interventions have been nearly all in the pacific direction; but which of them can we look back to with unmingled satisfaction? Are we proud of the morality or confident in the beneficence of the Treaties of Vienna? We tore away Norway from Denmark, in order to compensate Russia's robbery of Finland. How far did that iniquity contribute to the ruin of Denmark, in spite of us, in 1864? We gave Lombardy and Venetia to Austria : to what extent, by

that error or misdeed, did we not make ourselves
responsible for the long miseries and oppressions
which Italy suffered at the combined hands of the
Hapsburgs and the Bourbons? We created Greece,
and gave her an unfitting constitution and an imbecile king : have we had reason to be proud of our
creation, or to call it good? We separated Belgium
from Holland, and guaranteed our work : is it not
even now doubted by the shrewdest of our statesmen
whether that severance was not a political blunder?
And is there any doubt at all that that guarantee is
pregnant with embarrassments for us in the future.
Of our ignoble meddlings with the Polish and the
Danish questions it is safest not to speak ; but what
shall we say as to "the Eastern question?" Has
our action done good—real and permanent good—
there? We, in common with most Liberals, and
with many lovers of peace, thought in 1854 that the
case for intervention was a clear one. The great
body of the nation went heartily into the war.
What do we think and say now? Are we as confident as we were that our decision was a right one,
and that our interposition was practically beneficent?
Have not grave misgivings beset us ever since, and
are they not daily growing stronger, whether in
sober truth all our efforts to keep the Turkish
empire on its legs are not simply pouring water into
a sieve? Whether it is worth keeping alive?
Whether it *can* be kept alive? Looking to our
antecedent action, to distinct or implied engagements, to our traditional policy, to the preliminary
steps we had been led to take, it is not easy to see
how the war of 1854 could, *in* 1854, have been

avoided; but the question is, did we truly benefit
Europe, or truly save Turkey, by that war? Is the
saving of Turkey a benefit to Europe? We know
what the Crimean War cost us : can we say as
positively what it gained us? And if, in a case like
that, where our interests, our honour, and our traditions, were so closely involved, we can feel already
in doubt whether our intervention was wise and
useful, or not altogether an honest and generous
mistake,—what is likely to be our verdict in more
ambiguous cases? In plain truth, the difficulty,
or rather the impossibility, of foreseeing the ultimate
results of political action, is the strongest conceivable
argument against all action that is not distinctly
forced upon us. To do right, or to do good, one
may venture much, and labour much; but to feel
that what we do with the best intentions, and after
the most single-minded deliberation, may turn out
to be a mischief and a blunder, is enough to
paralyse the action of the most virtuous and courageous among statesmen.

There is yet another class of considerations, pointing in the same direction, which it may not be very
agreeable to dilate upon, but which it would be
simply foolish to ignore. The relative position of
Great Britain to the other Powers of Europe, singly,
or in their aggregate, is no longer what it was fifty
or sixty years ago. We are still, no doubt, the
richest nation in the world; but we are no longer
as decidedly and disproportionally so as we once
were. France treads very closely on our heels :
since the accession of the present emperor, it is

questionable whether her wealth and commerce have
not increased at a faster rate than ours.   Italy wants
nothing but security; and Russia, Austria, and Spain,
want nothing but that adoption of a sounder commercial and financial policy of which they have
already given indications, to develop and accumulate resources which will amaze even themselves.
Again, our commercial marine, our commercial
depôts, our commercial opulence, are still far ahead
of those of other nations, though France and
America approach us nearer than of yore ; but we
have lately had startling warnings that our commercial vulnerability is exactly in proportion to the
magnitude of our commercial transactions.   We
have seen that the smallest navy can make fearful
havoc with the greatest commerce ; and that under
the altered circumstances of the time *no* navy is
adequate to the protection of a foreign trade that
extends over the world, and sends its ships by thousands into every sea.   The days of convoys are
gone by : they never were very efficient, and no
commerce now could wait for them.   *Alabamas*
and *Sumters* may start up anywhere ; and *Royal
Sovereigns* and *Warriors* cannot be everywhere; and
too often, like London policemen, would be nowhere.
Thus in one sense, and a terribly practical sense,
our superior wealth is the measure, not so much of
our superior strength, as of our superior vulnerability.
We should suffer more than any other nation by a
war, just because our merchants are more enterprising, more wide-spread, more magnificent in their
operations, than those of neighbouring states, and
because our wealth is more dependent on our mer-

cantile transactions. Our enemies would have more
to prey upon; and a wider surface to attack. If, indeed, we could induce our benighted rulers and our
chief rivals to adopt the proposed doctrine of the absolute inviolability of private property at sea (when not
contraband of war), our position would become incomparably safer and more powerful; but we fear
that the latter are now too wide-awake, and the
former still too shrouded in antiquated fancies, to
allow us to hope for such a result.

But further,—our war navy, we may at once assume
or admit, is still the largest and mightiest in the world.
There are alarmists, and there are *frondeurs*, who tell
us we are mistaken in this idea, and that the efficiency
of our marine defences is by no means so certain,
either absolutely or relatively, as we fancy; and many
of their allegations have an uncomfortable air of
plausibility. But we will, for the sake of argument,
put their representations aside, and take the satisfactory statements of rival Lords of the Admiralty as
our guide. But granting all they say, the residual
fact is undeniable—our superiority at sea is nothing
like what it was in the period of our great European
wars. In those days we had actually no formidable
rival. The chief navies were those of France and
Spain: no others, except perhaps for a time those of
Holland and Denmark, were worth naming. We
had little difficulty in defeating and almost destroying
the combined navies of both our antagonists; and
after Trafalgar, England was undisputed mistress of
the seas. Let us forswear all vain boasting and illu-
sions: she is so no longer, and probably can never
be so again. Steam has told greatly for her in one

way, inasmuch as her coal-fields, her engineers, and her machine shops, are the first in the world.   But it has told still more against her in another way, inasmuch as it has neutralised what probably was the great source of her superiority, her special seamanship.   The resources of mechanical science are open to all nations, almost at last as unreservedly as to ourselves; and the greatly increased degree in which science enters now into naval warfare also tells against what used to be one of our special advantages—the superior dash and courage, the fondness for hand-to-hand fighting, the predilection for boarding, which distinguished our sailors, and led to so many of their victories, will be comparatively unavailable in future.

The new armaments, the fearful guns which will henceforth be in vogue, have done away with the days of battering broadsides, and "laying your ship alongside of the enemy," the tactics which Nelson loved.   "Boarding" is probably at an end for ever, and superiority in guns and gunnery, not in courage or in obstinacy, will decide naval combats for the future.

But *in what degree* is our navy still predominant in strength?   In an almost immeasurably less degree than formerly.   Our commerce is greater than that of any two other European nations.   Our outlying dependencies are more extensive than those of all other European nations put together.   Even by the admission of the Emperor of the French, our navy, in order to be *equal* to that of France, ought to be *double*.   Nay, it ought to be that, even if we were merely a European Power, since our army is so much smaller than that of Continental States.   Now what

are the facts? The comparison, of course, is in a
measure inconclusive, because we cannot give the
real effective *warlike capacity* of the different ships
—a matter which depends upon their armament and
the success of their various modes of construction,
which has yet to be decided. But at the end of
1863 (and *relative* positions have not greatly altered
since), *England* had afloat or in preparation 669
vessels, of which 566 were steam and 103 effective
sailing ships; *France* 489, of which 367 were steam;
Russia 310, of which 248 were steamers. The
number of officers and seamen were in England
(excluding marines) in 1864, 50,000; in France
39,000; in Russia 59,000. The entire number of
seamen at once available in case of emergency would
in England be 100,000, and in France 66,500. The
entire] naval estimates in Great Britain for 1867
reached £10,600,000, and in France, £6,000,000.
There is another element, too, to be taken into consideration : we have now a new naval competitor
and possible enemy to reckon for. The war marine
of America has hitherto been comparatively insignificant; it will henceforth be very formidable. She
has already 640 vessels of one class or another afloat,
and will have upwards of 700 by the termination
of the war. Nearly all of these are steam-ships,
and some of them of a very efficient and singular
construction. Already, therefore, there are three
nations, the combined navies of any two of which
would be stronger than ours, and any one of which
might give us much trouble. Do not let us fall into
the error of underrating the strength of our competitors. War, be it said in passing, is a different

thing from what it was, and to a certain extent a new thing. The conquest of Russia in the Crimean war tasked the efforts of the two greatest European powers, though she was taken at a disadvantage by being assaulted at the extreme point of her European territory. The slaughter and the cost of that short conflict were till then unexampled. They have been twice surpassed since. One campaign and two battles in the north of Italy, proved at least relatively more expensive and more sanguinary ; and the blood and treasure squandered in America have outstripped all previous examples. The seven weeks' war of 1866, again, half-revolutionised our notions of what future wars will be.

Again, our military requirements are greater than they were. The habitual average numbers of our standing army are increasing, and the recruiting field which is to furnish them is growing smaller. The present British army is 146,000 strong ; it used to be in time of peace about 100,000 or less. Before the mutiny we were satisfied with keeping from 20,000 to 40,000 European troops in India ; henceforth we calculate on 70,000 or 80,000. To keep up these numbers we need about 14,000 recruits every year. It is true that the aggregate population of these islands is slowly increasing, and is much larger than it was during the Napoleonic wars ; but, on the other hand, the demand for labour in every line of occupation is incomparably greater ; our manufactures and railways and other public works absorb increasing numbers every year, and emigration carries off something like 200,000 annually. The population of Ireland, which used to be our richest and readiest recruiting-ground, has fallen off by nearly three millions. It was about eight millions and a half in 1846; it is not more than five millions and a half now. Therefore, while our *total* population is larger, our *surplus* population is smaller than it was; and it is out of this surplus that our standing army in ordinary times has to be replenished.* No doubt we shall always be able to get troops and native troops when we need them, by higher pay, more liberal bounty, and wiser systems of enlistment and reward; but we shall get them at the expense of other necessary occupations—recruiting will *drain our industry* instead of merely *absorbing our idleness*, and the difference is a very grave one in regard to our national wealth and strength.

Without, therefore, laying ourselves open to the slightest charge of exaggeration, without trenching in the least on the province of the alarmists, without pretending to entertain any doubt that Great Britain will always find her spirit and her resources fully equal to meeting all inevitable dangers, all probable odds, and all clear and honourable obligations, it is indispensable that we should recognise the fact that, though still the greatest power in the world, she is no longer *immeasurably* such; that, though still

* We shall form a more adequate idea of the degree in which the diminution of the population in Ireland has reduced our nursery for soldiers, if we reflect that a population of 3,000,000 implies about 700,000 adult males, and that *two per cent.* per annum out of this would supply all the recruits we need in time of peace. Every year there leave our shores about 60,000 adult males, or as many as *one-third* of our whole army. It is true that the cessation of this emigration might at any moment provide us with the materials of a doubled army.

paramount, she is no longer unapproachably supreme
at sea ; that, though still far wealthier than any other
nation, she has drains upon her wealth which no
other nation has ; that she has duties and dangers
in prospect which may task her utmost strength ;
that, with all her courage and her might, she is not
equal both to the fancied claims of her traditionary
policy and to the irresistible claims of present and
future obligations ; that, in a word, she cannot continue to play the part of an imperial Providence in
Europe and in Asia both. She must make her
choice. She is mighty, but not omnipotent ; her
coffers are well-filled and easily replenished, but they
are not inexhaustible.

In the East we have a vast field of positive duty
and prospective usefulness, a field to task the
grandest energies, a field to satisfy the noblest
ambition. We hold there the double position of
lords paramount, and of a race of loftier and more
advanced civilisation. We incur there the double
and most solemn responsibilities of political supremacy and of intellectual pre-eminence. We cannot
abdicate our obligations, and it is scarcely possible
to avoid extending them. We are too, in Asia, in
Southern Asia at least, almost without a European
rival. Russia, it is true, has at times given us much
trouble in India and Persia, and has threatened some
in China ; but with all her skill in diplomacy, her influence and *hold* over the Asiatic races are not com-
parable to ours. Turkey, Persia, Thibet, and Siam,
are scarcely to be mentioned as powers. Holland
confines herself noiselessly to Java. Of the two

really great empires in the East, India is already ours; and China and Japan seem as if, in spite of ourselves, they would become ours.

In India we hold sovereignty, direct or indirect, over about one hundred and eighty millions of people, and people not savages or semi-savages like the Africans, but bound in the fetters of various and antiquated but most elaborate and highly-finished civilisations. They are of many races and many religions. The soil of India is one of the richest in the world; its productions are of the most various and most exchangeable kind; and several of the tribes show remarkable capacities both for industry and war. Altogether the resources of the country are immense. India to us is not a colony, and scarcely a dependency—it is an empire. We are established there as an Asiatic Power, and incomparably the greatest of all Asiatic Powers. We have to govern a conquered and a less civilised race, and we have to govern them as conquerors and as superiors. Our Indian revenue is considerably more than half our British revenue; in 1868 it was £49,000,000. Our Indian army, independent of the native armed police, is larger than the British army: it consists of 200,000 embodied troops, of whom 65,000 are English. Government, too, means a very different thing in India and in England. In India the Government is at once parent, despot, and proprietor. It is the sole owner of the soil; it is the protector and assistant of the people in case of great national calamities, such as hurricanes and famines; it is the undertaker of all public works; it is the dispenser from above downwards of such civil-

ising and educating influences as it can safely and
justly bring to bear upon the subject races.   In comparison with us the people of India are children—
passionate, wayward, ignorant, bigoted, suspicious,
—children with some of the irrationality of animals,
but with the passions and the strength of men.   The
task of ruling them is one needing singular delicacy
and tact ; the task of improving and teaching them
one of still more subtle difficulty.   We have to control them, to humour them, to civilise them, to administer at once justice and restraint, and, if possible,
never to startle or offend them.   A problem of such
knotted complication, one demanding such mingled
skill, caution, sound principle, and indomitable
courage, was never presented to any conquerors.
We will not for a moment pretend to fancy that our
rule, with all its drawbacks, is not a great blessing
to the people of India, and will not become a greater
one year by year. We have committed great wrongs :
we have made terrible blunders ; we have sometimes
been guilty of injustice, sometimes of oppression,
often of violence : though we have generally meant
well even in the past, and always mean well now.
But that we have a right to be where we are, and to
be there *as* we are ; that our position in India is not
that of intrusive foreign oppressors over a nation
striving to be free, but that of lords paramount over
a number of mutually hostile races, who, but for us,
would be mutual foes and mutual tyrants ceaselessly
at war ; that the Hindoos will have some alien
masters, and that we are incomparably the best masters they can have ; that our work in India is a noble
and a necessary one, and that, having undertaken it,

we cannot abandon or surrender it,—are all, practically, propositions that it is idle to doubt and needless to discuss. The conclusion which we wish to impress upon our readers is, that the work committed to our charge in India and in Asia generally, is to blend the two civilisations of the East and West, to graft progress on stereotyped forms and canonised stagnation, to let in light so that it will gradually dissipate the darkness, yet bring on no violent convulsions, to modify the new intrusive elements, so that they shall educe harmony and not confusion ; in a word, so to study and comprehend the Asiatic nature—its intrinsic differences, its special aptitudes and capacities, its distinct and indispensable needs, its original and incurable peculiarities—as, without risking either social or moral anarchy, almost insensibly to interpenetrate and imbue Oriental nations with as much of Western energy and knowledge as can harmonise beneficently with characteristics so inherently diverse.   That there are relations in which Europeans and Asiatics may live together with mutual benefit and comfort, we do not doubt.   It is our function to discover those relations, and to establish them in the most effectual and least painful way.

For, observe, our Indian Empire is not, and cannot be, a mere isolated possession, involving only limited responsibilities.   It renders us the chief power, the predominating influence, the universal referee, in the whole of Southern Asia.   England is the paramount potentate in all those Eastern seas. Our commerce, as well as our empire, helps to make us such.   Our ships of war, as well as our ships of trade, swarm in every creek and harbour.   Along

the whole of the Malay peninsula and islands, in
Borneo, to say nothing of China and Japan, the
English name is incomparably mightier than any
other for good or evil. We cannot evade either the
dignity or the obligations of the position if we
would.   It is forced upon us by the irresistible
sequence of events. Our merchants press everywhere, intrude everywhere, settle everywhere, and
our captains and consuls follow to protect, and if
need be—as it often is—to control them. Sir James
Brooke establishes himself at Sarawak, becomes a
native benefactor, then a Borneo potentate; he
achieves a sort of sovereignty there, or rather has it
in a manner thrust upon him; and being a true
Englishman, he, in turn, almost forces it upon his
country's government.   There is no doubt that ours
is one of the most beneficent and civilising sove-
reignties ever established over any savage races.
We certainly at first sought and dreamed of nothing
in China, except peaceful trade and security for
persons and for goods.   Nay, we have sedulously
striven to avoid any other relations.   What has
been the result? We have had to wage three wars
at least with the Chinese; we have had to storm
first their southern seaport, then their northern
capital; we have had to require the session of a
neighbouring island, where we have fixed ourselves
in perpetuity; we have had to force a treaty upon
them and to punish them for its infraction; and
lastly, we have had to save the government from a
desolating and almost overwhelming rebellion, and
to undertake the collection of a considerable portion
of its revenues.   Who can doubt that ere long we

shall have to do yet more to the great benefit of China, though at great trouble and with great re-luctance on our part? We need not have gone to Japan if our merchants would have let us alone; but having gone there, being there by treaty, the usual results are following :—first, outrages, which must be avenged, then little wars; then a stationed fleet; then an authorised residence; then troops demanded from India to keep hostile and lawless natives in awe. Who does not see the government —or at least the protectorate and the advisership of the government—of both China and Japan loom-ing in the distance? Seriously, we doubt whether any efforts can now save us from this ultimate issue : we doubt, almost as strongly, whether we ought to shrink from it : whether we ought not cheerfully and resolutely to accept the magnificent field of rescue and of service, whenever it shall be offered to us, or forced upon us by the logical current of events. Which of us doubts that we might in time introduce something like honesty and efficiency into the effete bureaucracy of China, and that every Englishman who replaced a Chinese or Japanese in the administration would be *pro tanto* an instru-ment and a step towards better things? In China especially, by universal admission, social and bureau-cratic corruption is so deep and general, that British influence would probably be the greatest blessing that could be vouchsafed to them, and perhaps their only way to permanence or safety. We do not of course dream of arguing that because we could govern China incomparably better than the Chinese, we should take the government out of their hands ;

but it is a reason why, if the government should
be forced upon us by circumstances which we do
not designedly prepare, we should not shrink from
doing a clear and a great good. " Manifest destiny "
sometimes points out manifest duty ; and to become
the governing race and caste in the far East appears
to us, we confess, as grand and beneficent a vocation as a people can be summoned to fulfil.

Some objectors will exclaim against the folly of
indulging in such dreams of magnificent activity and
boundless undertakings, as being far beyond our
strength, and tempting us into a field where our
powers would break down ruinously and discredit-
ably from pure inadequacy to the work. But those
who thus disparage British capacity and resources,
loose sight, we apprehend, of three considerations.
The first is that, as the only basis of these specula-
tions, we assumed (and argued in the earlier portion
of this paper) that Great Britain should restrict her
European activities and obligations, precisely with
the view of being able to venture on the more
profitable and more imperative field of Asiatic
enterprise and sway. The second is, that the main
portion of the great work we have sketched out for
British genius and energy would demand neither
troops nor treasure. It would be done through the
instrumentality and at the requisition of the aided
governments and the benefited nations. We should
supply the head, but only in a limited measure the
hands. We should furnish the integrity, the science,
the organising faculty, the indomitable and imperious
will, the administrative experience and adaptability,
but not the *materiel* of the system. We should

contribute the generals and the officers, but not the rank and file. Mr Lay's collection of the customs in China, Sir James Brooke's management of the Dyaks, did not cost Great Britain a shilling or a soldier. The same, or nearly the same, might have been said of Major Gordon's disciplined Chinese force which retook Nankin, and of Captain Sherard Osborne's steam squadron, which was to have swept pirates and smugglers from the Chinese seas. We do not propose to supply more than the governing class and the supporting influence. Before the mutiny, India was conquered and maintained at a cost to Great Britain of about one thousand civilians and twenty thousand soldiers ; and these were *paid* by India though *found* by England. The third consideration is, that our empire in India will afford us the means of realising all our dreams of paramount influence and ubiquitous beneficence and action in the East, without drawing on the mother-country for anything beyond an annual contribution of a few hundreds of her most intelligent and enterprising sons, whose ambition is already craving for a mission and a sphere. What India is to us—what vast power it confers upon us—what splendid resources for conquest or for rule it places at our disposal—all this was so lucidly and effectively shown in the *Spectator* * (than which no organ is so well entitled to be listened to on Indian topics), that we prefer to quote its words rather than substitute our own :—

" The resources of India, whether little or great, are absolutely at the disposal of the British Parliament, as absolutely at its disposal as those of Scot-

* October 1864.

land or Cornwall, Wales or Ireland. There is no elected legislature, no constitutional contract to stand in the way of action ordered from Westminster, no public opinion to be obeyed or conciliated, and no means of material resistance to be seriously dreaded. European opinion on the spot would, on adequate cause shown, sanction any orders on which Parliament was determined; there is no native opinion except in favour of internal order; and the only organised body capable of resistance is British, and comes home every ten years. The force thus absolutely at the disposal of Parliament is so great as to form not only an appreciable addition to the strength of Great Britain, but an addition more than equal to a first-class alliance. From Egypt to Japan, whatever the work to be performed, the aid of India is worth more in direct assistance than the aid of France. The revenue of England is calculated at seventy millions, but in any time of emergency it is a hundred and sixteen, for the forty-six million pounds of Indian revenue is absolutely at British disposal. The army of Britain is estimated at one hundred and twenty thousand, but it is really three hundred thousand, for every British soldier and Sikh auxiliary is available for action outside India. That army, moreover, can be raised to any numerical strength for which funds can be procured, to a million thoroughly trained troops for example, without the faintest difficulty, and within six weeks of the arrival of the order. No man who knows India doubts for an instant that, if the British Parliament decided to conquer China and Egypt and Japan all at once, India could carry out those orders, could garrison those countries, and could hold them for years against any force Asia or Europe is at all likely to employ in resisting such an enterprise. Or to bring the case nearer home. Suppose Europe contending for the heritage of the "sick man," India could, if stirred to vehement action, pour three armies of a hundred thousand men each into Asiatic Turkey, move, fight, and keep them there without assistance from England for at least two years. All these things may be, in our judgment would be, acts of wickedness or folly, but the potency of doing them comprehended in the possession of India completely alters our Asiatic position. We have in Asia, in fact, as an ally a first-class monarchy, with a revenue of European magnitude, an army all Asia combined could not resist, a fleet equal for transport purposes to any work demanded ; and this ally is so faithful that he never permits his policy to diverge from ours,—so devoted that, till we are crushed, his assistance is absolutely secure,—so humble, that he never expresses even an opinion as to the terms of peace, or the need of war, or the character of the operations to be undertaken. Have we such another ally on earth ? And this ally,—so patient, so faithful, and so prompt, —is in Asia supreme beyond all historic example, supreme as the United States would be if left alone among the Spanish republics, supreme as Napoleon was once over the Germanic Confederation. There is not a State in Asia which dare attack him, not one which would not be subjugated if he attacked it, not three in which an unreasonable demand on his part would not be followed by a servile submission on theirs. And his aid, which in a hundred years has failed but once, which in the nature of things cannot be granted in a half-hearted way, or after long delays, or upon conditions, costs Great Britain no revenue, and no exertion beyond the raising of a certain number of recruits, whom it is always within the competeney of this country to recall, and who till recalled not only do not cost it a shilling, but through their native auxiliaries count in every campaign as three for one. Wherever one British soldier is engaged, three Sikhs may safely and usefully be employed, and the Sikh, if not the first among soldiers in the world, is incomparably the first in Asia. India makes England a first-class power on two continents instead of one, without imposing on her the double obligations required to support the double rank."

Our preference of an Asiatic to a European field for political influence and activity is threefold :— First, because it is natural to our position, and is forced upon us ; because, if we neglect it, we may be interfered with in it, our position impaired, and our work marred ; and because we shall then have to do tardily, reluctantly, unsystematically, and at a disadvantage, that which we have such signal facilities for doing wisely and deliberately now. Secondly, because there, and there alone, can we be certain of doing good ; because our superiority to those we should influence and govern is, both intellectually and morally, so marked and so indisputable, that our supremacy, blunder as we might, could not result otherwise than in a preponderance of benefit to the subject and protected races ; and because with the experience we have acquired, and the stricter notions of political morality and the more solemn sense of responsibility to which we have at last risen, there is no reason to doubt that our future career will be far more judicious and irreproachable than the past has been. We *cannot* possibly be guilty of equal wrongs ; we can scarcely be guilty of equivalent mistakes. Thirdly, The reflex action on our national character will be far nobler and more elevating ; the magnificence and beneficence of the work to be done will tend to make high-minded and virtuous the men who have to do it; certain it is that whatever of truly great and far-seeing statesmanship Englishmen have ever shown for many generations, has been developed and run its course in the East ; certain it is, too (as has been well said), that " more than all our colonies, more than all our trade, the possession of India strengthens the English character, defends the English mind from yielding to its instinctive parochialism, and helps to turn a nation of selfish, if successful, industrials into a race of governing men.

But England occupies yet another political relation towards the world, independent of her European one. She has the largest and most populous colonial empire in the world. She owns more than forty dependencies ; one of them of almost, and another of quite, continental magnitude. They range over more than two million of square miles. Their aggregate population already exceeds *nine* millions, and will certainly be double that number before the century is out. Many of these colonies are tropical or semi-tropical, and most of them have

E

still vast tracts of unoccupied land of fertile character
and unknown resources. Towards all the more
important dependencies we stand in the position
less of a ruler and owner than of an indulgent
parent, who bears much, exacts little, and bleeds
freely. Notwithstanding momentary difficulties in
New Zealand, we may hope that all the sources of
probable quarrel or discontent between us and our
colonies are past or cured. The dream of taxing
them would never enter into the wildest fancy.
We never think now of even presuming to regulate
their tariffs, unless they are bent upon some monstrous folly which sets at once allegiance and
political economy at defiance. Slavery, with its
rich crop of discontents, is at an end. Transportation of convicts, which has endangered the loyalty
of so many colonies, is at last, thank God ! definitively abandoned. We have granted almost absolute
self-government to every colony, in which the elements of self-government existed. We help them
a great deal, and control them scarcely at all. There
is now no conceivable reason why any of our colonies,
properly so called, should wish for independence.
If they did seriously and persistently wish for it, we
should probably say, " Wayward children, go in
peace." There may be reasons why the mother-
country should at times wish to be free from the
obligations which this vast colonial empire entails
upon her, but they are not reasons which will ever
move her to take the first step towards separation.
It appears, therefore, nearly certain that our future relation towards Canada, Australia, New Zealand, the
Cape, and all real colonies, as distinguished from
mere dependencies like Ceylon and Mauritius, and

military stations like Malta and Bermuda, will be that of a central mother-country surrounded by independent kindred and attached allies, speaking the same language, governed by the same laws, enjoying all the privileges and liable to none of the burdens of British citizenship.

Now, can we imagine any rational ground why the people of countries thus situated, and thus treated, should wish for independence? It is inconceivable that they should deliberately wish to join any other State;—if they did, we are certainly enlightened enough to let them go at once, perhaps with something of natural mortification and regret, perhaps with a sarcastic smile. But by actual independence they could gain nothing and would sacrifice much. As a matter of pride, it must be more gratifying to be a portion of the greatest empire in the world than to be a small and weak State, incurring much danger and exercising no influence. The North American colonies are now blended into a confederation, and the Australian colonies will ere long follow the example; but in both cases they will still be greater if united with the mother-country than if independent, and assuredly not one whit less free. The only unsettled question between Great Britain and her colonies is as to the degree in which they should provide for their own defence. But if they were to separate, they would have to provide for the whole of it without any question at all. It may be said that by remaining parts of the British Empire they become involved in our quarrels, and are liable to attacks from *our* enemies, with whom they have no controversy, and suffer from the results of a foreign policy over which they exercise no control. Theoretically, there would seem to be much weight in this representation, and practically perhaps it was once true. But is it so now? The United States may no doubt attempt to seize Canada if they quarrel with Great Britain; but, whatever be the pretext now, their real reason we know would be less that they wish to injure Great Britain, than that they wish to possess Canada. Does not every one feel satisfied that Canada would be far more liable to and certain of invasion and annexation if she did not belong to England, but were independent, and with only her independent strength to rely upon? that she has *not* been over-run and absorbed long since simply because she was a British colony? and that for one danger to which the parent connexion exposes her, it saves her from ten? Look at the West Indian islands; does any one believe that if they were to separate from the mother-country and declare their independence, they would remain for a year unappropriated or unconquered by the greedy Republic of the West? We heard something a while ago of the project of Russia, in case our Polish correspondence with her had ripened into war, to concentrate a large naval force in the South Pacific, and pounce upon our Australian dependencies, which would thus have been made the victims of our European quarrels. The project sounds probable enough. But, in the first place, though the Russian fleet might have ravaged some of the towns and coasts of Victoria and New South Wales, it could not have retained possession for three months after the tidings of the raid had reached England. And, in the second place, what would be the position of either Australia or New Zealand if independent? Would

France and Russia covet those appetising gold-fields less than now? Would there be any consideration to withhold those Powers from attempting to appropriate them? for recent events have shown that wars of mere greed or spoliation are not wholly out of date. And what could the colonies do in their defence if left to their unaided strength?

It seems clear, then, that the obligations and responsibilities of Great Britain, as the head of a vast colonial empire, are as little likely to be taken off her shoulders by the separation of the colonies, as to be voluntarily surrendered or timidly abandoned by herself. It is probable even, and it is to be hoped, that they will become more solemn, more extensive, and more riveted every year by the increasing attachment, loyalty, and danger of these distant portions of our dominions. When, therefore, we look to the prospect of what we may be called upon to do and bear, in order that the promise of almost illimitable grandeur lying before our colonies, and ourselves in union with them, shall not be marred or blighted—of the inescapable and incalculable claims of our Indian possessions both upon our military and our administrative powers—of the work which is all but certain to be forced upon us in China and Japan,—and of the drain upon our strength and the field for our genius and enterprise which these several vistas open out before us,—may not we be considered to have proved conclusively and overpoweringly, that the more we can restrict and retire from European action, the stronger and more dignified will be our position, and the fitter and readier shall we be for the work which God has given us to do?

III.

DISPOSAL OF THE CRIMINAL CLASSES.

THE public mind has rarely been in so favourable a condition for dealing with this great question : in a condition which gave so good a chance of a hearing to the thorough and consistent thinker; in a condition which offered so hopeful an opportunity for action to the courageous and logical statesman. The nation has been gradually educated on the subject; and the difficulty which usually meets us on the threshold of such cases,— that of fixing attention and exciting interest,—is, therefore, already overcome. People are growing very uneasy, and consequently clamorous for prompt, decisive, and extensive proceedings, and little inclined either to count the cost or to cavil at the means. They are angry, with the wrath of fear, and, therefore, disposed towards severity ; and we all know that the prevalence of a morbid and fanatic tenderness has for years been one of the chief impediments to the adoption of a salutary system of criminal management and repression. They are in utter perplexity, and therefore prepared to hear with favour and to accept gladly any plan of action which is based upon a sound foundation, which carries completeness and coherency on its face, and which indicates, in the Ministers proposing it, an entire comprehension of all the conditions and all the requirements of the problem to be solved. Again : we have come to the end of all our contrivances for evading or postponing the difficulty, and are dimly conscious that it must now be met. We have exhausted all expedients, and are, therefore, at length in the state of mind in which alone, as all experience shows, Englishmen will search for or listen to a principle. Lastly, in our disgust at having crowds of liberated criminals perpetually let loose upon us, we have, accidentally and imperfectly, got hold of the idea which contains at once the suggestion and the key-stone of a better system.

It appears to the writer that a system may be sketched out so obviously just and impregnable in its fundamental idea as to receive almost universal concurrence ; a system whose undeniable difficulties will be simply difficulties of administration, agencies, and details, such as practical aptitude, and the experience of each succeeding year, will soon reduce to a very manageable minimum. If the principle be sound, the application will not baffle us ; and both for executive and legislative action, there is no strength so unassailable or so irresistible as that derived from standing on a principle.

Criminals may be divided into two classes, which it is essential to keep apart in dealing with this subject,—the casual, and the regular or professional offenders ;—those who lapse from innocence, and those who live in guilt. The former will be found everywhere, and at all times. No laws, however judicious, no police, however skilful or pervading, no average national morality, however high, will wholly eliminate them from àny community. The morally feeble, the undisciplined and the ill-trained, ·the sorely tempted, the vehemently passionate, will always exist, to present examples of outraged morals and violated law. But these are not the offenders who menace our peace and constitute our reproach, and the management and disposal of whom presents the problem which has so long baffled and perplexed us. The other class, the professional criminals,— who form, it is calculated, nine-tenths of the entire number,—belong to a different category, are acted upon in a great measure by other influences, and must be dealt with in a different manner. They are brought up to crime; they follow it as an avocation; they practise it regularly for a livelihood; it furnishes their daily bread; it is to them a profession with its regular steps, in which petty larceny is the lowest grade, and burglary the culminating honour. These offenders constitute that criminal population which can only exist in communities whose condensation is great and whose civilisation is complex, and their existence forms our present difficulty and danger. To this class, therefore, the following remarks will distinctively, if not exclusively apply.

And here we are met by the first practical question we have to decide—viz., how are we to discern and determine to which of the two classes any given culprit belongs? This can be done by one of two methods, or by a combination of the two. It is obvious that the nature of the crime can be no test. A casual offender may be detected in his first offence, and that offence may be a very heinous one.

A professional and regular criminal may, after a long course of successful and brutal depredations, be detected at last only in pilfering a handkerchief or snatching a purse. But we may either decide each case on such evidence as can be produced in court, or we may adopt some rough rule which shall err on the safe side, and which, though often inadequate, shall never be unjust. We may either, after conviction, accept evidence of the antecedents of the criminal, his haunts, his associates, his habits of life, &c., which shall satisfy the judge and jury that he belongs to the criminal class, and which usually would not be difficult to procure, nor be liable to reasonable suspicion; or we may, without any possible risk of harshness to the culprit, but with an absolute certainty of allowing numbers of regular offenders to escape, decide that a previous conviction shall in all cases be taken as proof that the subject of it belongs to the criminal population. The circumstance of coming a second time before the bar of justice affords an irrefutable presumption, either that the man has such inability to resist temptation and such proclivity to crime, that he either is, or is certain to become, an habitual offender; or that his first imprisonment has produced its usual consequences, and either fostered his proficiency in crime or deprived him of all avenues to an honest livelihood; or that he is an established member of the fraternity that lives by depredation. It would seem desirable to adopt both tests; to accept any reliable evidence in proof of the offenders belonging to the criminal class, and at the same time to regard a previous conviction as superseding the necessity of any other proof.

We shall wonderfully simplify our course of action if we adopt a clear and persistent idea of the light in which regular criminals should be regarded by the State. In the first place, then, they are not objects of vengeance. The State is not competent to take vengeance. Vengeance—that is, retributive infliction—is the weakness of the savage, the privilege of the Deity. The State is not competent to apportion punishment to individual guilt, simply because it can never be competent to judge either the degree of guilt incurred, or the severity of the punishment inflicted. As to moral criminality, with the inadequate means at our disposal for discerning motives, gauging temptation, and estimating antecedents, it is obvious that the most patient jury can never collect half the materials for arriving at a confident decision, nor can the wisest judge hope to do more than form a plausible conjecture. Moreover, the same penalty which to one culprit would be too lenient for a theft, may, to a differently-organised offender, be too severe almost for a murder. Vengeance, which repays, can, by its very term, belong only to that higher Intelligence which can estimate the debt to be repaid, and the value of the coin assigned for repayment.

In the next place, criminals are not to be regarded by the State as objects of compassion,—as patients to be cured,—as unfortunates to be pitied and rescued,—as " weak brethren," to be petted, and guided, and taken by the hand. They may be all this,— probably many of them are; and it may be quite

right that they should be thus viewed and treated
by individual members of the society they have outraged, and from which they have pilfered.   But the
State has a very different relation towards them.
It is neither a chaplain nor a schoolmaster,—except
incidentally, and with a view to an ulterior and more
selfish object.   Its function is neither to regenerate
offenders nor to forgive offences.

Society,—or the State, which is its organ,—has
only one concern with the criminal class, only one
light in which to view them.   They are its foes
and spoilers.   They live in a state of chronic hostility to all that is pure, valuable, and peaceable
within it.   They assail its members and prey upon
its possessions.   They are the enemies of society,
and society has nothing to do but to protect itself
against them.   It is possible enough that retributive
punishment, allotted after some rude conjectural
fashion of its own, or schemes of reformation and
education carried out according to the best system
we can devise, may be found the most effectual
means of affording society the protection it seeks.
But this is by the way.   The principle to be laid
down as the basis and justification of all our proceedings is, that society has in this matter one
object only to pursue, and in pursuit of it may discard all extraneous considerations.   It has to protect itself against crime; and it may do this in any
mode which, in its wisdom, it shall deem efficacious;
which, in its justice, it shall deem right; which, in
its strength, it shall find feasible; which its feelings
of mercy and humanity shall allow.   It has to
defend itself against its internecine foes; and it

must do this in the wisest and most thorough manner.

Now, what plan has been usually pursued for the attainment of this object ? In our endeavour rudely to proportion the punishment to the offence, we have sentenced far the largest proportion of our offenders to short terms of imprisonment. Out of 100,000 sent to gaol, 70,000 are confined for less than one month, and 30,000 of those for less than fourteen days. Yet it is notorious that short imprisonments nearly always send out the culprit worse than they found him,—certain to resort to crime,—almost certain to return to gaol. It is known that those once engaged in a criminal career can scarcely, under the present system, avoid relapsing immediately on liberation, even if their life in prison had created a desire to do so. In ninety-nine cases out of a hundred all openings to a virtuous course are closed to them, and their vicious associates are always waiting for them. Their first detected crime makes subsequent crime all but inevitable ; their first punishment may be said to be life-long, though intermittent. The fact that they come from gaol shuts the door of the family, of the workshop, and of the factory against them ; the same fact, on the contrary, is a diploma for the career of theft ; a life of larceny alone welcomes them and beckons to them. As things now are, their only chance usually lies between starvation and relapse.

It is known, further, that very few of the criminal population become criminals from sheer want ; nearly all are trained to theft from childhood.

Comparatively few become thieves in later life ; almost all have been "juvenile delinquents" before becoming hardened malefactors. Finally, we know that nearly every adult criminal,—usually when in prison, always when out of it,—is busy in training younger sinners. Among the convict classes, "the schoolmaster" is always "abroad."

It clearly follows from these facts, that we have habitually so acted as to defeat what is, or ought to be, our sole object. Having once got hold of our "enemy," we have secured his being our enemy for life. So far from permanently protecting ourselves against his enmity, we have insured our continuous exposure to it. We find him warring against us and preying upon us, and we forthwith proceed to confirm him in his hostility, and to improve his skill ; we leave him no alternative but a continuance of his depredations ; and we then turn him forth to wreak the one and to renew the other.

This has been our suicidal course,—followed in the absence of a distinct plan and an intelligible principle. What, however, ought we to do now that our object is defined to be the permanent protection of the community against the criminal class? Is it not obvious that, as soon as our enemy is delivered into our hands,—as soon as it is clear that he is our enemy, that he belongs, that is, to the population who live by depredation, and is not a mere casual offender, led astray by want or passion, —we should keep hands upon him till he has ceased to be our enemy? What should we do in any ordinary case of pertinacious and systematic hostility? Should we confine the man till a certain

space of time had passed ?—or till the hostile mood
of mind had passed ?   If we have seized a desperado
who, either from bad passions, or perverse insanity,
or untoward but resistless circumstances, hates us
or covets our possessions, and is virtually certain
to be always assailing us, or injuring us, or preying
upon us, and if we know that, as soon as we untie
his hands, he will be at us again,—do we ever
untie his hands ?   Should we not deem it madness
to do so, unless we could either remove him permanently out of our path, or change his disposition,
or incapacitate him from action, or in some way or
other secure ourselves against a repetition of his
former practices ?   And would not this resolution
to hold him fast be confirmed by the reflection,
that by so doing, we were preventing him from
training up new enemies to us,—that we were shut-
ing up his school ?   In like manner, is it not clear,
that when we have once got hold of a regular
criminal,—a member of that criminal population
whose treatment, defeat, and extirpation constitute
the problem we are set to solve,—we must never
let him go till we have in some way or other in-
capacitated him, till we have eradicated the inimical
and predatory will, or destroyed the inimical and
predatory power,—till his enmity be either disarmed
or extinguished ?

Assuming the correctness of the principle, then,
if means can be found for carrying it into practical
effect, not only will the existing race of regular
criminals be permanently disposed of as fast as we
can lay our hands upon them, but those of the
younger generation, whom these regular criminals

are now, in and out of prison, occupied in training, will be saved on the threshold. And if measures can be devised and adopted, as we do not doubt they may, for preventing the children of the neglected and dangerous class from growing up to recruit the criminal ranks, we may yet live to see our way out of this fatal question.

By what measures, then, can we effect the proposed permanent incapacitation, and how shall we know when we have effected it? Three modes suggest themselves. We may incapacitate criminals—

1. By deterring them.
2. By removing them.
3. By incarcerating them till reclaimed.

1. It is the opinion of all who are intimately conversant with the character and feelings of the criminal population, that the deterring effect of ordinary punishment upon them has been greatly over-estimated; and a few moments' consideration will incline all to this opinion. In the first place, crime is the profession of this class,—their walk in life,—the business by which they gain their daily bread. The gaol, the convict-ship, even the gallows, are among the chances of this profession, and as such have been familiar to their minds from infancy. These are to them just what capture and death are to the soldier,—contingencies to be avoided, indeed, but also to be hazarded; and which neither drive back on the threshold of enlistment the recruit of the army nor the recruit of crime, nor deter them from the ordinary risks and enterprises of the career they have embraced.

In the second place, we must remember that we are dealing with men engaged in, and trained to, a regular trade. It is possible, indeed,—or rather, it is conceivable,—that you might make that trade so hazardous and unprofitable that few would enter it ; but for those already in it to be deterred from pursuing it would be to be compelled to change their calling,—a thing which few men in any line can be induced to do, and which to the criminal is almost impossible, because, as we have seen, nearly every other occupation is closed to him. Probably the utmost that severe and special punishment could do in deterring the criminal population would be to drive them upon the less hazardous and less heavily-visited branches of their profession. This, however, would in some cases, be a great gain.

Thirdly, the mass of criminals are not men of quick or vivid fancies. Their executive and perceptive faculties are often preternaturally sharpened, but their contemplative and imaginative faculties are blunted or lying in abeyance. Yet a very considerable endowment of these is presupposed by the theory which lays much stress on the deterrent influence of penal inflictions. For, in order that punishment should be efficacious to deter ordinary and unimaginative men, it must possess three attributes,—it must be certain, it must be prompt, and it must be visible, or, at least, easily realisable. Now, our existing punishments do not possess,—perhaps can scarcely be made to possess,—any one of these essential qualifications. So far from being certain, they are problematical ; so far from being prompt, they are usually very distant and

very slow. The chances in favour of the criminal, especially in the slighter offences, are probably twenty to one. Some calculations give an
average of six years' impunity to the ordinarily
skilful thief. Every conviction represents many
offences. The depredator, therefore, in the pursuit
of his calling, is not braving actual detection and
retribution, so much as their remote and problematic contingency. Neither is the punishment,
thus indefinitely postponed, at all uniform or calculable when it comes. The practised criminal may
be detected in the most trivial of his larcenies, and
be treated with proportionate mildness. Even if
caught in the commission of a grave offence, the
sentence he may meet with depends greatly on the
accident of the judge who tries him, of the temper
of the jury, of the views of the Home Secretary,
who may mitigate his penalty. It is not too much
to say that the young villain who enters on a course
of crime has no reliable data on which to calculate
what fate he has to expect, nor when that fate will
overtake him. How, then, should he be deterred
by its contemplation ?

Nor are our punishments visible. In the majority
of cases, the convict is removed from the dock, and
never seen or heard of again by the spectators,
whose minds his penalty is supposed to terrify from
crime, till he emerges after the lapse of years. He
disappears,—that is all that is known of him. The
world is told that he is at Pentonville, or on the
public works, or at Bermuda, or in Western
Australia ; but what sort of existence these vague
words imply, the criminal himself did not know

F

when sentenced, and few who heard him condemned know either.   There are, indeed, three punishments to which it would be reasonable to attribute a powerful deterring influence, because they are cognisable by the senses, and are thrust upon our sight, viz., hanging, flogging, and working in chains. Yet every one of these, English feeling or English folly has eliminated, or is labouring to eliminate, from our penal code.   It is idle to lean on the deterring effect of punishment while we repudiate the only punishments which might really deter.

2. Transportation—once our favourite resource— is at an end for ever.   No colony will any longer submit to be the receptacle of the moral filth of the mother country ; and the resource of a new penal settlement, wherever situated, must be regarded as wholly out of the question.   As a refuge it would be ineffective ; as a place of punishment it would be costly and disadvantageous ; as a colony it would be unpermissible.   It would not present to the liberated convict, as did Australia, a land full of free settlers, anxious to profit by his labour, and therefore willing to forget his antecedents.   He would find no honest community to absorb him, no preponderating majority of respectable citizens among whom he might hide his head, from whom he might conceal his identity, whose prosperity would excite his emulative exertions, and whose character would react upon his own.   In a new penal settlement the only employers of labour would be the Government,—late his gaolers ; the only labourers, his fellow-convicts ; the only society, that of men as criminal and tainted as himself.   How

could the restoration to honesty and respectability
of the liberated 'convict be anticipated from a
community exclusively composed of his foes and
his fellow-vagabonds, his gaolers and his accom-
plices ?

If the new penal settlement be intended as a
place of infliction, it would simply be a prison with
many disadvantages. A prison—a gaol for the
purposes of punishment—cannot be too close under
our eye. It would be better on Wandsworth Common than at the Antipodes. It would be far safer,
abuses would be far less likely to creep in, and its
cost would be far less. Gaolers, officers, military,
police, must be more numerous for an establishment
at the Falkland Islands than in England, and must
be paid more highly. The ordinary needful cost
of a convict here may be taken at £25 a year,
of which his labour does or ought to repay a considerable portion ; his mere transport to Western
Australia costs that sum.

But suppose this objection got over or ignored.
Suppose that by painful efforts, and by slow degrees,
some isolated and ungenial spot of earth shall be
covered by the farms of these liberated convicts.
What sort of a community will have been created,
and what sort of a future can be predicted for it ?
You have sown with poisoned seed ; what sort of a
harvest is likely to be reaped ? You have selected
your ".pilgrim fathers"—the founders of a new
society—from the worst dregs of your vitiated
population, from desperadoes so bad that you dare
not keep them at home. Is this a deed which,
after past experience, England can repeat ? But

further,—either there will be no women in this
penal settlement, or these women must be the most
abandoned of their sex, for none other will go
there.   In the former case, we must lay our account
for the revival of all the unspeakable abominations
of Tasmania and Norfolk Island.   In the latter,
what will that community be whose fathers are
felons, burglars, and murderers, and whose mothers
are prostitutes, or worse ?

3. The only resource, then, since hanging can be
available to such a very limited extent ; since no
colony will now receive our convicts ; and since a
new penal settlement is not only inadmissible, but
would not supply the desideratum,—is that of indefinite incarceration.   We must imprison the corrigible
offenders till they are corrected, and we must imprison the incorrigible ones for life.   Or, to state
the proposition in its tersest, nakedest, most startling shape, we must incarcerate them all indefinitely,
liberating such only as we deem to be reclaimed,
and only when we judge their reclamation to be
genuine and complete ; restoring to them, in a word,
their power to war against and prey upon society
only when we have regenerated or subdued their will.

It does not seem easy to suggest any sustainable
objection to this practical conclusion.   It seems impossible to give any shadow of a reason why we
should not shut up for ever those habitual malefactors who are for ever unfit to be let loose,
or why we should not shut up all others till they
are fit to be let loose ;—nay, it seems almost a
self-evident proposition that it is not only very
silly, but very wrong, to do otherwise.   Some

offenders, it is well known, are incorrigible.
Either from bad organisation, or from inveterate
habits which have become as fixed as organisation,
it is a matter of moral certainty that, whenever
liberated, they will and must recommence their
hostility to society, and their depredations on its
members. Therefore, it is affirmed, the State has
no right to liberate them. It sins against the community by doing so, for it wittingly lets loose upon
it an insatiable and implacable foe. It sins against
the convict himself by doing so, for it deliberately
enables him to add to the number of his crimes,
knowing that he will avail himself of the facility it
grants. The great mass of offenders, on the other
hand, it is equally well established, are reclaimable,
—often after long probation, many failures, and the
disappointment of many hopes,—but still, reclaimable they are ; some by one means, some by another;
some by just severity, some by judicious kindness ;
some in a few months, some not for many years.
But we say of these, as of the others, that, till they
are reclaimed, the State has no right to let them
loose. It wrongs them, and it wrongs the community if it does so. It sins alike against those
whom it is bound to protect from injury, and those
whom it can protect from crime.

The public is quite right in complaining, as it has
long done, of the liberation, in a civilised and peaceable community, of crowds of professional malefactors whose reformation there is not the faintest
reason to surmise, and whose relapse into crime
there is every possible reason to predict. The
public is quite wrong in directing, as it usually does,

its indignation specifically against the ticket-of-leave men, who are perhaps no worse than thousands of others; who would probably be not one whit more safe or harmless had they endured the entire term of their nominal sentences; and who are not the agents of half the crimes imputed to them. The facts of the case are, that the number liberated on licence is about 2000 per annum; and that about 100,000 are annually liberated from ordinary gaols without any restrictions whatever. The public see the truth as to the 2000, but have not yet applied it to the 100,000. But the justice of their blundering complaint is the same in both cases. They perceive the error, and protest against the mischief, of liberating criminals while still criminally disposed, or by circumstances hounded back into criminal courses.

The principle, then, being morally just and logically sound,—and the public having got an imperfect, which might soon be converted into a perfect, grasp of it,—it only remains to notice one or two conceivable objections :—

1. Imprisonment for life may at first startle some unthinking minds; but such may be quieted by reminding them that in the great majority of instances the criminals who will undergo this punishment are those who used formerly to be hanged; that hanging was not abandoned because it was deliberately deemed that these offenders ought ever to be restored to society, but from religious and humane scruples; that if let loose, these men would soon again subject themselves to recapture; and that in any case, therefore, their life must be a long course of imprisonment,—with intervals in the one case,

without intervals in the other ; and finally, that their life, though it must be permanently passed in detention, need not be permanently passed under infliction. They are shut up, not for vengeance, but for the safety of society ; and, in course of time, much mitigation, consistent with safe custody, might be allowed them.

2. Other objectors urge that it is not the State's business to reclaim offenders, but to punish them ; and that it steps beyond its province when it undertakes the task of the chaplain or the schoolmaster, and attempts to proportion penalties to repentance instead of to crime. The reply to this objection is brief and conclusive. The State has one sole, clear, paramount duty in this matter, viz., to protect the community. We have already seen that this protection can only be effectually afforded by incarcerating all professional criminals for ever, or till they are reclaimed. Unless, therefore, the objectors are prepared to advocate perpetual imprisonment for all, their objection falls to the ground. But it will also be admitted at once that the State, in protecting the community, has no right to inflict any suffering beyond what is necessary for this protection ; it has, therefore, no right to retain in prison any who can be let out with safety. It can be shown, moreover, that it answers better—is wiser, more effectual, more economical, as well as more just—to keep convicts in gaol till they are reclaimed than to keep them in for ever. As far as the interests of society are concerned, the sooner a criminal can be turned into an honest and industrious citizen, the better ; the " protection " afforded is the

more complete, the more prompt, and the less costly.
We insist, therefore, on the direction of the State's
exertions to the transformation of the criminal,
simply and solely because thus can it best discharge
its special duty to the community,—thus can it best,
easiest, soonest relieve it of a burden, by liberating
an offender whom yet it must not liberate till he be
transformed.

3. A third class of objectors urge that, by taking
all this pains to reform and train the criminal, to
teach him a trade, to instil habits of industry, and
to inaugurate him in a respectable way of life, the
State incurs the risk of disheartening honesty and
encouraging crime. This is an objection for the
forum,—rather showy than substantial. A very
slight consideration of the facts of prison discipline,
and a very superficial acquaintance with the peculiar
character of the class of professional offenders, will
suffice to convince us of its futility. No one would
willingly select so circuitous and so painful a channel
by which to arrive at a respectable and self-sup-
porting position. Months of separate confinement,
entire and continuous seclusion from all old associates, severe and unremitting labour, monotony of
scene and thought, enforced regularity, abstinence
from all sensual indulgences, and the indefinite duration of all these conditions, constitute a picture which,
we may be sure, presents nothing that is attractive
to the criminal, nothing that can seem enviable to
the honest labourer. The most marked and universal characteristics of the criminal population are
self-indulgence and a hatred of order ; a scene where
hours are early and toil is regular,—where there are

no women, no tobacco, and no spirits,—is, in their eyes, little better than a hell.

4. The expense of the proposed system, if duly carried out, will be objected against it. This objection might, if it were desirable, be triumphantly disposed of by a series of detailed comparative statistics, which, however, would necessarily be more or less conjectural. But a reply which has nothing conjectural about it is, that these professional malefactors and depredators live at the cost of the community, alike whether in or out of prison; and we are perfectly certain that we shall keep them a great deal more cheaply than they can keep themselves.

The principle then being clearly seen and defended against all objections, the plan in which it is to be embodied, and by which it is to be carried out, remains to be explained. But, first, we must notice a corollary of the principle which, though a logical sequence, seems somewhat startling on its first enunciation,—and that is, that we must deal in the same manner with all the offenders we lay hold of, whatever be the particular offence which brings them under the grasp of justice. We are all the time speaking, it will be remembered, of professional and regular criminals,—permanent members of the criminal population. Now, we propose to take these into our continuous custody,—not because they have stolen a pocket-handkerchief, or broken open a till—but because they are organised and established enemies of the community, habitual depredators on its goods. The particular offence for which they are brought up furnishes the proof, but not the measure, of this habitual enmity and this predatory life.* The community equally needs to be protected against them, and they equally need to have their bad and inveterate propensities eradicated, whether the degree of their discovered depredation be great or small   Moreover, it will often happen that a great offender will be detected only in one of his smallest offences, or that a man who has committed fifty crimes, for which the cumulative penalties would be enormous, will be sentenced only for one.   Therefore, whatever be the special features of the case, it seems reasonable and righteous that all professional offenders should be dealt with in the same manner, and according to the same rule; the judge admeasuring his sentence rather to the proved character and antecedents of the prisoner than to the individual specimen of these furnished by the charge in the indictment.   To the very heinous, the notoriously incorrigible, the judge should award detention for life.   To those convicted of crimes of violence and brutality, he should award a given number of lashes in addition to their other sentence.   To all others, without exception, he should award a sentence in three divisions, varying merely in extent and in amount,—seclusion, atonement, and provision.

And this brings us to the difficult question,—on which, indeed, the whole matter must eventually hinge,—" How are we to ascertain when the convict is reclaimed and fit to be discharged ? and who are to determine his fitness or unfitness ?"

* The *Habitual Criminals Act* of last session was a step, though an incomplete one, in the right direction.

It must be avowed, at once, that no infallible test can be discovered. The utmost acuteness and the longest experience will sometimes be at fault, and, under any system, some criminals will be liberated while their reformation is yet imperfect or superficial. Those who relapse after having undergone the ordeal we propose, should, in the majority of cases, be classed with the incorrigible, and be detained for life. But it is believed that, with nine-tenths of the number, the test, strictly applied, will be found reliable and sure. It must be, in the main, a self-acting one; it must depend as little as possible upon the fallible sagacity of governor or chaplain; and the *onus probandi* must be thrown upon the prisoner.

1. Every convicted offender, then, as well in the ordinary gaols as in the convict prisons under Government control, should be subjected to a period of strict seclusion, cut off from all intercourse with old associates; exposed to an entirely new set of influences, visited daily by the chaplain, school-master, governor, and turnkey, but by no one else; seeing and speaking to none but those whose sentiments and interests are all on the side of law and virtue, as those of his former intimates were all set in the opposite direction. It would seem super-fluous to insist upon this,—to urge the entire and certain discomfiture and neutralisation of all reform-ing and deterring influences where prisoners in gaol are allowed to herd together, are shut up at night, and have free intercourse by day, with a number of other offenders, thinking and talking of nothing but their criminal experiences,—were it not that separa-

tion is still, we fear, in county gaols, the exception rather than the rule. It is utterly monstrous to expect any diminution of crime to arise from imprisonment as long as this self-evident and suicidal absurdity is suffered to continue.

The period of this seclusion should be not less than six months, nor more than twelve. Few regular criminals need less than the shorter, or can bear more than the longer term. Between the two, the judge must decide according to such opinion as the evidence of the prisoner's character which comes before him will enable him to form. The effect of this seclusion, according to the testimony of all who have watched it, is most powerful. It subdues and intenerates in a singular degree. The criminal propensities of the sequestered prisoner, fed by no fresh fuel, fall into atrophy or abeyance ; solitude and reflection, and converse only with the good,— an altogether novel and abnormal set of circumstances for him, — develop feelings and notions incongruous and antagonistic to his past, and he comes out of his cell at the expiration of the period assigned a wholly different man ; not reformed, but in a state favourable to reformation—weak, flexible, and impressible in the highest degree. Nothing, however, has yet been done, except in the way of preparation. The impressibility we have mentioned is the impressibility of almost childlike weakness. It is equal towards bad influences as towards good. With the latter it must now be our care to surround him ; if we were to liberate him on issuing from this first stage, his relapse would be a matter of almost certainty.

The remaining portion of the convict's sentence should be passed in labour. Of what description this labour should be, and how provided, there is no need to speak here. Handicrafts in prison, agricultural labour out of it, labour on useful public works, in fixed and movable prisons, may all be resorted to, and we need apprehend no serious difficulties of practice in carrying out these plans. They belong, however, to the domain of executive experience.

2. The prisoner, having now undergone the preparatory discipline necessary to correct and in a degree wipe out the past, and make him ready for initiation into a different career, enters on the second stage of his sentence. He has now to make atonement for his former depredations on the community, and for the expense which he has entailed upon it in providing for his maintenance and detention. He must work out this atonement. He must be sentenced to discharge such labour as shall be assigned him, at such rate of wages as the State shall fix, till he has earned the sum which the judge, on passing sentence, shall have named. The reflection that he is working in a manner for himself, and to hasten the day of his liberation, will stimulate his efforts and render comparatively easy and attractive those habits of incessant industry which else would have been difficult and irksome;—while the element of hope will greatly facilitate the maintenance of discipline within the gaol.

3. But even after a prisoner shall have been subdued and softened by seclusion, and taught skill and habits of industry by enforced but atoning and en-

couraged toil, it would still, in most instances, be unsafe to discharge him without any provision for his future, or any precautions for assisting him to place his new-born virtue in favourable circumstances,—in circumstances, at least, where he will not be surrounded by more than ordinary temptations. It should, therefore, be a portion of his sentence that he should further earn, before he can be liberated, such a sum of money as will suffice to enable him to emigrate to other shores, or to start to respectable industry at home.

Now, if the sums designed for atonement and provision are fixed at a sufficiently high amount,—and there is no conceivable motive for indiscriminate lenience,—the criminal, by earning them, will have afforded the best possible presumption that he can be discharged with safety. It is scarcely possible that a man who has passed many months in entire seclusion from all evil influences and all old associations, who has, by steady industry for years, repaid to society a fair portion of the sums of which he had defrauded it, and who has further provided himself with a fund in hand which makes him almost a capitalist at home, or will carry him to new scenes and new prospects,—shall not have undergone both such a real change and such a salutary penance as will make him anxious and able to pursue an honest course thenceforth, unless exposed to trials of unusual severity. *Il a fait ses épreuves;* he has had no motive and no power to deceive the chaplain ; the special representations of the chaplain and the governor as to bad conduct in gaol should be allowed a veto on his liberation, but no more.

Nor should the convict, when his term of sentence has expired,—or rather, when the conditions of his sentence have been fulfilled,—be liberated simply, and without precaution. To do this would be to risk the undoing of what has been so laboriously effected. The prisoner has been sequestered from the world, and in leading-strings, for years; he is necessarily unfit, at once, to meet it alone and unassisted; and the new world into which he is issuing —the honest one—is one of which, even formerly, he had small experience. In order to give him "a good start" much individual care and attention will be requisite. Police supervision, which, as Sir Walter Crofton recently showed, is often the liberated convict's best assistance, should surround his steps for a long period after his discharge.

Were it possible, it would, no doubt, be desirable that nearly all these discharged and reformed criminals should emigrate at once. Nowhere, at home, can they find such hopeful openings for a new career as in a new country; nowhere, at home, can they so surely and thoroughly get away from their unhappy antecedents. There may, however, be some difficulties in the way of the universal adoption of this resource. Government is pledged not to send any more convicts to our recalcitrant colonies; and to send liberated, even if reformed, criminals, might be deemed an evasion of this pledge. Some of our dependencies, it is said, refuse to receive any immigrants who have been convicted; but it is difficult to see how this tyrannical and discriminating injustice could be practically carried out. The discharged offender is a free man; by law he can go where he pleases; he pays his own passage, he provides his own outfit, and it would be all but impossible to distinguish him, either in Australia, Canada, or the United States, from the crowd of miscellaneous emigrants daily arriving. On the whole, it is probable he will be a more eligible citizen than the mass of these. The quantity of unoccupied land is so great in various quarters of the world, and the demand for labour to till it so continuous, and, at times, so ravenous, that it may fairly be anticipated that the difficulties in the way of emigration above alluded to, will be found rather theoretically formidable than practically or extensively operative. Nearly all well-disposed expirees would desire to emigrate, and all who wish should be put in the way of doing so.

For such as wish to remain at home or find insuperable impediments in the way of going abroad, much may be done by benevolent individuals or associations in helping them to employment. The first step, it must be remembered, is the only really difficult one. A man once settled can get on; a man once employed can have a character from his first employer; his antecedents need not be traced farther back. No one will be disposed to undervalue the assistance that may be afforded to the discharged criminal in this way, who is cognisant of the extensive and successful operations of the numerous " Sociétés de Patronage," spread over most continental countries, for finding places for discharged criminals,—an indispensable and most serviceable resource, which States unprovided with our facility of deportation have long since been driven to adopt. By a well-organised system of communication between gaol chaplains and associations of this sort, a large number of expirees might be provided for, direct from the prison doors.

Others might make their first step in the new life they desire to lead under the auspices of Refuges or Intermediary Establishments, such as that set on foot by Sir Walter Crofton, when Director of Convict Prisons in Ireland, at Smithfield, near Dublin, where men supposed eligible for conditional liberation are, as it were, filtered back into the world through the medium of a stage of provided employment and supervised freedom, described in his pamphlet. Their fitness for discharge and independence is here both exercised and tested; and many persons are willing to take inmates from a refuge such as this, who would scarcely have courage to try them direct from gaol.

There may still remain a certain number who cannot at once emigrate, whom no one will at once engage, and who cannot, unaided, at once establish themselves in work. For these, Government might, without violating any principle of justice or sound economic science, provide temporary employment; employment not artificially created for them, but profitable and desirable in itself. In the present normal condition of the labour market, there is no danger lest honest men should be thereby superseded or displaced; and we must bear in mind that in thus facilitating the restoration to virtuous courses of the liberated offender, it is the interest of the community at large, and not that of the criminal, that we are consulting. It would only be necessary to fix the rate of remuneration sufficiently low, to guard against the risk of the expiree remaining languidly or wilfully on the hands of the authorities.

It will be understood, it is hoped, that the writer claims no originality for his suggestions. If there is any merit of novelty in them, it must lie merely in the coherence of the plan, and the distinctness and irrefragibility of the two principles on which it is based.

IV.

RECENT CHANGE IN THE CHARACTER OF ENGLISH CRIME.

IT is one of the evils attending a system of government like ours, an evil incident indeed more or less to all popular and free governments, that party struggles so constantly postpone, hide and push into the background, the most important questions of practical administration and of national well-being. The controversy as to who shall hold the reins of power takes precedence of the incomparably more essential controversy as to the principles on which that power shall be wielded, and often even of the subjects to which it shall be applied. The attention of the governing classes to a great degree, and the attention of the individuals who constitute the actual or the expectant government to a still greater degree, are engrossed sometimes in the mere conflict for the possession of office, oftener still in proposals for constitutional changes, which are the weapons of party strife and the instruments of party victory, while prolific improvements in administrative machinery, questions of the deepest public interest, grievous sores which are eating into the heart of the nation, wrongs and sufferings which wear away the life and character of millions, are neglected or put by till a more convenient season, though in sober truth these are the very matters to which the others are but ancillary and subordinate—the ends in reference to which party struggles, the choice of rulers, the existence of government itself, are only means.

Now, as from time immemorial, *Delirant reges, plectuntur Achivi*, only that of old nations wept and groaned because their respective monarchs warred against each other, in our days the people weep and groan because their own chiefs war among themselves for the privilege of leadership. In contending which shall rule, they forget the purposes of rule and the urgent interests of the ruled. It is so much easier to get up the steam for an organic change than for an administrative reform, to grow enthusiastic over the merits of a man than over the details of a measure, to excite that popular passion which is the motive power in politics about an extension of the suffrage or the abolition of the Irish Church, than about an improvement in the poor law, or in criminal justice, or in national education. The storming, or the badgering, or the defence of the Treasury Bench, would almost seem to be the daily work, the main business, the routine function of parliamentary politicians; the supply of the people's needs, the redress of the people's wrongs, the control of the people's faults and passions, only occasional and intrusive interruptions to the monotonous oscillations of the party pendulum.

It may seem strange that this should be so under a popular form of government, especially under one which is every year growing more democratic. The explanation, however, is simple and obvious.

In the first place, the fighting instinct of men is very strong and prompt when they find themselves opposite one another with a common prize in view; any politician can be a combatant, but it needs something of a statesman to look to the cause and the object rather than to the detailed strategy and tactics of the battle, and the honestest of men, when a little heated, easily persuade themselves, first, that they can do the needed thing better than their rivals, and then that it is almost more important they should do it than that it should be done well. In the next place, even where the governing classes know well what they want and where they suffer, and where the mass of the people are the governing classes, *they are never the governing individuals :* they have to rule and act by deputy'; and their deputies, the moment they step into the arena, forget their constituents in themselves, and the aim, motive, reason of their existence in the exciting details of that existence. And, strange to say, their constituents as often sympathise with them in this forgetfulness as not; and so long as they are allowed to choose the men who are to govern them and look after their interests, they fail to perceive how wretchedly they are governed, and how ill their interests are looked after.

Now, there is one grave matter in our present social condition which ought to receive more attention than, perhaps, any other, yet which, it is scarcely too much to say, actually does receive less, viz., the protection of society from violence and crime. Of late years two remarkable changes have come over us, which it behoves us to signalise and well to understand, if we would not go backward in the main features and the first conditions of civilisation. The relations between the protectors and the assailants of social order have been disturbed, and occasionally almost reversed, and the characters of both crime and punishment have gradually undergone a singular and somewhat analogous alteration. They are branches of one subject, and have a strong mutual bearing on each other; but we shall comprehend them more clearly if we look at them separately in the first instance.

In the first place, then, the turbulent and rebellious, those who seek to violate the law and to set authority at defiance, have become far more daring than of yore, and the agents of law and authority— its " myrmidons," as it is the fashion to style them —have grown (relatively at least) less resolute and efficient. The roughs are both stronger and bolder than the police. They were always, perhaps, the more numerous; but, of late they have become practically the more powerful also. Possibly, it may be, they always were so, if they had only known it or believed it. But the change that has everywhere come over them is this—that whereas formerly they *evaded* justice, they now *defy* it. They used to conceal themselves from the eye and the strong arm of the law; they now set both at naught. They used to *fly;* they now *resist*. Wherever, on recent occasions, order has been assailed by considerable numbers, wherever the mob has come into collision with the authorities or the police, the mob has had the best of it; the defenders of law, and of the Queen's peace, have either been

ludicrously feeble and inadequate, or afraid to act,
or overpowered when they did act.   The outrages
that were committed in open day, in the most fre-
quented streets of London, with absolute impunity,
a year or two ago, on the occasion of the march of
a militia regiment from one end of the metropolis
to the other; the Hyde Park riots; the avowed
retirement of baffled magistrates and police before
the Wigan colliers; the shameful Murphy atrocities
a year ago at Birmingham, and repeated only the
other day at Ashton; the invasion of the Home
Office by Fenian sympathisers not many months
since;—all told the same tale, and taught the same
lesson, a lesson neither party has been slow to learn.
The roughs, as we have said, have everywhere
proved stronger than the police, than that repres-
sive force which society brought to bear upon them;
and the inevitable consequence has been, that the
roughs have grown audacious, the police and the
authorities have grown timid, and both are thoroughly demoralised.

The mischief is terrible, and needs to be rectified
at once, but the explanation is not far to seek.   It
is not that society is weaker, or that malefactors are
really stronger or more numerous than they were;
it is not that, truly and in the last resort, the relative
force of the two parties is in any material degree
changed; it is simply that the arm of the law has
lost its terrors, and that the prestige of authority has
been grievously impaired.   Formerly there existed
low down and deeply rooted in the minds of the turbulent and dangerous classes the consciousness that
Government was too strong for them; that the

orderly and peace-loving and law-abiding elements
of society had something of omniscience and omni-
potence at their command, an overwhelming force
against which it was in vain to strive, and which it
would be well to avoid rousing ; and that signal
punishment would be certain to crush all who set
themselves against it. Therefore, only the desperate
or the fanatical ventured to measure arms with the
recognised delegates of the great Social Will. The
ostensible material forces with which society maintained order and executed its decrees were positively
smaller, and, relatively at least, as inadequate as
now ; but, in the background, there was the vague,
undefined, illimitable *reserved* strength of the nation,
known to be irresistible, and believed to be ready if
there were the least need to call it forth. It would,
of course, be impossible, without an intolerable burden and an utter dislocation of our complicated civilisation, to maintain in every district a police force
physically adequate to cope with the elements of turbulence and disorder which exciting times or sedi-
tious malefactors might array against it. Nor is it
necessary, so long as it is recognised and *felt*, in the
lowest as in the upper ranks, that the police force,
however scanty, is merely the representative of a
might which, though latent, would be absolutely
overwhelming if compelled to show itself. But—
and this is the practical conclusion which we are endeavouring to drive home—if there is no such conviction, if this saving truth be not recognised and
felt, if this salutary and restraining certainty shall
have been weakened and destroyed, either by the
proved incompetence of the authorities to organise

on occasion the needful powers, or by the unwilling-
ness of a parsimonious or suspicious middle class to
entrust them with adequate resources, or by a flabby
and maudlin sentimentality on the part of society
which shrinks from inflicting the indispensable severity of punishment, then the physical and ostensible
force required to defend peace and order must be
everywhere quadrupled.   If the roughs are not
controlled by terror of the law, they will have to be
controlled by actual material weapons, by greater
numbers and superior arms to their own, by
revolvers in the hands of multiplied constables, and
by the sabres and muskets of the military; and
the process will be found a far costlier and more
sanguinary one in the end.   Until the wholesome
dread of punishment, and a conviction of the absolute
certainty of defeat in case of resistance—which are
" the cheap defence of nations "—shall have been re-
established in the minds of the " dangerous classes,"
every mob which ventures to defy the law and its
agents must be dispersed and repressed at any cost
of life or money, and with that prompt and peremptory severity which is the truest and the earliest
mercy.   A few more examples, like those to which
we have adverted, of legitimate authority retiring,
baffled, beaten, timid, and disgraced, before a
triumphant crowd of roughs or insurgent workmen,
and the process by which society will have to be
saved, and its authority to be vindicated, may become something from which even the most resolute
reflecting will shrink back aghast.

   The other change in the character of crime which
we wish to notice is analogous, both in its nature and
its cause, and points to a similar relaxation in the

moral fibre of the national mind.   Heinous crimes
are committed on far slighter provocation and from
far feebler motives than of old.   Resentment for very
small injuries, irritation at very ordinary degrees of
thwarting, desire of very scanty gains, seem sufficient
to bring about the most deliberate murders.   It
would almost appear as if slaying had ceased in the
eyes of thousands to be a serious matter at all.   Men
assassinate now to revenge a wrong, or to express an
anger, which formerly would have at most been held
to warrant a blow.   Two recent illustrations recur
to the memory at once.   Three or four weeks ago a
railway porter coolly shot the station-master in his
own office, simply because the station-master had
rebuked and threatened to report him for some
neglect of duty.   The superintendent was murdered
for doing what it was right and necessary he should
do, and what every employer of labour is forced to
do, and does, as a matter of course, every day.
Again, a couple of months previous, a handicrafts-
man at Todmorden, not of bad character, and by no
means without education, with circumstances of
revolting brutality killed his clergyman, the clergy
man's maid-servant, and his wife, who had just been
confined, and whose death involved that of her infant.
The offence which these four murders were committed to avenge was simply that the clergyman had
refused the murderer permission to "keep company"
with a young girl in his service, on the fair plea of
her extreme youth.   The murderer was not deprived
wholly of opportunities of seeing her, and was able to
correspond with her freely; he was merely required
to wait, and was forbidden to visit on the footing of
an accepted lover.   The master, here again, had

done nothing but his duty—nothing more than masters and mistresses do every day; the assassin had encountered nothing beyond a very common disappointment; yet he brooded over the offence, and considered himself so deeply wronged that wholesale bloodshed seemed not at all too severe a retaliation on all concerned. Death, in his estimation, was not a disproportionate penalty for having opposed his wishes.

Now, in the whole of this class of cases, the phenomenon which should arrest attention is not that the impulse to crime should have been felt, but that it should have been yielded to. There are always scattered through society a number of unregulated tempers, whose egotism is so extravagant and morbid, that the least obstacle to their desires, or the least scratch to their *amour-propre*, assumes the dimensions of the sin against the Holy Ghost—an offence " for which there is no forgiveness, neither in this world, neither in that which is to come." There are also, and always have been, thousands of men, weak in intellect, strong in passions, dull in feeling, and of brutal instincts, whom cruelty and violence attract rather than repel, and to whom crime of any sort comes easy when there are no retributive terrors in the background. But in ordinary times, and in well-governed communities, both these classes are withheld from yielding to their impulses of anger or vengeance by the certainty and the fear of punishment. The consideration of consequences comes in aid of the feeble reflective powers they may possess ; or the rag of conscience or compassion which may be left to them, turns the balance against crime, saves them from going over the precipice, and prevents the volition ripening into the deed. They will obey the impulse, if they can do it with impunity ; they will resist it, if they know that punishment, and condign punishment, will follow.   The motive may be small and the temptation may be languid, but they will be sufficient, provided the dread or the belief in retribution be weak also. And herein lies the explanation. The whole course of facts, the whole set of manifestations of public feeling, of late years have tended to generate, and could not fail to generate, in the minds both of actual and of potential criminals—of that class, we mean, who are ever trembling on the brink of crime, and need to have an opposing weight thrown into the right scale—the conviction that impunity is probable; nay, that escape—escape at least from the punishment of death—is so probable as to come encouragingly near to certainty.   Formerly the difficulty was to save any criminal from the gallows; now the difficulty is to get the worst criminal hanged.   Crime grows insolent as justice grows tender, and for some time back we have shrunk from the infliction of all those penalties which criminals most dread.   Society has selected as its favourite punishments (which are simply its weapons of self-defence) those which itself dislikes least, instead of those which its enemies dislike most.   Ruffians are peculiarly averse to being hanged or flogged, and are most effectually deterred from brutal violence by the fear of these results ; but unluckily society is peculiarly averse to them also, and society considers its feelings in preference to its safety. Murderers have a thousand chances of escape—so many chances that the law has almost lost its terrors.   Either the evidence is inadequate for a feeble-minded jury, or some subsequent doubt as to the completeness of the proof arises in the public mind, and is urged passionately on the Home Secretary; or extenuating circumstances are discovered or imagined ; or that class of fanatics who object altogether to capital punishment, even for capital crimes, put all their machinery in operation to rescue the criminal and to foster the crime. Brutal ruffians may not reason closely, or observe the public mind minutely, or calculate averages accurately, but the general impression made upon them is precisely the same as if they did. They see that a great part of the nation—and far the most active part—practically hate hanging more than they hate murder ; and they are vaguely but undoubtingly conscious of the fearful fact which was some months ago announced on the authority of Blue-books, and which, in conclusion, we will repeat by way of clenching our argument. The figures relate to 1866 :

Indictable offences committed,	50,000
Persons apprehended for ditto,	27,000
Sent to trial for ditto,	19,000
Convicted,	14,700

It is believed, moreover, that on the average nine out of ten offences committed escape detection altogether. The statistics of murder are still more agreeable— to murderers :

Verdicts of murder by coroner's juries,	272
Murders reported by police,	131
Persons apprehended for these,	124
Committed for trial,	94
Actually tried for murder,	55
Found guilty,	26
Hanged,	12

That is, not one person hanged for every ten murders undeniably committed, and not one in five found guilty.

V.

TRADE Unions, having been for the last three years a subject for general discussion, will probably soon become a subject for legislation likewise. The sittings of the commission of investigation, and the astounding revelations which it brought to light, are still fresh in our memory, and it will be long indeed before they can be forgotten. But it is of the last importance that the indignation and horror which has been aroused in the public mind by the appalling disclosures at Sheffield and elsewhere, should not be misdirected, and wasted in consequence of misdirection. There has been a somewhat general, and by no means an unnatural, inclination on the part of the press to regard the outrages that have so shocked and scandalised us all as peculiar to Sheffield in their essence as well as in their atrocity ; and trade unions throughout the country are eager to favour this impression, to disclaim any connexion on their part with any similar proceedings, and to separate themselves in the clearest manner, as far as words can do so, from the slightest sympathy with or participation in principles and doctrines which could probably or logically lead to such startling results. It is to prevent the public mind from being led away from the realities of the case to any false issues of the sort, that it is essential to go to the heart of the question. We must not forget that the inquiry which has led to these disclosures, was instituted in consequence of a demand from the trade unions authorities in the very town which was the scene of the chief outrages, and in order to vindicate themselves from the suspicion of being the authors of them or connected with them; that Broadhead, the master ruffian of the band and the instigator of all these crimes, joined conspicuously and coolly in the demand for the commission; that he even offered a reward for the discovery of the assassins whom he himself had hired; that he had been for many years the most trusted and powerful official of the most notorious of the trade unions of Sheffield; and that after these outrages had begun to excite public suspicion and disgust, he was appointed treasurer to the National Association of Trades Unions, numbering 60,000 members.

There can be no doubt whatever that the vast majority of these associations—their officers as well as their members—are wholly incapable of such outrages as have come to light at Sheffield, and would be as much shocked as any of us at being even remotely mixed up with them. It is probable that even at Sheffield most of the workmen who knew, or never doubted, that such things were done, and were done in the interests of their respective trades, would yet have shrunk from deliberate murder or arson, and may now be horrified when they see in what excesses the minor violences which they were cognisant of and sanctioned were nearly sure to culminate. It may be true, moreover—indeed, I believe it is true—that the unionists of Sheffield, and the artizans there generally, are too ready to proceed, and have habitually proceeded, to extremities of violence which have become rare or obsolete elsewhere, and which artizans generally throughout the country would indignantly repudiate. But it is important we should realise that Sheffield, if abnormal in these matters, is abnormal only *in degree;* that trade outrages there may have been more daring, more numerous, more systematic, and more brutal than in other places, and may have been continued to a later date, but that wherever trade unions have been rampant, powerful, and well-organised, the same results have followed ; that acts of violence directed by them and committed in their interests have been frequent and habitual, and have at last culminated in deliberate assassination, planned and executed in furtherance of the objects of those associations.

It is needful also—and it is here only that I expect to find·myself at issue either with journalists or other friends of the operative classes—that the purposes for which these combinations of workmen were originally formed, or at least to which they are now directed, are *essentially* injurious and unjust ; that they are hostile to the interests of the community at large as well as to those of the artizans themselves ; and (what is more to the present purpose) that the objects they have in view *can, from their very nature, only be secured by proceedings intrinsically illegal and oppressive*, commencing by

intimidation and "social pressure," practically and
naturally advancing to assault and battery, vitriol-
throwing, blinding, maiming ("laming," as it is
technically termed), and logically and actually leading up to murder, whenever the parties are sufficiently bent upon their ends and sufficiently exasperated in their feelings to *insist* upon success.

Perhaps the most startling feature of the Sheffield
disclosures is, not the *business-like* character of the
assassination and blowing-up system ; nor even the
number of the band—six at least were named and
proved—who were ready for their hideous work ;
nor their anxiety to "get the job;" nor their willing-
ness to "lame" or shoot men against whom they
had no spite, and whom they scarcely knew person-
ally, for a few pounds—but the *autocratic* coolness
of the secretary, pondering what it would be well to
do—*i.e.*, who should be slain or mutilated—for "the
good of the trade," or for the "salvation" of the
union.   Once appointed, his employers took care to
know as little as possible of the details of his pro
ceedings; he evidently regarded himself, and was
regarded by them, as a kind of dictator, whose business it was to see *ne quid detrimenti respublica
caperet :*—that was his sole rule of action, and he sat
thinking how it would be best carried out, who was
contravening the rules of the trade, and whose
"job" had better be done first.   The same feature
is recognisable in every case of union outrages
where the facts have been made public.   The
secretary or chairman, or more usually a small and
secret committee, sit to do the best they can for the
interests of their body, and the sense of combined

H

secrecy, power, and responsibility seems to turn
their heads ; they feel like a sort of providence to
whom is committed a great cause with ample means
for ensuring success, and the perception of right and
wrong ; the very notion of *crime* seems to die out of
their minds.   Those who wish to satisfy themselves
on this head, and to find ample confirmation of the
above remarks, will do well to study the first and
second reports of a select committee of the House
of Commons on combinations of workmen, which
sat in 1838, with Mr O'Connell in the chair.   It
originated, I believe, in the feeling excited by a
deliberate murder committed during a long strike
by the cotton-spinners of Glasgow ; and the evidence taken contains full details not only·of that
murder, but of a host of minor outrages all issuing
from the same source and directed to the same
object.   In the same Blue-books are many analogous
and equally atrocious cases connected with the
Dublin trades ; and the murder of Mr Ashton,
during a strike at Hyde in Cheshire, in 1830, is
another precisely similar instance, which many of us
have too good reason to remember.   Thus Lancashire, Lanarkshire, and Dublin, as well as Sheffield,
have had their calendar of blood, and the details in
all the cases are shockingly similar.   The evidence,
especially, of the then Sheriff of Lanarkshire, Sir
Archibald Alison—who, though a deplorably inaccurate historian and economist, was a good officer
and lawyer—throws great light upon the practice of
suborning and concealing crime then in vogue at
Glasgow, as well as upon the extent to which crime
was carried.   A man was shot by order in·1825,

and died; another murder of the same sort was attempted in 1827; a third successful one in 1837. The evidence relating to Dublin, and particularly to the Builders' and Sawyers' Trades Association, is almost all of the same sort; the actual murders are only one or two, but severe beatings, many of which might well have ended in death, are almost countless. It is true that these atrocities all date thirty or forty years back, whereas those at Sheffield belong to yesterday. But this is really about the only difference between the cases.

The avowed aims and recognised modes of operation of trade unions are to raise and maintain the rate of wages; to prevent or diminish competition, as far as practicable, among workmen; in their respective trades to make labour dear by making labour scarce; to limit the amount of work done by each artizan, and the number of artizans who are to do the work. The practical means employed to effect these objects are equally well known and are almost as frankly admitted, though the terms in use to veil and euphonise the plain truth may be somewhat varied. They are "persuasion" first, argument, "social pressure"—a rather comprehensive term; then menaces; lastly, personal violence where persuasion and intimidation fail of success. The moment personal violence of any sort or in any measure is recognised—and it is notorious that there are scarcely any trades in which it has not been, and but few in which it is not still, resorted to and regarded as more or less legitimate—the extent to which it may be carried, and the form it may assume, become mere matters of degree, varying according to ·the

exigencies of the case and the exasperated feelings
of those engaged.   It is first "rattening," "picket-
ing," hooting, and the like; then beating or "laming;"
then blowing up ; then murder.   In saying this I do
not go one step beyond the facts as established by
‛evidence before the Sheffield and other Commissions,
and as almost, if not quite, admitted by the parties
themselves and their advocates.   The murder is, of
course never contemplated in *the outset*, nor the
blowing up, nor always even the beating; but the
" social pressure" and the intimidation are; and
what I wish to point out is, that the rest follow
naturally, logically, and almost of necessity, as the
plot thickens, as the drama is evolved, as difficulties
grow more obstinate and serious, and as men's
passions become excited in the conflict.

I say nothing here as to the beneficence or legiti-
macy of the objects aimed at.   All I seek to show
is that, as they *can* only be secured by, and as, in
fact, they depend upon and consist in, acts of coercion
exercised over the free will and free action of other
men, whose interests or wishes are in opposition
to those of their coercers, they necessarily *involve*
oppression, and *must* be carried out by force, or the
threat of force—by punishment, or the fear of punishment.   When this is clear, the whole argument is
irresistible and conclusive ; for force exercised or
menaced by a tribunal which has no legal authority
must be secret, irresponsible, and certain to degenerate into excesses.   The trade unions, or the trade
union official, or the " system," which begins by
imposing its will upon recalcitrant or intrusive workmen, by intimidation or by " rattening," is certain to

proceed to beating and laming, and can never say that it will not proceed to assassination where the case requires strong measures. If it is to succeed, it must proportion its penalties to the gravity of the occasion and the obstinacy of the offenders. It is sure, and indeed is almost compelled by the necessity of the case and the obligation of triumphing, to adopt measures at last from which it would have recoiled horror-struck at first. The moment coercion is recognised—and coercion lies at the very basis of the system—acts of violence proceed *gradatim* and *crescendo*, and neither union nor committee, nor even secretary, can say to themselves or to their tools, "Thus far shalt thou go, and no farther."

Every one of the details of the objects of these unions *implies* pressure and coercion, as may be seen by taking the three most ordinary cases that union interference assumes. They are all, *in their nature and essence*, distinct acts of violence and oppression. The first and simplest is, where a more than usually skilful and diligent workman, who could easily earn 5s. a-day, is forbidden to earn more than 4s. He is robbed of the odd shilling; nay, more, he has to pay probably 3s. or 4s. a week to the organisation that thus robs him, and for the benefit of inferior or less energetic artizans in whose fancied interest he is thus mulcted. If he is a young man who seeks to rise, or a burdened man with a wife and family whose comfort depends upon his earnings, he naturally objects to and resents this iniquitous and foolish oppression. Perhaps he resists it, and refuses to submit, in which case he is "rattened," or otherwise molested, or turned out of the union; and if he be obstinate he is threatened, and the threats in due time are executed.   The unjust regulation against which he kicks can only be upheld by coercion, and by coercion which in case of contumacy leads to violence, and is idle and ineffectual unless it does.

The next case is that of men who refuse to belong to the union, who do not wish to submit to its dictation, and do not choose to waste their hard earnings by subscribing to its funds.   The unionists refuse to work in the same shop or at the same job with these " free lances ; " they give notice to their employers that they will strike unless these men are dismissed ; and their threat is too often effectual ; they deprive them of their bread because they will not consent to join an organisation of which they disapprove, or they force them into it by intimidation.   Is not this coercion ?   And if violence of some sort, or the dread of such,—a dread which must be kept alive by occasional examples,—were not employed to enforce this coercion, it could not succeed ; the most skilful and the most independent men would be all non-unionists, and the union would fall into powerlessness and contempt.

The third and most common case is where workmen—non-unionists—take work under a master against whom unionists have struck, or for wages which unionists have refused ; and when, in consequence, these workmen ("knobsticks," as they are termed) are watched, threatened, " picketed," beaten, or blinded by vitriol, or sometimes shot if they persist in their intrusion.   This is the form the action of trade unions has most commonly assumed in the

cotton districts, and a distincter case of interference
to prevent men doing what they will with their own
cannot be conceived. The men are poor, sometimes
almost starving ; they are willing and anxious to
work for the wages offered ; their wives and children
are clamorous for them to accept the employment
placed within their reach. Of course, therefore,
they do so, or would do so but for the influence
of terror—that is, the well-grounded anticipation of
personal injury. If that terror were not produced,
and that injury threatened or inflicted, the trade
unions would in most cases be set at defiance and
would be unable to attain their ends. But the mills
are picketed, the "knobsticks" are watched to and
from their work in dark winter days, and too often
the unhappy men have been compelled to succumb,
not from dread of the violence that has been offered
to themselves, but in consequence of outrages perpetrated on their defenceless families while they
were out at work.

Now, in all these instances the unionists rely
upon intimidation to procure obedience to their
commands, and could procure it in no other way,
for the simple reason that these commands are
onerous and injurious to those on whom they are
enforced, and are tyrannical interferences with their
legitimate free action. Intimidation means violence,
or the threat of violence ; and the threat, we all
know, would do nothing without the perfectly understood reality behind it. Therefore, I say that the
power of trade unions is not only directed to illegitimate and oppressive objects, but is upheld by
violence, and can be upheld in no other way. It is

idle to deny or disguise the fact; it is an insult to
our knowledge and our understandings to talk of
restricting the interference of such organisations to
"moral suasion;" we know that it never stops there,
and would be laughed at if it did; and we see every
day instances of the extent to which the sense of
crime and wrong dies out of the minds of both
instruments and leaders, who soon learn to consider
their "trade" as sacred as their country, and to
regard everything done for it as hallowed and
warranted by the importance of "the cause." Unless, then, I am wrong both in my facts and my
reasoning, the very existence of trade unions, as
they have been and as they are, signifies and is
the pursuit of objects which justice and morality
never prompted, by means which they can never
sanction.

Thus much for the intrinsic culpability of these
associations. Their intrinsic mischief is the next
point to consider.

The objects which the trade unions have in view
are hostile to the interests of the community, and in
the end injurious to the work-people themselves;
and one collateral proof of this is that, as I have
shown, these objects are pursued, and can only be
successfully pursued, by breaking the laws of the
community, and by oppressing and coercing individual workmen. Of course, in speaking thus I
have reference to trade unions properly so-called,
and not to those few and simple associations which
confine themselves to assisting their members when
ill, or in distress, or casually and involuntarily out of
work, and which are in truth sick clubs and mutual

insurance societies, rather than trade unions properly so called.

The objects which ordinary trade unions propose to themselves, and which, as we have seen, they pursue with singular directness and determination, are to raise and maintain the rate of wages in their respective trades, by preventing any one from accepting less than the established scale, or by restricting the amount of work done by each individual, and the number of individuals competent or allowed to do it. They effect this latter object in two ways: they limit the number of apprentices allowed to be taught, and they discourage and prevent the competition of outsiders. Now, the first point that is obvious—and nearly everything I have to say in this matter is obvious, and does not require proving or arguing, but only *stating*, in order to make its character and bearing clear—the first point that is obvious is, that by this means the quantity of every article produced is diminished, and the cost of producing it is enhanced. Things are made scarcer and dearer, and the community is injured in two ways: fewer people can purchase the article or purchase enough of it, and those who do purchase it have to pay more for it than they otherwise need have done. In the case of saws, or fenders, or such similar articles as are made at Sheffield, the effect is not very perceptible, but there are three cases in which most persons feel the operation of the proceedings on which we are commenting, and suffer from them. The rent of houses, the price of books, and the cost of coals are all greatly increased by the trades unions respectively concerned. In all the building trades—masons, bricklayers, sawyers, and carpenters—these organisations are peculiarly strict and powerful, and probably add indirectly ten or twenty per cent. to every poor man's rent. The same may be said, though in a less degree, of paper-makers, printers, and binders. But the case of the colliers is perhaps the strongest and the clearest. Few of us have any idea, or get anything beyond occasional glimpses, of the degree in which the supply of coal is curtailed, and its price enhanced, and the comfort and health of every poor man thus interfered with, by the colliers' unions, which enable them often to work only three or four days a week, to fix the maximum quantity of coal which shall be raised, and to keep willing outsiders away from the field of action ; but probably it would be no ex-aggeration to say that were every miner free, and every collier employed and allowed to work as long and as regularly as he pleased, and were he to work full hours whenever he was not drunk, the price of coal might in many places be reduced nearly one-half.*

The second point to be noticed is, that this en-

---

* Mr M'Donald, President of the Miners' National Associa-tion, in January last, at a meeting of delegates of Scottish miners, told his hearers that their combination "had in nine months obtained for them £544,000 increase of wages" (of course mainly out of the price of coal), and *recommended them to* "*keep down the stock of coal* as the best means of keeping up wages." In the same number of the *Times* (January 5, 1867) which contains this paragraph is the report of a speech by the Recorder of New-castle in reference to a miners' strike which had recently termi-nated. That gentleman stated that, assisted by various unions, 10,000 or 12,000 men had been kept on strike for a long period, and at a clear loss of wages of £300,000.

hancement of the cost of articles not only greatly reduces the amount of necessaries and comforts which can be purchased by the family income,—a reduction which, of course, the labouring man feels more keenly than any one else,—but menaces the national prosperity, and bids fair to transfer to other countries that industrial supremacy of which England has so long been proud, and from which so large a portion of her strength and influence is derived. We have heard something of late of the danger to which we are exposed in respect to the iron trade from foreign competition, and it is beginning to be whispered that even in cutlery our superiority is no longer unquestioned ; but whatever may be said as to these particular instances (into which I will not enter, because I am anxious to state only what is undeniable and admitted), one thing is certain, viz., that every trade union, whether among colliers, iron-miners, iron-workers, machine-makers, builders, railway engineers and drivers, or ship-wrights, adds its percentage—often a large one—to the natural cost of production of every article we fabricate and export, and by so doing is enabling other nations to meet us and to beat us in neutral markets, and sometimes even in our own, and is thus steadily sapping that supremacy in the industrial arts on which the members of those trade unions depend for the bread they eat, the comforts they enjoy, and the position they abuse.

The third point, as to the admission of which there can be no demur, but the importance of which has never been realised or *calculated out*, is that though trade unions may, and probably do, raise the *rate of wages*, it is by no means clear that they raise the aggregate *earnings* of the workmen, and it is absolutely certain that these earnings are subject to deductions for the maintenance of trade unions whose total amount would astonish and appal the payers were they to be added up.   The contributions levied by more or less compulsion and " social pressure "—often, as we now learn, by actual outrage—on the members of the union, range from five to twenty per cent. on their weekly earnings ; and how much of these contributions is expended in " strikes," in payments to officers, in the hiring of bravoes, and in the maintenance in idleness—*i.e.*, the buying-off—of competing applicants for employment, we shall never know with accuracy.   But every now and then a few facts leak out, which give us a glimpse of what the truth may be.   We know that unemployed workmen will constantly apply for work, and will accept work in all trades at lower wages than those prevalent, unless frightened away or bought off, and that the means resorted to are usually a mixture of these two systems.   We are told that in the case of one of the most notorious unions at Sheffield, the rate of wages has only been kept up at the cost of maintaining " on the box," *one-third* of the whole number of those engaged in the trade— *i.e.*, paying them for being idle.   In the case of the colliers, many thousands of unemployed men are thus permanently supported on the earnings of the employed, in order to prevent them from competing, and I am informed on very high authority—indeed, I believe the fact is quite notorious—that in several cases the contributors to this " buying off " fund are

miners who themselves will only work four days a
week, and are habitually drunk the other three.
Again, some months ago the *Economist* published
some very careful, and apparently moderate, calculations of the cost of "strikes," as compared with
their achievements even when successful, showing
that in nearly every case the loss of earnings to the
operatives by the time they were on strike, added
to the contributions levied upon them for the purpose of enabling them to strike, came to a sum
which it would require many years of the enhanced
rate of wages to make good.*   And this was in the

* We append these calculations in a note, in order not to in-
terrupt the current of our argument.

"We now wish to call attention to another invariable circumstance connected with strikes, which, though not so often or
so completely forgotten, has, perhaps, seldom, if ever, due weight
attached to it.   It is this :—there is great reason to doubt
whether. strikes—except in the rarest cases—ever raise the
aggregate or average *earnings* of the artizans concerned, even when
they succeed in raising or maintaintng the *rate* of wages.   It is by
no means certain that they do not, usually, and, in the end,
actually, depress both wages and earnings.   Our impression is,
that they do.

" The point that we wish to enforce admits of being stated in
very short compass, and will be all the clearer for being thus
briefly and roundly stated.   During strikes there is an entire
cessation of earnings, and as artizans, as a rule, have no savings
of their own, but habitually live from hand to mouth, strikes, it is
clear, could not be maintained for more than a week or two, unless
funds were provided beforehand for supporting the workmen,
tant bien que mal, while out on strike.   These funds, of course,
must be provided, and, as we know, are, in fact, provided by
regular weekly contributions or deductions from the earnings of
the labourers while in full employment.   These weekly contributions constitute a large and perpetual tax on the income of the
artizans—a tax varying with the trade and the time, but always
serious, and sometimes heavy.   We have no means of knowing

case—comparatively rare—of successful strikes. When they fail, of course the loss is total, uncompensated, and often frightful.

the proportion it bears to their earnings, but there is reason to believe that it often reaches 5 per cent., and occasionally 10 per cent. It is needed, too, in many instances—as should never be lost sight of—not only for the purpose of supporting workmen when on strike, but for paying the salaries of their leaders and emissaries, and the ordinary and extraordinary expenses of the organisation, and occasionally also for the more illegitimate purpose of maintaining in idleness supernumerary or redundant workmen who would otherwise (it is feared) compete with the contributors and unionists for employment, and lower wages by such competition.

" It is obvious, therefore, that the workmen's contributions to the trades unions funds must often be heavy. Assuming that in trades where strikes are contemplated or are probable, they reach usually 1s. in the pound, they virtually reduce the earnings of the artizans to that extent. Now, do strikes usually or ultimately raise or keep up wages to that extent ? Let the matter be looked at by the light of concrete figures. Take the case, *first*, of a successful strike—a strike (say) for an advance or against a reduction of 10 per cent., where the average wages are 30s. a week—an unusually advantageous supposition. The strike lasts two months, we will say. The workman gains ten months' earnings at 30s. a week instead of twelve months' earnings at 27s.,—or £66, instead of £70, 4s.—*i.e.*, he is a loser on the year of four guineas. But to gain this loss he has contributed for ten months 1s. 6d. a week, or £3, 6s., and he has received from the union funds during the two months he is on strike (say) 5s. a week, or £2. His total *loss* is, therefore, £5, 10s. on a balance of the whole transaction.

" 'Take the case, *secondly*, of a still more successful strike, a strike in which eight weeks' abstinence from work secures a 10 per cent. advance of wages for *two* years. The two years' contributions amount to £7, 4s., and eight weeks' receipts from the fund amount to £2, showing a loss of £5, 4s. But against this he has to set ninety-six weeks' wages at 30s., instead of 104 weeks' wages at 27s., or £144 instead of £140, 8s. In a word, he has gained in the two years £3, 12s.,

When, therefore, we sum up the matter, and consider, first, the degree to which the cost of every
article, and thereby the cost of living in the aggre-

and lost £5, 4s., showing a net loss on the transaction of 32s.   If
these calculations are correct, it would appear that even an abnormally successful strike does not pay ; and our impression (derived
from considerable experience, but, we admit, without figures at
hand to prove it) is, that strikes which extort a 10 per cent.
advance are seldom so short as two months, and that it rarely
happens that an advance thus gained is maintained unbroken for
two years.   It will generally be found that a slack trade, or a commercial crisis, or a war, or some equivalent occurrence, enable the
employer to take back the whole or part of the advance in some
shape or other, before two years are out, and that the advance has
been the indirect cause of short time.   Add to this that strikes
often last sixteen or twenty weeks, instead of eight—we have just
seen the end of one that lasted nineteen weeks—and that the
means of maintaining a vigorous and obstinate strike nearly
always require that the workman should continue his contributions, not for one year nor for two, but for several—perhaps for
all his career—and it will scarcely be held that we have stated
the conditions of the problem unfairly *against* the trades union
view of it.

"There is another very grave consideration to come in here,
on which we only wish to throw out a suggestion, and not to
dogmatise.   In how many of the cases of *successful* strikes would
not the desired advance have been obtained with equal certainty,
even if, *perhaps*, somewhat more slowly and somewhat less decidedly, without either strikes or trades unions, by the simple
operation of masters in times of brisk trade competing with each
other for an inadequate supply of workmen?   Is it not probable,
to say the least, that where the number of labourers is insufficient
to meet the wants of the special industry in question, wages must
and will rise without adventitious aid from combinations?   And
is it not more than probable—is it not certain—that where the
number of workmen is redundant, *i.e.*, beyond the wants of the
trade, no combinations and no strikes can *permanently* raise wages
or prevent them from falling, and that if they do this for a time,
they do it illegitimately, and they do it at the cost of an augmented subsequent collapse?

gate, is increased by the operation of trade unions ;
secondly, the diminished demand for labourers consequent upon the limitation of the consumption of
the article they produce caused by the enhancement
of its price ; thirdly, the heavy tax levied in the
form of contributions " to the box " on the earnings
of the artizans ; and fourthly, the encouragement
thus given to foreign competition, whereby the
demand for British productions, and for the labour
of the British workmen, is reduced and endangered
—is it not as certain and as plain as anything can
be, that trade unions are a miscalculation and a
gigantic blunder, looked at even from an artizan

" But passing by these suggested considerations for a while—
or, rather, relegating them for the private rumination of unionist
operatives—take the case, *thirdly*, of an *un*successful strike of
eight weeks' duration, in the trade and under the circumstances
above referred to.   In such a case, the loss of the operative on
the year by the transaction will be eight weeks at 27s., or £10,
16s., *plus* his year's contribution to the union funds, or £3, 6s.,
and *minus* his pittance of 5s. a week while on strike, or a balance
of £12, 2s. against him.   By the same calculation, his loss on *two*
years would be £16.

" Now, we do not put forward these calculations *ex cathedrâ* as
conclusive and unassailable.   It is possible they may be open to
cavil and correction in some particulars.   We only put them
forward as specimens of the sort of calculations which workmen
meditating, or honest leaders advising, a strike ought to make for
themselves, and may make with much more full and precise data
than we can pretend to possess,   It might also not be quite irrelevant were they to endeavour to estimate some of the more
indirect expenses incident to strikes, such as the ultimate cost of
debt incurred, and of credit from shopkeepers (which is, ultimately, taken out in the quality or price of the article supplied),
of goods pawned, and the like.   But these are points on which
we can offer nothing but the vaguest hints, real and important as
they indisputably are."

point of view; and that, on the whole, a more grievous folly never was maintained at a more deplorable cost, or by means more utterly condemnable—alike in defiance of sound economic principles and of the simplest dictates of morality ?

How to meet the case is a question on which I do not wish to enter. No one would wish to re-enact the combination laws, or to prohibit associations of workmen for all legal, recognised, and avowable objects. It is notoriously difficult, if not impossible, to prevent intimidation, or to protect effectually the intimidated ; and this fact gives great cogency to the arguments of those who plead, that *therefore* we ought to denounce and place beyond the sanction of the law organisations that are pretty sure to operate through intimidation, and notoriously *can* operate successfully in no other way. Public opinion and recent disclosures will do much : unionist committees and officials and members will be shocked when they see their deeds put in plain words, and reflected in other eyes ; education and discussion will do something to show the workmen how ruinously costly the system is and must be to themselves, but the first and most essential thing to be done is so to improve the detective keenness, the omnipresent force, and the retributive severity of the law and its instruments as to make violence, coercion, and menace a difficult business and a losing game. When trade unions can no longer compel or coerce, they will cease to be effectual, or to be worth maintaining, and will either die out or be restricted to legitimate and beneficent aims.

"Ought there, then," it will be asked, "to be no

I

trade unions, no organised combinations to raise wages and regulate modes of working ? " I certainly would not forbid them, but as certainly I believe that they never can do good, and must always do harm. If there is a deficiency of hands in any trade, wages will rise naturally, and no master can prevent it. If there is a redundancy of hands, wages ought to fall, and trade unions can obviously only prevent them from falling by supporting the excess of work-men in idleness at the cost of the others (which of course renders the apparent increase of wages a mere delusion), or by driving them out of the trade, which can rarely, if ever, be effected without menace or coercion. On the other hand, trade unions must, by the very nature of their operations, if successful, increase the cost of the article produced, and there-fore limit the consumption of it, and therefore diminish *pro tanto* the number of workmen that might be employed in producing it. They must curtail the demand for labour at the very time they are striving to enhance its remuneration. Thus they fight against the clearest economic laws, and undo with one hand what they endeavour to do with the other.

The above line of argument has been impugned by two controversialists, who, however, I do not think have succeeded in weakening its cogency. One of them, Mr Morley, adopts and repeats the fallacy, or rather the oversight, which trade unionists all hug to their hearts, which lies, in fact, at the very root of their ideas and their system, and which probably can never be completely extirpated or rectified so long as clever men like Mr Morley can

be found to aid the delusion they ought to dissipate.
He admits that trade unions do enhance the price
of production and the cost of living generally, but
he argues that the producers gain more than the
consumers lose. " The restrictions imposed by the
unions check production, it is true. So far their
operation is injurious. They limit the quantity of
enjoyable things in the world, which by itself is a
misfortune. They lessen the purchasing power of
money. But then—and this is the important point
—they increase the amount of money received by
the artizan in a greater proportion than that in
which they lessen its purchasing power. The
artisan pays more for his articles, but the increase
in his wages much more than covers the difference
between the new prices and the old. The evil of
the enhancement of cost is spread over a very large
surface—the whole community. The boon of the
rise of wages is concentrated upon the wage-receiv-
ing part of the community. . . . And I maintain,
in spite of arguments which your correspondent
somewhat too serenely pronounces self-evident,
that a process which increases my income by, say,
ten per cent., and at the same time only makes me
pay, say, two per cent. more for the things which I
want to buy, is very distinctly a process to my
advantage." Here is the old fallacy of the corn-
law advocates reproduced in all its naked selfishness and shallowness on behalf of those in whose
name, and on whose just demand, the corn-laws were
repealed. The producers are the men to be considered and protected; the consumers may go to
the wall. Let every trade be fenced round and

fostered as far as may be, and then all workmen will be well off; and when all the working classes are well off, what more can we desire ?

The oversight which lies at the root of this fallacy, which vitiates it as a plea, and the exposition of which disperses it at once, is that Mr Morley and his clients forget that all labouring men are consumers as well as producers, and that every producer must in fairness allow to every other that enhancement of the price of *his* article which he claims for himself.

Let us take the first case that comes to hand. The bricklayer, say, by his union, contrives to raise his *rate* of wages (not, observe, his real net aggregate *earnings*) 10 per cent., and only raises the price of his house 1 per cent. But the brickmaker has his union as well as the bricklayer; so has the mason, so has the plasterer, so has the carpenter, sawyer, painter, and glazier, and each adds a decimal or two to the cost of house rent till the many decimals soon mount up to an integer or two. But the bricklayer, when he has got into his dearer house, and is paying perhaps 2d. a week more than he need otherwise have done, or is crowded into unwholesome quarters, must buy clothes, and the tailors' union (to say nothing of the clothiers and the dyers) levies its small tax on the coat of the man and the cotton and linen gar-ments of his wife and children. Then he must have shoes, a hat or two ; and the enhancements come in here also, for both hatters and shoemakers have or might have unions. Printers have unions, and so have paper-makers ; so his newspaper or his book costs him a trifle more in consequence. Colliers, too, manage to curtail the supply of coal, and railway drivers help to increase the cost of transit, and the

two between them, though Mr Morley cannot conceive how, do manage to make the bricklayer pay a
few additional shillings per annum for his fires. All
this, however, may, it is argued, not amount to anything very serious in the aggregate, for happily food
is free ; there are no trade unions among graziers or
ploughmen or agricultural labourers, and we have
forbidden landowners to fence themselves round with
the sort of protection which trade unionists claim and
enforce for their respective crafts.   " Thank God for
that ! " exclaim Mr Morley and the combined bricklayers and builders.   But where is the justice of
making the poor tiller of the soil pay the increased
price for his coal and his house and his clothes, and
refusing to let him charge you a corresponding increase of price, brought about by similar restrictions,
for the wheat and the bacon or meat which he grows
for you ?   And if this increased price were put upon
food, and all the artizan consumers of food were
forced to pay it, what an outcry we should have from
all the trades, and how much of their boasted 10
per cent. rise of wages would remain to the fore ?

But the other part of the truth still remains.   The
rate of wages, as I said, may be raised, but not necessarily nor nearly so much, if at all, the net earnings.
There are the expenses of the union officers; there
are men to be supported during strikes; there are
competitors to be maintained in idleness ; and all
these things make a formidable item *per contra*, and
often raise the contributions of members to a height
which perhaps Mr Morley is not aware of.

And this is my reply to the criticisms of another
adversary, " A Consumer," who says that " if trade
unions do really raise the rate of wages," my reason-

ing falls to the ground, and I have admitted the whole case of the men. Not so; I do not myself believe that trade unions do in the long run raise even the *rate* of wages beyond the limit they would attain from the natural increase of demand for labourers consequent upon the thriving state of each special trade. I believe that, as a rule, any advance obtained by union action is usually lost as soon as trade grows slack. I have little doubt, moreover, that in the end the action of unions actually tends to *depress* the rate of wages by reducing the demand for the article produced. But of course it is impossible to prove this, especially to working men, who can seldom be expected to look beyond the immediate effect of their proceedings. But if, as I am nearly certain (though here again, positive proof, exact calculations, are impracticable), the *net* average earnings of the individual workman are not increased, and if, as I feel quite confident, the *aggregate* earnings of the whole body of artizans of each class are not increased, then the working men are not gainers by the unions, and my arguments remain untouched. Now, my position is, that even if the unions do increase the *rate of wages*, and yet (as I maintain) do not increase the *net earnings* of the workmen, they do them a balance of mischief; *they succeed in raising the price of the article they buy, and fail in raising the price of the article they sell.*

"A Consumer" may say "these are generalities." So they are; but I apprehend they are sound ones; and close proofs, such as can be set down in figures and balance-sheets, are unattainable by us outsiders, though if working men kept detailed accounts of revenue and expenditure for eight or ten years, they might solve the problem.

VI.

INDUSTRIAL AND CO-OPERATIVE PARTNERSHIPS.

THE publication of the report of the Royal Commission on Trades Unions has once more recalled public attention to this subject, than which scarcely any one is more important or more urgent. Never, probably, since the days of the great Poor Law Inquiry, has any Commission issued by the Crown done its work so thoroughly, or paved the way for so much practical good. The facts it has brought to light, both criminal and economical, and the unusually temperate and searching discussions which have taken place upon them, have enabled every one to understand the subject, and will, it may be hoped, have paved the way for an agreement among all parties as to the legislative and administrative measures which must be adopted in reference to it. This is a rare result of such investigations and such controversies, and is one for very sincere self-congratulation. The better portion of the skilled artizans and the subsidiary workmen—the rank and file of mining and manufacturing craftsmen—are learning to know, what they had long felt painfully but imperfectly, the extent and severity of the coercion exercised upon them by trade unions, and the wrong done to them in many ways by these associations ; while, at the same time, they hear now, what perhaps they never suspected, that in a great number of cases, if not in most, the members of those unions, those who in the name of the trade or handicraft exercise this pressure upon their free action, are only a minority of the whole number engaged. The honest and respectable among the unionists have now been forced to *realise*, what probably they often feared, but did not like to admit, even to themselves, that the objects for which they banded themselves together, and in furtherance of which they had spent and suffered so much, were habitually pursued and could only be effectually secured by coercive measures against their fellow-workmen, indisputably illegal, often criminal, always harsh, sometimes cruel, and not unfrequently culminating in murder. At the same time the brutal and the bad have had their brutalities and outrages brought to light, and exposed in naked fact and language with no softening disguise to hide them, and may perhaps learn to regard themselves in a true light, by seeing how they are regarded by others.

On the other hand, the general public have learned with much surprise, and, probably, with some shame, the existence, in the very midst of our orderly and law-loving society, of a system of organised oppression, terrorism, and violence, equally discreditable to the Government which has allowed it to grow up and become dominant, and to the temper and sense of justice of the classes among whom it originated ; while, at the same time its objects are at variance with every sound principle of economic science, and injurious alike to the interests of the community which endures it, and of

the special set of workmen for whose benefit it is
designed. Many of the facts which have been
brought to light were, of course, well known to the
parties more immediately concerned; but the extent
and full bearing of the system were not fathomed
even by them; while both the public and the Administration may be said to have been wholly ignorant of the matter. By the light that has thus been
thrown upon the whole question, all parties, both
workmen and the nation at large, have been prepared to act and legislate; the workmen, because
the whole inquiry has sprung out of the demand for
the legalisation of their unions; the general public
because a state of things has been revealed which
obviously renders prompt and decisive legislative
action necessary. At the same time, moreover, the
artizans and the upper and middle classes have
begun to understand each other's feelings and
objects far better than before. *We* see distinctly
what are the precise purposes which created these
unions, and the ideas which justify their action to
the artizan mind; and the working men see the
impressions of horror and of condemnation which
the tyranny and violence of these associations have
made on the minds even of those most disposed to
sympathise with and assist those below them in the
social scale. We are not without indications that
the capitalist is beginning to recognise what is just
and natural in the demands of the labourer, and the
labourer to recognise what is fixed and right in the
moral and economic doctrines of the capitalist.

But we have gained much more than this. Not
only are all parties prepared to legislate, but we are

perhaps not over-sanguine in fancying that all are
prepared, or will 'shortly be prepared, to legislate
mainly in the same sense. The country is now ready to
concede all that any honest and fair-minded unionist
can demand, all that any decent artizan will avow and
put into plain words as his object, all that any educated friend or advocate of the working classes would
dream of asking on their behalf. On the other hand,
even the most audacious unionist—whatever be his
real object and desire—far less any respectable
mechanic or partisan or patron of operatives in the
upper ranks, would not venture to demand deliberately and distinctly anything clearly unjust or oppressive—any right to coerce his fellow-workmen, for
example, or to use violence towards them. As soon
as it came to speaking out in detail and in plain
English before a respectable audience in any rank
of life, there would be found little *avowed* difference
between the parties. The free right to combine and
act in concert for the purpose of extorting higher
wages must be conceded by the community. The
claim to prevent other workmen from working for any
wages they please must be surrendered by the unions.
The duty of the State to protect the one set in their
right to work, and the other in their right to refuse
work, and of all to decide the terms and conditions on
which they will work, must in like manner be recognised by all. No man dare distinctly to ask for power
to bully his fellow-workman ; he would be laughed or
hooted out of court at once. No man would dream
of refusing a legal status to any trade union which
steered clear of coercion, terror, and oppression ; he
would be told at once that the time for that sort of

injustice was gone by. In fine, neither Parliament
nor the nation would now refuse any demand on behalf of trade unions which those unions would venture to make or defend in broad daylight, and before
a decent assembly of their countrymen. I am scarcely
stating the case too strongly, though it may seem so
at first sight; for the public is certainly prepared to
concede to those associations every legitimate freedom of action, and to give them the aid of the law
(which was what they originally asked) in the assertion of every right which does not involve an illegal
and unjust interference with the similar rights and
liberties of others. And the unions could not venture
to object to any legislation or to any administrative
action of which the sole object was to prevent and
punish coercion, or to protect the willing workman.
To do so would be to unmask themselves, and avow
themselves enemies of law and justice.

The case, therefore, is very clear both for legislative and administrative action; and, as far as legislation is concerned, it is easy as well as clear. The
first thing is formally to legalise trade unions established for the purpose of raising wages, regulating
the hours and terms of labour, or any other legitimate object of desire; to give them the same power
over their own members as any other voluntary
association; to allow them to sue or be sued as a
corporate body, to give them a simple legal remedy
against defaulting subscribers or defalcating officers.
They would, of course, have a perfect right to make,
as a body, any bargain they pleased with capitalists
who treated with them, and to appeal to the law to
enforce their regulations on their own members, in-

asmuch as those regulations, once adopted by the
body, are of the nature of *contracts*. As long as a
workman was a member of the association he must
be bound to obey its rules and submit to its fines.
More than this (which would give a perfect legal
status) I do not see how any fair-minded unionist
could ask, or how any educated advocate of unions
could ask for them. All that would be needed to
prevent abuse would be, that no coercion of any sort
should be used to compel a workman either to enter
into the union or to remain in it if he wished to
withdraw. In a word, the law and the Government
must protect, equally and efficiently, both the unionist and the non-unionist in his rights and liberties.

The next—and perhaps the only other necessary—
legislative step must be to make a broad distinction
between *strike* societies and *benefit* societies ; *i.e.*, between associations for the purpose of raising wages,
regulating terms and hours of labour, &c.,—in a
word, fighting the capitalist or employer—and associations for the purpose of mutual assistance in sickness or old age. These objects are now almost
invariably mixed up together, and professed or pursued by the same unions ; and the combination is
not only a great injury to the workman, but—however unintentionally—a distinct and cruel fraud
upon him. The *Economist* some time ago did good
service by calling attention to this mischievous
system in two or three careful papers. The severance I have indicated is demanded by the clearest
principles of integrity and equity, and is for the
obvious interest of the workman himself. As long
as the two wholly distinct objects are combined, and

undertaken by the same bodies, and carried out by means of funds raised from the same subscriptions, the unions, *quâ* benefit or insurance societies, must necessarily be insolvent. The money that has been subscribed by the operative in order to secure a stipulated provision of so much per week in sickness and old age—which are *calculable* casualties—is spent in maintaining him when out of work from strikes or suspended trade—which are *incalculable* casualties; and when he needs it, therefore, in his day of *natural* distress or want, it is no longer forthcoming. In a word, the funds provided by the members of the association for one purpose originally have been diverted by the managers of that association to another purpose; and though this diversion has been effected with the full sanction of the members, or of a tacit or avowed majority of them, and though the managers are therefore exonerated from the blame of breach of trust, yet it is not the less true that virtual deception and injury have been practised on the subscribers, and that the mode of action makes it simply impossible for the association to meet the inevitable claims upon it, or to carry out those engagements with its members which were their chief original inducements to becoming members. They do not get the principal thing they bargained for, because their funds have been wasted in a secondary object which they never ought to have bargained for in the same breath.

Nor is this disappointing and often cruel consequence a contingent or accidental one: it is an inevitable one, and results from the very facts of the case. It is clearly brought out by the evidence taken before the Commission, that *all* trade unions, even the richest and best managed, are at this moment insolvent; that is, they are, or will certainly be, unable to meet the claims of their members for the stipulated payment in sickness and old age; their accumulated and *calculable* assets being quite insufficient to discharge their regular and *calculable* liabilities, present and future.

Another evil arising from the mixing up of strike societies with benefit societies—of unions for the object of maintaining contests for higher wages and trade regulations, with unions for the object of mutual insurance against age and sickness—is that the combination tends greatly to encourage strikes. These associations, especially the younger ones, whose assets come in freely and largely, and whose liabilities are all *deferred* ones, find themselves flush of money, and fancy themselves, therefore, to be rich; and they have a natural, and often irresistible, temptation to employ those means in endeavouring to extort more liberal remuneration from their masters. In doing this, as the *Economist* has pointed out, they are not only injuring and defrauding the subscribing operatives, but they are acting in contravention of one of the main arguments they put forward in their own defence. They are not in truth (as they would allege) fighting the capitalist employer with the capital provided *ad hoc* by combination among the labourers, but with the labourers' *insurance* capital, which is all, or most of it, *mortgaged to future claims*, which claims the strikes prevent from being ever liquidated. They are fighting the antagonistic capitalist not with their own capital, nor even with borrowed capital, but really and virtually with *peculated* capital.

The remedy for all this is quite clear. Benefit societies and sick clubs are perfectly legitimate and most useful institutions. Strike societies are perfectly legitimate also, whether useful or the contrary. Every legal facility and privilege should be secured to both. Only, in common fairness, in simple honesty, they must be kept distinct. Let the workman who subscribes to a benefit or friendly society know that he will obtain that provision for age and sickness on the faith and for the purpose of which he so subscribes ; and let the rules and tables of that society be drawn up so as to secure this object. Let the workman who subscribes to a strike society, again, know that he is giving his money for the purpose of placing himself in a position to contest questions of labour or wages with his employer, whenever his leaders think it desirable to do so. The funds subscribed will then in both cases be applied to the purposes for which they were designed. As it is, the leaders of a strike are carrying on their struggles with the money of the widows, the orphans, the aged, and the sick—not exactly *stealing* it indeed, but using it recklessly, wrongfully, and cruelly.

The next thing to be done—an object which must follow the other, but which probably is still more important and imperative—needs not legislative but administrative and executive measures. The non-unionist workman and his employer have to be protected against the interference, violence, and dictation of the unions. These bodies, having been legalised and secured in their legitimate rights, have to be prevented from assailing the corresponding and equally sacred rights of others. The non-unionist workmen (who are often the majority, though they may not know it, and being unorganised, are comparatively weak) must be defended against all attempts to force or frighten them into the unions, and must be protected effectually in their indisputable right to work for any master they please, during any hours they please, in any fashion and with the aid of any machinery they please, and at any rate of wages they please. And the employer must be secured in turn in *his* liberty of making any bargain or contract with any set of artizans he chooses, and who may choose to contract with him. No unionist worth reasoning with or considering can or dare openly object to this, or distinctly avow that he desires and demands to forbid or prevent these things. He would not be listened to for a moment in Parliament or in the country if he did ; nor would he find decent advocates to back up his preposterous pretensions.

Now, for the securing of these necessary and righteous ends no new laws are requisite. The common law of the land ought to suffice ; only that law must be administered in a very different way from the present one, and the Government must fulfil its obligations with a vigilance and resolution of which we have had few examples in time past. The life, liberty, property, and social and civil rights of the subject must be effectually guarded against all assaults. In a word, the administrators of the law and the guardians of the public peace must simply do their duty, and must take whatever means and spend whatever money may be necessary for the purpose. We do not need new laws; we only need to execute the old ones. Every outrage, every interference, every act of intimidation against which either workman or employer wishes for protection, is already denounced and prohibited by law. Every right and freedom they claim is already, theoretically, theirs by law, or will soon be so. Only, the law is feeble, because its administrators are timid or incapable; it is inoperative, because there is no adequate machinery to set it in operation. The outrages and intimidations and interferences which have lately come to light, and which have so long been the curse of nearly every trade and handicraft and the disgrace of the community, have been rendered possible only because magistrates took a very inadequate and lenient view of their inherent atrocity and their extensive mischief, because no competent or sufficient police force was on foot to control or to detect them, because lawyers and juries were too often inclined to strain both evidence and law in favour of the criminal; and lastly, because the central Government, wholly unconscious of the gravity of the case, and slumbering on its far Olympus, displayed a torpid ignorance and inaction that were at once sinful and imbecile. Hence the Sheffield and Glasgow murders, the Manchester and Dublin maimings, the outrages of the mines and the " Black Country," and the astonishing power and range which the system of terrorism, lately unveiled, was suffered to attain. What we need, and what we must have without

K

delay if the mischief of past neglect is to be undone, and if decent security is to be obtained for the future, is a far more powerful, cleverer, better organised police in the manufacturing districts; energetic and capable magistrates, more alive than existing ones to the exigencies of the hour; a greater disposition on the part of all who administer the law to be satisfied with moral certainty in cases where, from the peculiar circumstances of the offence, full technical evidence is difficult to arrive at; and a resolution on the part of the Government that a system of organised crime and oppression so dishonouring to the executive shall not be suffered any longer to bring obloquy and danger on the country.

But when all this has been done, when the law has been made strictly just and impartial, and its prompt and vigorous execution provided for, one thing yet remains as essential as either of the others. We shall only have half done our work unless we can carry the general good sense and feeling of the working classes along with us in what we do. The original source of the evil will still remain unless we can succeed in extinguishing the present sense of antagonism between capital and labour, and make the employer and the employed *conscious*, as well as, what they are and always must be, *actual* and unavoidable co-operators and partners. There has been much mystification on this subject, and in the heat of strife the real facts of the case have almost escaped attention, or been altogether misconceived. The workmen wish to be *partners*, they demand to share in the profits of the concern in which they are engaged, in the profits which they join the capitalists in creating. The wish and the demand are perfectly just and reasonable; the only part of the matter which is not reasonable is, that the workmen do not recognise the fact that they *are* partners already, and that they *do* share in the profits, though they have not yet come to understand the precise footing of this actual partnership. What, in fact, they ask is not to be made partners, but to change the character of the partnership. The case is perfectly clear, and may be made intelligible to the operatives themselves in a very few words.

The profits of any business are the joint production of capital and labour—of the wealth and sagacity of the employer and the skill and efforts of the artizans. These profits ought to be, and as a rule perhaps practically are, pretty fairly divided between them. But profits are not *realised* till goods are made and sold, and the returns are actually in hand—that is, not for a year or more, perhaps, after the work is begun. Now, the workmen not being capitalists, cannot wait for this distant date; they need to receive their share of the profits at once and *before any profits are realised;* nay, when it is not yet certain that any profits will be realised at all (for all businesses are not always profitable, especially at the outset); they therefore require the capitalist, their employer, to *advance* them their share, and to advance it, so to say, *on guess.* He does so; but in consideration of doing so, in consideration of his paying them a year or two beforehand, and paying them what he may possibly never realise himself, he pays them somewhat less than the share which would accrue to them if they could have waited as he has to do ; and it is obviously quite just that he should do this, for in the first place he loses the interest on the wages advanced, and in the second place he takes upon himself the entire risk of the *uncertain* issue.

This is the *first* point or peculiarity in the partnership between masters and men in its existing form; the *second* point and peculiarity to be noticed is this : the artizans, not being capitalists, not only cannot wait till profits are actually realised and in hand, but they cannot put up with *fluctuating* profits, or with the possibility of no profits at all (as sometimes happens). They therefore require the capitalist employer to guarantee them against this fluctuation, to *commute* their share of the varying and contingent profits into a *fixed* sum or stipend, *i.e.*, to pay them regular weekly wages in lieu of an irregular amount at the year's end. He does this ; and in consideration of doing this, of giving them a certainty while he himself has only an uncertainty, of securing to them an average while he submits to the ups and downs of fortune, he makes a further moderate deduction from the share which would have accrued to them had they been able to venture on a fluctuating income. And it is, again, obviously fair that he should do so, for a certainty is always preferable to an uncertainty, and the deduction from the workman's *theoretic* share is the premium which he pays for the insurance of that share.

It is plain, therefore, that the workman is already an actual partner with his employer, and a partner on perfectly intelligible and equitable terms, and perhaps on terms which are as pecuniarily beneficial to him in the long run as any others would be ; although sometimes his precise percentage of the joint profits may not be as large as he desires, or would have bargained for, or might, on a readjustment of the partnership, obtain. But now a large number of workmen, or of persons who speak in their name, are asking *for different conditions of partnership*, some reasonably and some unreasonably. In a word, they desire *fluctuating* instead of *fixed* profits; they claim to share in the varying fortunes of the business; and they allege, probably with perfect truth, that until they do thus share its chances and changes, they will never feel satisfied that they obtain their fair proportion, and will never take that vivid interest in their work which alone can secure the maximum of profit to both capitalist and labourer. I believe they are quite right in this conviction, and I am satisfied (as, indeed, has already been proved by several successful experiments) that this modification of the ordinary partnership arrangement between masters and men is in many cases practicable enough. Not until artizans feel that every added effort and care and attention on their part will redound to their own advantage by increasing their share of profit will any business be made to yield all it might yield; not till they benefit by good times and suffer by bad times will there exist that ready sympathy between them and their employer which is so necessary to the comfort and well-being of both; and not till they obtain remuneration in some way calculated according to the varying net returns of the business will they, as a rule, believe that they have quite fair play. Their demand, therefore, is rational, and I believe its adoption would be beneficial to all parties. Only, it may be put in a reasonable or in an unreasonable form, and as most of the workmen, and nearly all their advocates, are inclined to put it in the unreasonable form, I must add a word or two on this point. It is plain from what has been already said, that the workman can have no right to claim *both* a fixed and a fluctuating share, any more than he could claim both an *advanced* and *deferred* share ; or, rather, he must not demand the same share, or as large a share, if he has already received *commuted profits in advance*, as he would be entitled to if he had waited and taken his chance. He cannot, that is, expect his master both to pay him his usual wages in advance (or his *anticipated* share of profits), and his usual fixed wages (or his *commuted* share calculated on an average of profits), *and* a share of profits at the end of the year besides. If this were done, it is plain he would be paid twice over, and therefore in excess (supposing always that the original calculation had been a fair one). It is plain, again, that if this proposed modification is adopted, and the workman is paid *according to the actual and varying profits realised*, he cannot wait for that realisation any more than he could under the old system, and he must still receive at least the principal portion of his share in advance. It is almost equally clear that, as matters now stand, and will remain till the workman becomes himself in some degree a capitalist, a master could not come upon his operatives and ask them to refund what he had advanced to them in the form of wages, in those years when there were very small profits, or no profits at all, or perhaps a heavy loss.

It is clear, again, that to ask the capitalist to share profits with his work-people in profitable years when they cannot share losses with him in losing years, would be distinctly unfair,—supposing them to have received their *full* wages—*i.e.*, their equitable and calculated share—in advance. It follows, therefore, that in order to render strictly fair and reasonable the demand of the workmen for a share in the profits at the year's end—*i.e.*, for a *fluctuating* share varying with the varying gains—they must in the first instance have *foregone some portion* of their regular wages, or their *fixed and commuted share* paid in advance. That is to say, if a workman's fair share, commuted and advanced, is 20s. a week, and he believes (correctly) that his fair share, uncommuted and unadvanced, would be 23s. in good years—still, as in bad years it would often be only 10s. or 15s., he ought to begin the new system by accepting 18s. a week, in lieu of 20s. in advance, or he would run the risk of undesignedly defrauding his employer. In other words, if he wishes for fluctuating profits *as well* as fixed wages, his fixed wages must be smaller than if he were content with them alone. He must, in fact, leave in the hands of his employer a margin to meet contingencies. This will be best for him in the long run, because his fixed income (which he would spend) is smaller, while he has fluctuating receipts to look to in the future (which he probably will save), and his *aggregate* earnings will be unquestionably larger.

How *this* form of partnership or genuine and fair co-operative system can be made to work is a mere matter of detail.

It is not easy to exaggerate the good effects that might be expected to flow from anything like a general adoption of plans for rendering manufacturing operatives sharers in the *fluctuating* profits of their employer's business, in addition to, or partially in lieu of, a fixed remuneration calculated on the *average* profits of that business.   First of all, it would make them conscious, which few of them now seem thoroughly to be, that those profits *are* fluctuating, and would make them more often than at present willing to submit to a reduction of wages when bad times clearly call for such a sacrifice on their part.   Next, it would greatly tend in the majority of cases to correct their extravagant estimates of those profits, and induce them to be more reasonable in their claims upon them.   Then it would increase those profits by offering an inducement to all workmen to put forth their best exertions, to avoid waste and damage, to suggest and carry out economies, and the like. Again, it might be expected nearly to put an end to strikes, because strikes reduce the profits in which the operatives would have become sharers, and because, if the state of trade be really and truly such as to warrant and demand an advance of wages, that advance would, in any event, come to them at the year's end in the shape of increased bonus instead of in the form of an increase of fixed remuneration. It would almost destroy the mischievous influence of trade unions, and leave only their beneficial operation (if there be such) ; artizans would no longer consent to turn out or quarrel with their employers at the command of secretaries or secret committees, since to do so would be cutting their own throats, and refusing their own bread and butter, even more clearly than it is now. And, finally, it would tend to render workmen more fixed in their habits—less willing, that is, to change masters on slight provocation or inducement ; and it might also help in time to make them capitalists, if they could be persuaded to lay by the lump sum which would stand to their credit in the firm's books at the end of the year.

There are many forms in which this system of paying the operatives, substantially or partially, according to the varying profits actually realised, might be, and indeed is, carried out. They may, partly by subscribed and partly by borrowed capital, set up for themselves, and become their own employers—a plan which has been attempted, with varying success, in Leeds, Rochdale, and elsewhere. The principal difficulty of this scheme is, that a manufacturing business can never, or most rarely, be carried on successfully by a committee ; and operatives have not always the good sense and sagacity to place their affairs in the hands of one manager in whom they can repose confidence, and then to leave him unhampered by jealousy or suspicious interference. Another difficulty is, that it is always unsafe to work with a large amount of borrowed capital, and that they can seldom raise by shares among themselves a sufficient sum of their own to carry them through years of loss or stagnation. Still, the experiment has been tried, and has not always failed. In some cases, indeed, their success appears to have been remarkable. Co-operative *shops*, we know, have often answered admirably. A return, dated in 1866, enumerates 417 of these associations, with 148,586 shareholders, an

aggregate paid-up capital of £761,313, realising profits equal to £279,226, and paying 35 per cent. to
their members, after allowing 5 per cent. on all
borrowed moneys.   But beside these—which, though
most useful and successful enterprises, such as the
middle classes may soon, in pure self-defence, be
driven to imitate, are not *employing* or productive
enterprises—I have a return lying before me, given
in the *Industrial Partnerships Record*, of eight manufacturing co-operative firms, all I believe in Lancashire, yielding on an average 24 per cent. net profit
on the capital subscribed—a sum equal to the wages
actually paid (which must, we apprehend, have been
fixed at rather a low rate)—having a paid-up capital
in the whole of £365,121, besides loan capital of
£146,495, and having invested £352,000 in buildings
and machinery.   These are the published results,
and even after every possible allowance has been
made for over-sanguine calculations or accidental
prosperity, it must be admitted that they are most
encouraging.

Another plan, which I believe has been adopted
with great benefit in several cases, is to give a bonus
at the end of the year (say of ten per cent. on the
net profits) to all workmen employed, over and
above their regular wages, and in proportion to their
wages, as a sort of free gift and as an inducement to
harmony and diligence.   It is found to answer to
the employer to surrender a portion of his gains in
order to increase those gains upon the whole ; and
when the operatives can trust their employer to calculate and divide fairly the stipulated bonus, the
motive no doubt would produce a good result.   But

it is obviously an imperfect and only tentative and inchoate form of the co-operative idea, though one which the great employers of labour would do well to adopt, and perhaps the only one which is suitable to the most gigantic industrial concerns.

A third plan is that which has been introduced, so far with most satisfactory results, by Messrs Briggs in the coal trade, and Messrs Crossley in, I believe, the woollen business. These gentlemen have converted their concerns into joint-stock associations (retaining, I understand, the practical management of them), inviting their workmen to become shareholders in preference to others, and holding, of course, a large number of shares themselves. The operatives in both cases have become shareholders gladly and to a great extent, and in both the shares are at a considerable premium—as, indeed, they well may be, with a dividend in Messrs Crossley's establishment of twenty, and in Messrs Briggs's of twelve, per cent. In the latter concern the second modification of the co-operative idea is blended with the joint-stock plan; that is, besides the ordinary dividend, a bonus of five per cent. on the wages is paid to all mere operatives employed, and ten per cent. to working shareholders.

In addition to these large manufacturing establishments, a number of smaller ones are daily springing up in less important trades, where the experiment can be tried on a smaller scale, and on the whole the results are most encouraging. Basket-makers, frame-gilders, clothers, fire-brick makers, and others, have formed industrial partnerships in various places, and I see no reason why they should not achieve the suc-

cess which all sincere friends of the working class
must wish them.

In the three directions here indicated, then, must
be sought, and may be found, the remedy for the
present unsatisfactory state of the relations between
capital and labour, and the solution of the most difficult and urgent social problem of the day.   Legislation must do its part in giving to trade unions a
full legal status, and enforcing their separation from
those benefit or mutual insurance associations, with
which they have no natural, and can have no legitimate connexion.   The executive administration
of the country, central and local, must do its part in
enforcing the law with the most unsleeping vigilance
and the most stern severity, and the public opinion
of the nation must support justice and its agents.
And the working men themselves, and all their true
friends, must aid the result by carrying out, wherever
possible and under whatever form may be best
adapted to the special circumstances of each case,
those co-operative principles whose experimental
adoption alone can fully convince both employers
and employed that their interests are identical and
in harmony, and render them cordial fellow-workers
where now too often they are suspicious and jealous
antagonists.   Nothing but a general neglect and
abnegation of duty on all sides could have brought
matters into their present disastrous condition.
Nothing but a general resumption of deserted or
unrecognised obligations can set us right.   The
soundest doctrines of morals, of jurisprudence, and
of economic science, all point in the same direction,
and dictate the same course of action.

VII.

THE ECONOMIC PROBLEM.

WE are sometimes in danger of drawing the most erroneous conclusions from the most admitted facts and the most unimpugnable statistics, merely from overleaping in our haste some essential step in the reasoning. And occasionally this step will be the most important in the whole chain, and the mistaken inference at which we in consequence arrive may be one affecting the most serious issues of our social condition or our daily life.

For example:—There is no doubt that, as a nation, we have advanced enormously in all the essentials and elements of civilisation in the course of the last four or five centuries. All the world has improved, and England as fast at least as any other people. All the wheels of life have been oiled, and the standard of living has been astonishingly raised. The wealth of the country, and its possessions in nearly everything that wealth can purchase, have been at least quintupled since the days of the Edwards and Henrys. The poorest cottage is now provided with appliances and conveniences which were scarcely to be met with in the richest then. The humblest classes are now fed and clothed, and comforted with articles procured in curious abundance from countries which were not discovered in those earlier times. Our fields are incomparably better cultivated than they were, and yield a three-fold produce. Our flocks and herds have multiplied incalculably in numbers, as well as improved surprisingly in quality. Woollen and linen clothing, which were scarce and dear then, and cotton, which was altogether unknown, have grown comparatively cheap and abundant now. The art of medicine has been vastly improved, and has been brought within reach of all ranks in a way our ancestors never dreamed of. The discovery and working of coal mines have furnished us with abundant supplies of cheap fuel, unknown in those ruder ages. Yet it would be a great mistake to infer from these notorious and indisputable premises that the mass of our people—the agricultural labourers, for example, the largest class of all—are better off, fare better, are more comfortable, more able to enjoy life, than they were in the fourteenth century. By the common consent of all historians who have investigated the question, the exact contrary is the case. The peasant in those days—in common with the merchant and the squire—was more rudely housed, more coarsely clad, worse tended and worse taught, than at present; but he was far better fed, had an ampler supply of the necessaries of life, was less anxious about the future, and more able to provide for it; and—what probably is the right standard of measurement—there was incomparably less difference between his material condition and that of his lord than exists in this nineteenth century. We need not adduce authorities—the fact is admitted and indubitable; and it is at once the most shame-

ful fact in our social state, the saddest conclusion
our researches can arrive at, and the knottiest as
well as the most urgent problem our statesmen have
to solve.

Again : the marvellous stride in the general
prosperity and the aggregate wealth of Great
Britain in the last five-and-twenty or thirty years
is notorious to all, and demonstrated by a hundred
proofs. The national savings have been lavishly
wasted on the most foolish schemes, as well as
courageously spent on the most useful undertakings,
yet they are still on the increase. The augumented
income of the country may be partially measured by
the difference between the assessment to the pro-
perty-tax in 1842, when it was first imposed, and in
1867. It was in England and Wales £227,000,000
in the former year, and £316,000,000 in the latter—
an increase of *forty* per cent. in a quarter of a
century. The trade of the kingdom has trebled in
the same period.* Every harbour is crowded with
ships from every quarter of the globe. We have
had to build countless acres of new docks. We
have had to pull down our barns and build greater.
The produce of foreign lands is poured into our
warehouses with an abundance never known before.
Manufactures have increased in a similar ratio, as
every town in Lancashire, Yorkshire, and Cheshire
can testify. One entirely new species of industry,

* The *real* values of our imports and exports have only been
recorded since 1854, but since that period they have increased
from £268,000,000 to £501,000,000, or nearly doubled. Between 1842 and 1858, the last year for which the *official* values
(or measures of *quantities*) are given, the increase of these was
from £177,000,000 to £444,000,000.

source of wealth, and lucrative' investment has
sprung up, and reached a marvellous development
in the lifetime of a single generation, viz., the railways. The construction and working of them has
given employment to a vast amount of skilled and
unskilled labour ; and, till stupid and criminal mismanagement began, they yielded a very liberal
profit on the capital employed. Colossal fortunes
have been made both by contractors, speculators,
and investors in them, and not always lost again.
The building trades, too, have been surprisingly
active : nearly every town has expanded its area ;
some have doubled theirs. Round the metropolis
there have sprung up what it is scarcely an exaggeration to call a crowd of affiliated cities—streets,
squares, crescents of new houses, stretching far into
what was once country, and raising in the mind of
every beholder the question—" Whence can the
people come who fill these dwellings, and how can
they afford to live here ? "—for most of them imply
and would require in their occupiers incomes of from
£500 to £2000 a year. Yet, in spite of this enormous supply, house-rents everywhere are rising
instead of falling, and nearly every house is taken
as soon as finished. Moreover, we are habitually
living in a style seldom seen a generation ago, and
indulging in luxuries at which our fathers would
have held up their hands in disapproval and dismay.
The expenditure of the upper and middle classes is
lavish beyond example—often tasteless, usually unwise, and sometimes simply criminal. The *appearances* of society would indicate a community bursting
and insolent with newly-acquired gains, revelling in

ease, gorged with abundance, and with no recognised need for economy or foresight.

Nevertheless, these appearances are to a great extent fallacious; or it would be more correct to say that the inferences naturally drawn from them are only partially true, and must be accepted with great modification and with many drawbacks. There is a reverse to the medal and a dark background to the picture. The degree in which comfort and well-being are diffused through the community can by no means be measured by the aggregate wealth of the nation. The critical question is—How is that wealth distributed? And in England at the present moment it cannot be denied, and, indeed, is most painfully felt and most bitterly complained of, that, notwithstanding the swelling riches and indisputable prosperity of the country as a whole, it is for a great proportion of the middle classes more difficult to live than it used to be; requirements are greater, and the means of meeting those requirements have not risen in proportion; in one word, and in the common phrase, "*living*" is dearer than it was a generation since; it is more difficult " to make ends meet;" and the career of these classes, instead of being easier and more unanxious than it was, offering more leisure and leading to richer rewards, has become, and we fear is still increasingly, a ceaseless struggle from marriage to the grave to preserve comfort and respectability on inadequate resources —a struggle in which thousands break down utterly, and thousands more have their tempers spoiled and their domestic life embittered, and talents and character meant for enjoyment and achievement, yet

L

attaining neither, frittered away in simply " keeping
the wolf from the door." This is most true, no
doubt, of the recipients of fixed incomes—the Government *employé*, the commercial clerk, the humbler
class of professional men, schoolmasters, clergymen,
and the like ;—but it is true also of the smaller
tradesmen, of nearly all, in fact, except great merchants, well-established retail houses, or manufacturers on a large scale. In fact, it is the common cry
of most men and of nearly all wives whose incomes,
whether fixed or fluctuating, range from £250 to
£2000 a year.

Now, why is it that, while England has grown so
very much richer, the classes which so largely contribute to England's riches have grown, if not
positively, yet relatively, poorer—so much so as to
be truly and distinctly what they have been called,
" the uneasy classes ?" There seem so many
reasons on the surface of matters why they should
be better off than formerly, that we desire some
clear explanation why they are worse off. Many
circumstances contribute to the unsatisfactory result, and they are neither far to seek nor hard to
decipher. In the first place, the general *standard of
living* has been raised ; and this is probably the
most powerfully operating of all the causes we shall
have to name. We all of us live far less frugally
and simply than our fathers did ; we habitually
indulge in luxuries and comforts which they rarely
allowed themselves ; we have accustomed ourselves
to think many things necessary which to them
were superfluities ; our *ideas* on the subject have
undergone an insensible revolution in obedience to

the practices we see around us. We must have
newer things, fresher things ; we must have our
holidays, our easy chairs, our French wines, and
the like. This alteration in the standard has per-
colated downward, partly from the upper ranks, and
partly from the *nouveaux riches* among the middle
ranks. The increase of population, the augmented
wealth of the higher mercantile classes, and, perhaps
more than anything else, the railways, have vastly
improved the incomes of the landed aristocracy,
and they live in consequence decidedly more
lavishly and elaborately than they used to do, and
are imitated in this respect, of course, by those who
aspire to rival or to equal them. But a far stronger
influence has been exercised in this direction by the
number of great fortunes that of late· years have
been made in trade, in railways, and in speculation,
often suddenly, often, too, by men who have little
taste or education to teach them how money can be
spent creditably and wisely — who, therefore, as
abundance poured in upon them, have launched
out into every species of vulgar, self-indulgent,
ostentatious extravagance, and by so doing diffused
at once high prices and bad taste around them—
made it, at the same time, more necessary for those
in the same circles to live well and more difficult for
them to do so. Many of these successful men
belonged to the same class and even to the same
families with the great majority of those of moderate
means and fixed incomes, and their example naturally
spread among their former associates, who had the
same desires without the same power to gratify
them ; for, unfortunately, we are a very *aping* and

imitative people, and are fond of aspiring to rival "our betters," even in the things in which they are least better than ourselves. In this way the whole daily life of hundreds of thousands of the middle classes has been demoralised. They have fancied it incumbent on them (and we admit that it is not easy to resist and repudiate the fancy) to live "as others do," according to the imbecile phrase so current in the mouths of most of us, without the right so to live, or the means of so living.

In the next place, the incomes of the middle class have not risen as the incomes of the class above them and the class below them have done. They have participated to some extent in the prosperity of the country and its swelling affluence, but by no means in the same proportion as either the landed aristocracy, the large capitalists, or the artizan. The rent of land and the price of land have both risen greatly as cities have spread, as railways have been constructed, as towns have stretched out into the fields around them, as successful tradesmen and manufacturers have required villas in the country. The new commercial policy inaugurated in 1842 gave an enormous impulse to mercantile enterprise, and opened fresh and inexhaustible fields for its reward; immense wealth was thus won, and the profits of trade vastly increased; but these great prizes fell chiefly to the men of capital, and to a few lucky individuals who rose from the ranks. In life, as in Scripture, the rule holds good: "To him that hath shall be given." Vast joint-stock companies abounded, but *some* capital was needed to become shareholders;

and shareholders were ruined at least as often as they were enriched, while the *large* gains were usually monopolised by the directors and the magnates. Commercial grandees grew grander, commercial fortunes grew more colossal and more numerous, small capitals grew into large ones ; but the salaries of commercial clerks rose little and rose slowly. The business of lawyers increased as the country grew busier and richer, and their fees became occasionally almost fabulous ; but the payment of the scriveners and the law-stationers increased slightly or not at all. The Government spent more, and employed greater numbers ; but the salaries of civil servants have not been revised for a generation, have only in particular instances been raised, and their emoluments as a whole have in some cases even been·reduced. They, and the clergy, the especial recipients of "fixed incomes," stand in point of money payments nearly where they did. Meanwhile, the artizan class—the whole body of working men, apart from the agricultural labourer — has materially improved in position. The wages of labour, especially of every sort of skilled labour, have risen at least twenty-five per cent. in the aggregate. Railways and other engineering works, public and private, have called quite a new industry into existence ; augmented Government expenditure in dockyards and arsenals has contributed not a little to the same end ; shipbuilding and manufactures, which received such an enormous stimulus from our free-trade policy, have done still more ; the increased demand for houses, and for houses of a better sort, has spread a similar improvement over all the artizans connected with the building trade, while extensive and systematic emigration has come in, not directly to produce any effect on wages, but to prevent the effect arising from these other causes being counteracted by the competition of rapidly-increasing numbers. And here, probably, we get a glimpse of the real reason why the middle classes, the recipients of moderate and fixed incomes, have participated so scantily in the general prosperity. The working classes have emigrated — *they* have not. They had not the means of going to the colonies as purchasers of land or small capitalists, and they were unwilling or unfit to go as labourers. They could not farm, and to dig they were ashamed. If the families of clerks, clergymen, half-pay officers, and Government *employés* had thinned their numbers by wholesome depletion, as the artizans have done, it would have been simply impossible for their social and material position not to have improved along with that of other classes. In this busy, striving, struggling, thriving land, they, and they only (along with peasants and single women), are redundant in numbers, and therefore ill-remunerated and uneasy.

But independently of these explanations, it is certain that the price of the actual necessaries of life, and the inevitable expenditure of middle-class families, have greatly increased of late years, and are still augmenting in a degree which threatens to make "uneasiness" both chronic and universal. Labour enters largely into the cost of every article —indeed, the labour of producing it may be said to constitute its cost,—and we have seen that the

wages of labour have risen probably one-fourth.
This affects, directly, shelter, clothing, food; and
indirectly, nearly everything we consume or need.
House-rent has risen more than anything else—probably 50 per cent.;—not only because enhanced
wages render building dearer, but because the price
of land has risen everywhere, and in the neighbour-
hood of towns more decidedly than anywhere else;
—and every fresh City or metropolitan "improvement" raises the rent of dwellings more and more,
by a process only too familiar to us all. Furniture,
probably, is not really dearer in itself, but a more
costly style of furniture prevails; and this practically
comes to the same thing. Then rates are far
heavier than they were; local taxation has grown
more and more burdensome, while imperial taxation
(per head and per article) has been growing easier.
Poor-rates, police-rates, sewerage and lighting rates,
and general rates have, especially in the metropolitan districts, swollen almost beyond endurance; and
though possibly, in comfort, in appearance, and in
protection we receive back some balance for what
we pay, still, as the payment is obligatory, the augmentation in our expenditure is unescapable. Clothing we might expect to be cheaper, but in fact it is
not; some vestiary materials have become more
abundant and lower in price; others, such as leather,
and of late, cotton, are considerably dearer;—and in
all cases the increased price of labour, and the large
profits of retail trades (a point we shall recur
to presently), prevent any reduction in wholesale
values from reaching the consumer. Meat, as we
all know to our grief, is far more costly than it used

to be ; the supply is scantier in proportion to the
demand.   Bread ought to be cheaper, but we question whether any middle-class family (not baking at
home) finds it so.   Wheat averaged 57s. a quarter
the seven years before the abolition of the corn
laws ; in the last seven it has averaged 50s.   The
more universal luxuries which may be classed under
the general head of groceries are no doubt cheaper,
and considerably so.   Tea and sugar (the wholesale
prices, duty paid) have fallen 30 per cent.   Light
wines have fallen even more ; but they do not enter
largely into the consumption of the uneasy classes.

We have just alluded to the fact that in many
cases the consumer does not get the benefit of the
unquestionable reduction which has taken place in
the articles consumed.   For a long series of years
the Government has been perpetually lowering or
altogether abolishing duties on imported, and excise
taxes on manufactured, commodities ; yet the reduc-
tions seem scarcely to be felt in the retail price.
Tea, coffee, wine, and sugar, are perhaps the only
exceptions.   The duty on glass and bricks was taken
off in Peel's time ; yet glass and bricks appear no
cheaper, or, at least, their cheapness is not perceptible in the cost of our houses.   The timber duties
are gone, and gone in vain for the middle-class
householder.   Raw materials of all kinds are
exempted from duty ; yet manufactured goods seem
no cheaper for the exemption.   Cattle and provi-
sions are imported free ; yet they rise in price.
The corn laws, which so long helped to starve the
people, were swept away ; yet the four-pound loaf
costs on the average, we believe, just as much as it

used to do.   In all these essential instances *the consumer appears to be helpless in the hands of the retailer.*
He intercepts the whole, or the greater part, of the
designed and desired relief.   The working classes
in Lancashire and Yorkshire became conscious of
this fact some years ago, and in consequence instituted those co-operative stores, at Rochdale and
elsewhere, which have achieved such a wonderful
success; and at last the Civil Service, recognising
the same incongruity, and feeling it still more
severely, has followed the salutary example.   What
is the explanation ?   It is our system of *distribution*
that is in fault.   Mr J. S. Mill long since pointed
out that in this country retail traders—that is *distributors*—were far too numerous in proportion to *producers.*   In a word, and to speak plainly, they are
too thick upon the ground to live at once honestly
and well.   They perform a necessary and most useful and respectable function in the community, and
render services which could not be dispensed with ;
but there are too many of them, and in consequence
the *clientèle* (to use a French phrase)—*i.e.*, the
regular customers of each—are too few for adequate
and honest profit.   The *modus operandi* is too obvious to need pointing out.   If a small tradesman
turns over £20,000 a year, he may be satisfied with
five per cent profit.   If he turns over only £5000,
he cannot live on less than ten.   If a baker supplies
regularly a hundred families, he can afford to sell his
bread a halfpenny a pound cheaper than he could if
he only supplied thirty.   Again—if a costermonger
or a grocer in the poorer districts has few competitors, and drives a roaring trade, he can sell an

honest article at a fair price. If otherwise, he is
driven to the villany of adulteration and short
weights. In higher circles we see a different phenomenon, but one equally unrefreshing for the consumer. The rich man seems as powerless as the
poor man in his contest with the distributor. The
profits of the latter are there believed to be enormous. The raw materials of a lady's or gentleman's
wardrobe have probably fallen in price considerably
since our fathers' and mothers' days, but both men
and women not only spend more in dress than they
did, but pay more for each individual article. There
can, we fancy, be little doubt that the cost of the
actual substance and the actual labour in a silk dress
or a frock-coat scarcely accounts for more than half
the price we pay for either. The difference goes
partly in the plate-glass window, partly in the carriage, and partly in the suburban villa of the fashion-
able milliner or the celebrated tailor. In the same
manner, the middle-class housekeeper finds the
wholesale quotations of meat in Smithfield market falling week by week, but can get no reduction
in the price of his leg of mutton or his rib of beef.
Wheat goes down, and so does flour, though less
decidedly; but the baker charges him as much as
ever for his loaf. Butchers and bakers must live;
and as there are too many of them, they must either
cut each other's throats, or prey upon their customers. They must live, and so they live on us.
It scarcely seems as if mere ordinary competition
could effect a cure; competition—unless fierce and
internecine, which it rarely is—often only reduces
the *clientèle* of each rival, and so augments the mis-

chief. We do not recommend the French plan—
and it would be impossible to introduce it here; but
each baker in Paris, for example, having his own
district and no rival, and the price of flour being
known and published from week to week, the tradesman makes his regular and reasonable profit, and the
consumer gets the full advantage of every fall in
price; and if occasionally he has to pay more instead of less, at least he has the satisfaction of
knowing why. For us, for rich and poor alike,
there is no remedy except in co-operative stores—
at least till we have fewer retailers and distributors,
and a more numerous body of customers for each;
and, indeed, what are co-operative stores except
retail shops on a large scale, and able, therefore, to
be content with small profits? To amend, purify,
and, if necessary, reconstruct our DISTRIBUTIVE SYS-
TEM, is for us all the great social and family problem
of the day.

VIII.

THE duty of political consistency has attained a paramount position in the minds both of politicians and of the public generally, which, though natural and explicable enough, would seem not to be quite defensible by sound reason. The idea which lies at the root of it is intrinsically professional, and is apparently borrowed partly from the army and partly from the church; unwavering allegiance to party associates and political opinions is regarded as a matter of personal fidelity, and renunciation of that allegiance is treated much as desertion is treated by military law or apostasy by ecclesiastical canons, as morally iniquitous and mean, punishable by death in the one case and by damnation in the other. The conception is simple enough, and the application of the doctrine has always been found too convenient for its justice to be deliberately questioned. It has descended to us from days when a political career was a fight, and a fight on the issue of which life, liberty, and property were often put to issue; and when, moreover, the questions and interests at stake were for the most part too clear and simple, too little susceptible of doubt or *nuance*, too certain to be looked at solely from one side or solely from the opposite, to render it probable that a perfectly honest man could either waver or change. The idea, again, is sustained and strengthened by the common and recognised weaknesses of human nature—weaknesses partly intellectual, but principally moral. There are so few men mentally capable of seeing both sides of a question ; so few with consciences sensitively alive to the obligation of seeing both sides ; so few placed under conditions either of circumstance or temper which admit of their seeing both sides. On that account it is true, and has been practically recognised as true, that for one man who changes his opinions or deserts his standard from sincere conviction, ten men change principles and party for sinister objects or from selfish motives ; while among the waverers and apostates in the political arena as to whose honesty no question could be raised, so many have been obviously men of unsound judgment or infirm wills, that the world may be held fairly warranted in its rough and ready decision, that any marked inconsistency in public men, any distinct conversion of creed on great subjects, any deliberate desertion of the party with whom they have been accustomed to act, does raise a *primâ facie* case of indisputable plausibility against either their wisdom or their purity.

Thus far we may safely go with the ordinary public impression. But there are several considerations, some obvious, and all undeniable as soon as pointed out, which should lead us to mistrust this rough and ready judgment, which completely rebut the *primâ facie* probability, and show that in our days political inconsistency—those changes, at least, of principles and opinions, of party allegiance and practical statesmanship, which pass under that opprobrious name—may be not only justified, but imperatively commanded, by the purest patriotism and the soundest sense. The *onus probandi*, of course, must in every instance rest upon the accused ; but the proof is not difficult and the burden is not heavy.

If, in the first place, we look at the historical fact, we shall find that few indeed of our more eminent and really intellectual statesmen during the last two generations—during the epoch, that is, of those great political convulsions, transitions, and maturing problems which try the consciences of men—have ended life where they began it, at the head of the same party or in the profession of the same opinions. Some have gone one way, some another ; some may allege, with perfect truth, that circumstances had so altogether altered that it is the landmarks by which we measure their position that have been removed, rather than themselves who have shifted their ground; others may plead that the change has been their party's, not their own. But the broad apparent fact of change remains, and cannot be impeached. Pitt, who began as a Whig and a zealous and daring parliamentary reformer, was for the last fifteen years of his life the chief and mainstay of the Tories. Burke, incomparably the wisest and deepest thinker of his or almost any day, a systematic and enthusiastic Liberal, the earnest defender of the liberties of America, of the rights of Catholics and Irishmen and slaves, abandoned his party and separated from all his most cherished friends on the question of the French

Revolution, and ended his career the almost fanatical devotee of the aristocracy. Canning, an eager and thoroughgoing Tory in his youth, became almost a Liberal, and at least had gained the support of the Liberals, before he died. Peel, as we all remember, on two of the greatest of public questions, and on two several occasions, abandoned or broke up his party, but yet rose steadily in public esteem in spite, or perhaps in consequence, of his conversions. Lord Brougham, for the first fifty years of his life almost a Radical, was for the last thirty something very like a Tory. Lord Lytton, who was early distinguished as a *prononcé* Liberal, subsequently sat as Colonial Secretary in Lord Derby's Cabinet. Mr Disraeli, recently as Prime Minister the Tory leader of the House of Commons, entered, or tried to enter, that assembly as an advanced Radical—not perhaps an instance likely to bring the virtue of political inconsistency into credit or into fashion. Lord Palmerston, who grew more respected and more powerful as years rolled on, began his official life among the Tories as Secretary at War under Lord Liverpool's Administration; he served under Canning, with whom he was a favourite; he was the Foreign Minister of Lord Grey, Canning's fiercest assailant; he was the colleague at one time of Lord Chancellor Eldon and at another of Lord Chancellor Brougham; and he died the Liberal Premier, the most popular man in England, and at the head of one of the most powerful parliamentary majorities that any Minister had wielded since 1832. Lord Derby, so lately the acknowledged chief of the Conservatives, was an hereditary, and for a long time, in his way, an

ardent Liberal; a Whig and a reformer till 1835, a
reactionary Tory since 1846; a daring assailant and
retrencher of the Irish Church in 1833, its resolute
and outspoken champion in 1866.   And lastly, Mr
Gladstone—who, whatever may be thought of his
wisdom or his moderation, stands in the very first
rank for purity of character and splendid abilities—
commenced his political course as a Tory, and the
nominee of that Duke of Newcastle who "did what
he would with his own;" adhered to Peel and advanced with him *pari passu* while he lived, and has
gone far beyond him since; the colleague of the
Duke of Wellington, and the colleague of Mr Bright;
the champion of "Church and State" in 1839, the
surrenderer of the Irish Church in 1869.

But *argumenta ad homines* like these have never
more than a disputable, and, as it were, a preliminary
value.   They only serve to show that proceedings
common to so many eminent, able, and honourable
men must be susceptible of a decent explanation
and of at least a plausible defence.   If, however,
we go a little deeper, and consider the matter dispassionately, and without the mist which popular
prejudice has gathered round it, we shall find that
political inconsistency may be assigned to so many
good motives that it is nothing less than unphiloso-
phical, as well as uncharitable, so habitually as we do
to attribute it to bad ones.   Perhaps it is scarcely too
much to say that, in our times and under our parliamentary régime, for a politician to profess the same
opinions, and to act steadily with the same party and
the same associates, from first to last, establishes a
strong *primâ facie* probability *against* either his con-

scientiousness or his sagacity, or both. Let us glance over a few of the rational and creditable causes from which change of party and of opinion may spring. In the first place, half our views, as we all know—more than half in the case of all of us who are not abnormally inquiring and reflective—are inherited, not acquired. It is always so in religion; it is nearly always so in politics; and it is neither surprising nor discreditable that it should be so. We naturally adopt the doctrines, the prejudices, the moral tastes, the intellectual ideas, the modes of approaching questions, of those who brought us up, and among whom we live. We even are fed almost exclusively upon their knowledge. We *imbibe* our conceptions from the mental and moral atmosphere we have breathed in our early and most susceptible years, and it is not till we get among an entirely different set of circumambient influences and opinions that we begin to question the invariable soundness and certainty of our parental teachings. Our young legislators go into Parliament just as our young divines go into the Church, sworn—or, if not sworn, bound by ties of honour nearly as binding as an oath—to articles of faith, none of which they doubt, because none of them have they ever examined. They are enlisted into particular ranks, range themselves round a particular banner, vow allegiance to a particular chief, as a matter of mere hereditary routine. They do not choose; they are chosen. They are born Tories or Whigs—just as others are born Churchmen, Catholics, or Quakers; and what they were born, that they remain, till awakening reflection and observation, some convulsive crisis, or

M

some commanding statesman, startles them first into misgivings, then into investigation, then into conviction, then into apostasy.   It is scarcely too much to say that numbers of our young members of Parliament never fairly recognise how strong is the case against their own side of a question till they hear it discussed by capable debaters in the House of Commons.   Till then, they have never heard the opposing views expounded, except through a hostile medium.   Parliament is *the* school—here almost the only real school—for politicians ; and it is unreasonable to expect students—young students at least—to enter school already taught.   Whether it is right or wise that immature minds should occupy legislative benches, and that the supreme governing assembly of the nation should be made the arena in which so many of our rulers learn the alphabet of their art ; whether the interests and destinies of a mighty people ought to be the *corpus vile* upon which skill is practised and experience acquired—are altogether different questions, on which we need not enter here.

A second very valid and frequent cause of change of opinion, and therefore of the charge of political inconsistency, is simply the flight of years, and the modifications of mind and temperament which years bring with them.   The majority of our public men enter life young ; fewer now than formerly, but still the *stock* of the House of Commons consists of those who, from taste or position or family considerations, embrace politics early as a career, and prosecute it, in one or other House of Parliament, till old age.   Now the views of youth and age—or

rather the modes of viewing things, the spectacles
through which aims and measures are seen in youth
and age—are intrinsically different, must usually be
so, ought always to be so. Youth is susceptible,
imaginative, and excitable ; sees grievances quickly,
feels wrongs acutely ; resents injustice vehemently ;
fancies that all evils can be remedied and all dis-
orders cured. It rushes, therefore, ardently into
the cause of Reform, and is the motive power of
progress. Age—by which we mean mature life—
tempered by long experience and a slower pulse,
recognises that grievances are not always injustices ;
that some evils can only be remedied by encounter-
ing dangers greater than themselves ; that unquestionable good can occasionally only be purchased at too high a price. It is, therefore,
essentially disposed towards Conservatism—rather
inclined to endure the actual than to venture upon
the unknown. Youth is sanguine, and sees few
difficulties and no dangers ; age is timid, and prone
to exaggerate both. Youth appreciates the object ;
age counts the cost. Youth commonly sees things
too vividly to see more than one side of the question ; age, if it be worth its salt, sees both, and
perhaps weighs them too nicely in the balance.
Youth burns for the achievement of good ; age is
content if mischief can be warded off. The calm
and mellow reflectiveness of age—the mere faculty
of *recipiency* which the death or the deadening of
early passion brings with it—sees a thousand modifying and restraining considerations on every subject
which escape the blind and rash impulsiveness of
youth, and weighs far more soberly, and very differ-

ently, what is seen by both. Thus, even if circumstances remain the same, it is scarcely possible that a competent and thoughtful politician at fifty should take the same view of public questions and measures that he took at five-and-twenty; still less is it possible that, if he be honest and courageous, he should not avow and act upon the change.

Again : views and standards of public duty and Parliamentary obligations vary considerably in the course of a generation. They are modified, ripened, enlightened, widened. At the beginning of this century comparatively few members of Parliament conceived that they were in any way called upon to think for themselves. The chiefs decided on the line of policy; the bulk of the party adopted it as a matter of course. A party was an army; the ruler decided on the war, the general directed the tactics, the rank and file simply did as they were bid. There was no third section in the House; there were few "independent members;" there were almost no crotchety ones. With the Reform Act of 1832 a great change passed over this aspect of public life. A number of fresh politicians gained entrance into the assembly; men accustomed to think, argue, and inquire ; men not broken into the old official formalisms and conventionalisms as to public duty which passed current in a shallower and less earnest age ; men with an individual conscience and an individual intelligence ; men who could no more take their politics from the Treasury bench than their creed from Lambeth or the Convocation. Constituencies, too, had their own views, and expected their representative to be able to defend his

upon the hustings. Now, when a man has to defend his opinions, he is forced a little to examine
them, to ascertain their foundation, to think what
can decently and logically be said for them. He
often begins to see that this is in truth far less
than he had fancied. He grows ashamed of maintaining tenets for which he can make out no respectable case. New questions, too, came up, as to
which no stereotyped party doctrine had yet been
consolidated or established; and on these, individuals were in a manner left to make up their own
minds; while at the same time, by some such process as we have sketched, it began to be found that
there were no longer only two sides to a question.
Gradually, then, a new theory as to the obligations
of a politician grew up and gained adoption; so many
senators insisted on thinking for themselves that it
soon became incumbent upon all to do so: and thus
men got into the habit of exercising what (as Lord
Westbury says) "they were pleased to call their
minds" upon each topic as it arose, in a fashion
which was very inconvenient and often very exas-
perating to their leaders. In this way arose infinite
confusion among hereditary opinions. Men found
that they had been born on the wrong benches, or
were sitting for the wrong constituencies. Tories
discovered with surprise that they had an unsus-
pected Whig corner in their minds, and Liberals
that they had a strange amount of Conservatism
lurking at the bottom of their hearts; they mutually
avowed their discoveries, and were called "renegades," "apostates," "flagrant examples of political
inconsistency, and tergiversation," in consequence.

Inconsistency of this sort—and it is the commonest of all sorts—is but the legitimate growth and outcome of a raised and improved standard of patriotic obligation, of a more diffused intellectual activity, and a developed purity of conscience.

But this is not all. Circumstances change as years pass on, and they often change widely within the lifetime of a statesman. The same measures, nay, the same principles of action, which were sagacious and appropriate at one period, may become injudicious and unsuitable at another. There is a time for pressing on, and a time for holding back—a time for almost revolutionary daring, and a time for almost obstinate resistance and reaction. It is for a calm and courageous statesman to weigh and measure the requirements of the actual hour, and to refuse to be bound to, or influenced by, the deductions drawn by others from his previous professions and avowals, even though he may in earlier life, or under other contingencies, or amid different surroundings, have announced general principles too wide or unmodified for the occasion that called them forth. He may have been rash in announcing such broad fundamental rules; but he would be something worse than rash if he suffered himself to be coerced by them, under pain of being accused of " inconsistency," into a line of action logically imperative, but practically unwise. Pitt could with perfect plausibility and honesty of conviction, if not with irrefragable soundness of judgment, refuse in 1793 to carry out, or even to discuss, that wide plan of parliamentary reform which he brought forward in 1784. Organic and popular changes on a great

scale, which were perfectly safe and fitting in the
dull stagnation of Lord North's administration,
might be utterly unsuitable and unsafe in the midst
of that wild democratic excitement which succeeded
the French Revolution of 1789. Peel may have
been unwise in resisting Catholic emancipation for
so many years, as most of us think he was; he may
have been wrong in conceding it as he did in 1829,
as many even still contend. But it is not correct
to charge him with "inconsistency" because he
altered his course when the dangers of the course
he had hitherto pursued became too menacing to
be encountered. He changed, not because he had
abandoned his former convictions as to the grave objections to the concession claimed, but because under
the circumstances of the conjuncture the evils of
concession had come to outweigh the evils of continued resistance. It had always been in his mind a
question of balance, and the balance he was forced to
recognise had begun to incline in an opposite direction.

There is yet another quite unimpeachable cause of
political inconsistency, or what is commonly though
loosely called by that name. From time to time, as
we have said, new questions come up, as new ideas
slowly make their way from the closet of the student
through the various classes of the community, or as
the nation traverses new phases in its history.
These new questions are like a shell falling into the
serried ranks of party, scattering them in all directions and separating chief friends. There may be
no real inconsistency in the line taken by any one
of the statesmen whose course is disturbed by the
introduction of the fresh element into political life,

because none of them had previously any settled or declared opinion on the subject; but there is apparent inconstancy and change, because men cease to act with their former associates, and join the camp of their former opponents. The French Revolution was an example of this sort of convulsing novelty in the last century, by the ideas and objects which it originated, ripened, or involved. Democracy, socialism, universal equality, and their derivatives, had not till that outburst—in modern times, at least—come to the front ; and politicians, therefore, were not committed upon them, and indeed for the most part had never been called upon to form any views in regard to them. The abolition of the corn laws, and the principles of free trade generally, may be taken as an analogous example in our days. They had been discussed by philosophers for some years, but they can scarcely be said to have become a practical public question till 1840, or thereabouts ; and at that time there were very few among our statesmen and politicians who had either really considered them, or held any clear and deliberate opinions in reference to them. They were as new to the Whigs as to the Tories, and (party conflicts and interests apart) were almost as likely to find converts on the one side as on the other. It was a Whig Premier who declared, " before God," that the project of extinguishing the corn laws " was the wildest and maddest scheme he had ever heard of." It was a Tory Premier who, three or four years later, persuaded his followers to surrender them. It was on this new question that Lord Stanley, a Whig by birth, finally went over to the Conservatives and became their leader, and that Peel and Gladstone definitively embraced those progressive doctrines which broke up their party, and have now made the last-named statesman the hope and chief of the most advanced Liberals. Yet it would be inaccurate and unjust to charge any of these public men with inconsistency in consequence of the line they respectively adopted in reference to free trade.

Nor, to conclude, can a politician be fairly accused of inconsistency merely because he chooses to stop short in the career of retrenchment and reform. He is not bound to pursue his course to its furthest ultimate results, or to draw the extreme logical consequences from the principles he has adopted as the practical guide of his life. Everything in politics is a question of occasion, of balance, of degree. A man may be a daring and aggressive Reformer as long as certain grievances and abuses against which he has set his face are unredressed, and become a resisting Conservative the day after, and yet be a model of deliberate consistency. The attitude of assault one moment may be quite in logical harmony with the attitude of defence and resistance the next moment. A politician, pledged to an extension of the suffrage is not bound to vote for a five-pound franchise because some time ago he voted for a ten-pound franchise. A politician who has been open-mouthed against extravagant expenditure is in no way called upon to object to expenditure which, even if increased, has ceased to be *extravagant*. Because he quarrelled with a revenue of seventy millions, he is not bound to continue his crusade against a revenue of sixty. Lord John Russell once said, and said within a very few years—" I was a zealous reformer when I entered public life; I am a zealous reformer still." Taken nakedly and broadly as it was said, this seems much like saying, " I was ravenously hungry before dinner. I have had a full meal since —but I am ravenously hungry still." For when Lord John began his career, borough-mongering was rampant; the middle classes, as well as the populace, were excluded from the franchise; the pension-list was gross and shameless; the Test Acts were still in force; Catholics were unemancipated; Dissenters were met at the threshold of the House of Commons by an oath they could not take; in short, all kinds of abuses which existed when the veteran statesman made his first declaration had ceased to exist when he made his second. There is a legitimate and there is a bastard consistency; true political consistency—-real harmony and steadiness in a statesman's life—lies not in always holding the same language, defending the same measures, acting with the same men—but in always having your country's good distinctly and singly in view—that good being estimated, no doubt, on certain definite first principles; in striving for the same end, not in using the same means; in going five miles to reach your goal, not in going ten to overshoot it. There are men who fancy themselves consistent because they are always combatant and aggressive; purifiers of the temple because they are always wielding the knotted cord; reformers, because always indulging their iconoclastic propensities;—while in truth it is only their tempers, and not their politics, that are consistent.

IX

THE PARLIAMENTARY CAREER.

A CHANGE would seem to be creeping over public life in England, which, if it be real, it is especially important to signalise and understand. The change has been gradual, but promises to be rapid. It began with the Reform Act of 1832; it has been growing ever since; and, if we are not mistaken, it will be accelerated and consummated by the electoral measure of the session before last. It springs out of a combination of circumstances, and is aided by many influences, and will assuredly entail many grave and potent consequences. In a word, a Parliamentary career is no longer what it used to be; it is entered upon by a different set of men; it is sought from other motives; it is used for other purposes. The rewards it offers are fewer than formerly; and the cost and sacrifices it involves are greater. It is still nearly as much desired as ever, and it must always be an object of ambition; but the ambition which aspires to it bids fair to become less pure and lofty than it was and than it should be—less hallowed by the character of the arena in which it plays its part—less ennobled by a consciousness of great purposes and great power. The change we speak of is not completed yet, and therefore we see only a portion of its operation; but it is

not the less indisputable or significant on that
account. It is insidious ; it may be slow ; it may
be inevitable and incurable ;—but at least it ought
not to be unconscious.

The change we refer to is briefly this :—The
House of Commons is growing less attractive and
less easy of access than of yore to the best men,
while it retains all its charms and opens wide its
doors to the worst men. Those whom we most
need there are not those who can most easily get
there, or who most eagerly seek to be there. Those
whom the country could well dispense with in such
a position flock to it in scores, and step easily over
the threshold. Those who have personal, professional, or class *interests* to serve have every motive
for entering Parliament. Those who have only
great public objects to serve, and great principles to
propound and promote, are beginning to discover
that their exertions may be far more efficient and
secure much prompter success in other careers and
on other platforms ; the seed they sow will ripen
faster and bear richer fruit in other soils ; while
nowhere and on no stage is it so difficult for a
labourer in the public vineyard to keep his conscience pure, his eye single, his attitude upright and
unbending, and his course unswerving and direct.
The price you must pay for the House of Commons
as a stage on which to exert your powers and promote your ends (supposing those ends noble and
unselfish) is disproportionately great ; while the
success you can achieve (practical and unselfish
success we mean) is disproportionately small—and
too often soiled and mutilated as well as small.

Macaulay long ago described Parliamentary strife as " a career in which the most its combatants can expect is, that by relinquishing liberal studies and social comfort, by passing nights without sleep, and summers without one glimpse of the beauties of nature, they may attain that laborious, that invidious, that closely-watched slavery, which is mocked with the name of power." The description, true enough even in his day, is incomparably truer now. The sacrifice of comfort and leisure is more complete, the toil severer, the slavery at once harsher and meaner, and the power immeasurably scantier and more illusory. But we must enter a little more into detail.

Of course, a seat in Parliament is still, and will long continue to be, eagerly sought by large classes, and by many individuals who have special interests to defend, special causes to serve, special objects to gain. It will be sought, too, by numbers who deem it a fit appanage or a natural corollary of their social position, as well as by those who hope through it to attain or assert a social position which is not theirs by general consent or hereditary right. Thus, there will always be plenty of country gentlemen— sufficient, it may be hoped, to leaven the mass with a due infusion of the genuine old genial Conservatism of England—whose standing and influence as great landed proprietors and representatives of ancient families point them out as fitting representatives also of an order still powerful and respected. Many of this class, moreover—though fewer than formerly, and fewer perhaps year by year—will be able to secure their return, through the felt but unasserted influence of combined character and rank, without resorting to those humiliating means of canvassing or cajoling, or the still more humilating means of intimidation, which deter the more scrupulous natures from the strife. What effect upon the success of candidates of this sort may be wrought by the votes of the new £12 constituencies who reside in and about small unrepresented towns, it is too soon to judge, and is not worth while to guess. But that they will always come forward in great strength for election, and be returned in considerable numbers, we may be certain, for they feel instinctively both that they have a right to be in Parliament and that their presence there is essential, and increasingly essential, to defend the interests of their order and to assert their due weight in the general councils of the nation.   We need not fear, then, that country-gentlemen members will shrink or fail—at all events, not for some time to come, nor till the prevalent tone and temper of the whole people have undergone a great change.

Partly for the same reasons, and partly for special ones applicable to themselves alone, the sons of noble families will still appear freely as candidates. The old sentiment—whether logically sound or not —that their wealth and social standing entitle them to a large share in the county representation, still lingers both in their own minds and in the minds of a considerable portion of the electoral body. A young lord will always be a formidable rival on the hustings and at the poll.   Two considerations, especially, will always operate powerfully in urging them to come forward. It is felt that not only the

interests of the aristocracy, but the especial national
policy grateful to its tastes and principles, are more
efficiently and more gracefully defended in the out-
post of the House of Commons than in the citadel
of the House of Peers. If anything of selfish claim
mingles with the conflict, the selfishness is more dis-
guised. If anything of bigoted or narrow sentiment
is involved in the policy maintained, its unen-
lightened character is less offensive when shared and
manifested by a popular assembly. The Lords are
as well aware as the Radicals that all their battles
will be most wisely and most safely fought in the
Lower House; and it is there, in consequence, that
till their native sagacity altogether deserts them,
they will seek to strengthen themselves. The other
consideration is more personal. Every heir to a
seat in the House of Lords is conscious that he
will enter that House under a great disadvantage
unless he has enjoyed a preliminary training in
that other assembly where the mighty questions of
national policy are debated with a fierceness and a
closeness, an intensity of purpose, and an unspar-
ing hostility, supposed to be unknown in the gentler
and more decorous controversies of the Senate. It
appears to be universally acknowledged that, with
scarcely an exception, all who aspire really to be
distinguished leaders in the House of Lords must
have won their spurs in the House of Commons.

The squirearchy and the aristocracy, therefore,
will never be lacking among the aspirants to Parliamentary honours. The same may be said of
lawyers. Their professional knowledge will always
be useful and always needed there; and there

seems a certain propriety in the arrangement by which those who are to administer laws help to make them. Barristers, too, are seldom very fanatical or enthusiastic devotees on public questions; their views and feelings are professional rather than political; they can more easily than most men, and with less conscious insincerity or wear and tear of conscience, bend their somewhat flexible opinions to the requirements of this or that constituency; the practice of pleading any cause in court is a capital training for the task of defending any measure in the Senate; while, their whole life being habitually one of controversy and contention, they will not be deterred and disgusted, as many quiet men are, by the rough battle of the hustings. But besides all this, according to our present system—a system open, no doubt, to the strongest and gravest objections, but not perhaps on that account the more likely to be rectified—a seat in Parliament is a necessary step to the highest honours of the legal profession, and therefore certain to be sought and obtained by all its keener and more ambitious members. As long as attorneys and solicitors-general, chief justices, and lord chancellors are chosen exclusively from Parliamentary lawyers and political partisans, so long shall we always be secure of a sufficiency of barristers on both sides of the House of Commons.

There is yet another class of men who, so long as legislative processes remain unchanged, will always abound and superabound in St Stephen's Chapel— viz., railway directors and the managers and chiefs of other great companies. Their appearance there, indeed, is a phenomenon of very recent date. A very few years ago they were looked upon with especial dread and dislike by nearly all the sections which then preponderated and ruled in Parliament. But now they have made good their footing there, and as we all know, are far more influential than is desirable for the public well-being. They have every motive for entering the House of Commons, and every facility for winning entrance. They are often enormously rich, and can wield many of the subtler influences which decide elections. Like lawyers, their aims, when once elected, are personal rather than political; the questions which stir and guide their Parliamentary action are local ones, not public ones; they acknowledge closer allegiance to their company than to their party, and are supposed to think more of their commercial than of their electoral constituents. They form, or may form—and when they act, as must be anticipated, in a compact body, will form—that most pernicious element in the Parliamentary system, a fluctuating phalanx, a shifting weight, a mercenary band of guerillas, which can be used to determine public and party questions on other than public and party grounds. It is possible —we do not say it is probable, but it is certainly conceivable—that, under the influence of a number of combined magnates of the class of which we speak, some of the gravest and most critical measures of national policy, such as reform, emancipation, retrenchment, nay, even peace and war, might in an evenly-balanced state of parties find their fate to depend upon such wholly irrelevant questions as whether the Government should purchase a par-

N

ticular line, or whether the control of the State or the Parliament over railway management should be augmented or relaxed. The prospect is an obvious one, and the evil a grievous one enough ;—nor is it likely that the numerical strength or the sinister influence of the directorial interest in the House will ever be materially lessened until either the State takes the entire railway network of the country into its own hands, or till railway supervision and legislation are committed to an independent and permanent tribunal.

Another class of men, at least as undesirable, will always crowd the avenues to the House of Commons, and force, buy, or beg their way into it in swarms, namely, the *nouveaux riches*,—those who have suddenly grown wealthy by lucky speculation or exceptional sagacity, and who wish to obtain by membership the one thing which mere money cannot purchase. It gives them social position, the pleasure of associating on ostensibly equal terms with their superiors in rank, manners, and education, an entrance, to some extent at least, into circles which no other key could open to them. It gratifies the vanity of many ; it is the first round of the ladder of ambition to a few. It is worth their while to pay any price for a seat in Parliament ; and they will easily outbid nobler and more intellectual competitors, for the object to them is more essential, and the price is a smaller consideration ; they can afford to pay higher both in purse and principle, and what is great promotion for a *parvenu* is but poor temptation to a gentleman. Even the social reward involved in the position of a member of

Parliament is on the decline ; but it is still sufficient
to dazzle and attract the class we speak of. A
worse or less worthy class of politicians it is impossible to conceive ; they have had no liberal education to enlighten or enlarge their minds; they
have had no political training to teach them wide
views of public questions or a high sense of public
duty ; their opinions will be the mere shibboleths,
not even of a party, but of a section ; and they will
be peculiarly accessible to the less pure and dignified
influences which haunt the purlieus of Parliamentary
life. They can contribute little to the wisdom of
the Senate, nothing to its dignity; while, on the
other hand, they will be among the most effective
agents in bringing about that slow degeneracy in
its tone and reputation which we augur and deplore.*

---

* An analysis of the new House of Commons strikingly con-
firms the above remarks. It contains 45 heirs-apparent or pre-
sumptive to peerages, besides 65 younger sons of noble families,
and 94 near blood-relatives of the peerage,—giving nearly one-
third of the entire assembly belonging to the aristocracy. Besides
these, there are found 63 baronets, actual or expectant, and a large
number of wealthy but untitled squires. Altogether nearly half
the House of Commons belong to the landed nobility and gentry.
The commercial class is represented by 116 members, of whom
4 are contractors ; and though the directorial element has been
somewhat reduced, there are still 121 railway directors. The
professional and intellectual class, " men of ideas rather than of
means " (leaving out the ministerial politicians *par excellence*, like
Mr Lowe and Mr Gladstone), numbers scarcely over 50. There
are about 100 naval and military officers, but most of these belong
more properly to the aristocratic or landed class. Add to this
summary a classification of ages, and the analysis is complete.
Thus, about 40 members are under 30 years of age ; 150 between
30 and 40 ; 368 between 40 and 60 ; 100 above 60. Certainly

But while all the classes we have enumerated
will press into the House of Commons as eagerly as
ever, there is another class to which it is yearly becoming at once less accessible and less attractive, —
a class which, to our thinking, is more needed there
than ever, and more needed than any other—those
who enter it as educated and disciplined politicians,
intending to become ministers and statesmen ;—
young men of independent minds and means, who
embrace public life as a noble career and a liberal
profession, hoping no doubt to rise to fame and distinction on that arena, but hoping yet more ardently
to do good service to their country in the widest
field which it offers to a noble ambition, and to
govern and guide it to destinies not unworthy of the
historic past.   To take a part in the administration
of the State, Dr Arnold long ago pronounced " the
highest earthly desire of the ripened mind ;" and he
was right; the profession of politics, rightly estimated—all its grander possibilities fully realised, all
its solemn obligations adequately felt, all its legitimate prizes valued at their intrinsic worth—is the
noblest a citizen can embrace ; and as such, used to
draw within the sphere of its attractions all the
finest minds and the most superb abilities of each
successive generation, its purest patriotism, its
loftiest aspirations, its profoundest practical sagaci-
ties,—Burke and Canning, Pitt and Mackintosh,
Peel, Macaulay, and a host of minor but still shining

the analysis is, in one sense, reassuring.   It does not seem as if
any one of the three great elements of rashness and revolutionary
aspirations would abound — youth, poverty, or unrecognised
ability.

lights.   Now, to men of this sort, unless indeed
gifted with splendid and exceptional oratorical
powers, Parliament will become, is already becoming,
far less easy of access and far less desirable than
of yore.   The fact can scarcely be doubted, and the
reasons are not far to seek.

In the first place, to a really intellectual man, the
House of Commons can scarcely afford an intellectual treat.   It is more likely to prove a perpetual
intellectual irritation.   The occasions when great
minds rise to great emergencies, and put forth their
finest efforts in a worthy cause, are few and far between; and even on those occasions one hour of
genuine mental enjoyment is usually purchased by
three or four of deplorable annoyance.   The attendance exacted is pretty close and constant, and is most
often mere hard endurance.   Four nights out of five
are occupied with matters of business and detail,
with the particulars of the estimates, with local
questions, with the fancies of special members like
Mr Whalley, with squabbles on important but unin-
teresting concerns, like the Metropolitan Markets
Bill; and any drearier occupation to cultivated
natures cannot well be imagined.   But what is even
worse and more provoking is that, even when really
great questions come on for discussion, and when
the gravest political issues are at stake, the debates
for the most part are disappointing and disheartening in the extreme to all whose intelligence qualifies
them thoroughly to measure the magnitude and
depth of the subject in hand.   There is no *fathom-
ing* of the matter; no true measuring and meeting
the opponent's case; three-fourths of the controversy

ride off upon side issues ; the most exciting moments
of the conflict are invariably those of personal incrimination and retort ; arguments are used in the heat
of rhetoric which no qualified dialectician would venture to adduce in writing, and which no candid dis-
putant could read with patience ; the best efforts of
the best speakers consist far oftener of appeals to
passion and to interest, than of pleas addressed to
sober thought ; for one hour of real reasoning, you
have five of clap-trap, of injurious sophistry, of
windy declamation, of eloquence unquestionable
but irrelevant, of statements that will not bear a
moment's investigation, of logic that a moment's
calm reflection would scatter to the winds.   It is
doubtful whether any man ever mastered any question by merely listening to a Parliamentary debate ;
and it is difficult to read one in " Hansard " without
grief, shame, and weariness of spirit.

There was a time when Parliament was the chief
arena and instrument of power, when it was necessary to sit there in order to carry measures, or to
dictate or determine policy.   It is scarcely so now.
It has become rather a court where the decrees of
the nation are registered and reduced to shape, than
where they are originated and concocted.   It reflects
and ventilates the national conceptions, and desires,
and volitions ; it never creates them, it seldom guides
or controls them ; it only partially and occasionally
modifies them.   Formerly, even within our own
day, a Minister could usually procure the enactment
of any measure he brought forward, with no very
material changes.   Now, even popular and powerful Ministers can never feel confident of doing so.

Ministerial power, now-a-days, is subject to the condition of persuading 658 individuals, a far larger
proportion of whom than formerly feel called upon
to think for themselves, without always being more
truly qualified to think. Individual members, again,
bent upon great objects, or going into Parliament in
order to carry measures on which they have set
their heart, find it next to impossible to move that
inert mass, except by going to the fountain-head of
the constituencies. Enthusiastic senators have touching tales to tell of the obstacles they encounter when
they take in hand a public cause which they have
thoroughly mastered, and endeavour to make it prevail in the House of Commons ; the obstacles from
honest but impenetrable stupidity, from pure inertia,
from local interests, from class opposition, from lower
motives still. It is far easier, and a far speedier process, to influence Parliament by exciting and indoc-
trinating the nation, than by the more direct process
of labour within its walls. Cobden made little impression upon the House of Commons till he took
to lecturing and arguing out of doors. Let any one
bent upon a great social reform, or an unquestionable and much-needed administrative improvement,
attempt to interest the Minister most immediately
connected with his project, and to enlist his exertions in its favour,—and ten to one, the Minister
will tell him it is idle to bring it forward, unless
" pressure from without" shall have forced it on
public attention, and given Government power to
carry it through a torpid or reluctant House.

There is no doubt that if a man is a born orator,
Parliament affords him a magnificent, almost an

unrivalled pulpit. He addresses there a selecter audience directly, and a wider audience indirectly, than he could obtain on any other arena. But even then he wields power rather through and over the outside world which he convinces or persuades, than in the assembly which first hears his words. He is heard by a vastly more numerous circle than he could reach probably in any other way, while the immediate gratification to pardonable vanity and honourable pride is incomparably greater. Indeed, there is perhaps scarcely in life a delight equal to that of the orator, who has fully mastered the minds, and is really for the moment wielding the sympathies, of an intellectual audience like the House of Commons. But unless in these rare and exceptional instances, the mind of the age—and especially the temporary, fluctuating, practical phase and fragment of that mind which we call "public opinion," and which politicians most seek to mould—is far more easily and more deeply, as well as more widely, influenced by the writers than by the speakers of the day. The Press exercises, moreover, a far more extensive and more powerful, as well as a prompter, empire than formerly over the mind of the nation. Larger numbers take a vivid interest in politics and social questions; larger numbers can read; the mental food provided for them is stronger in quality as well as incomparably more abundant. For one magazine that our fathers had, we have ten. For one newspaper of the ante-Reform generation, at least five flourish now; and many of those five are daily instead of weekly, and sell for a penny instead of sixpence, and circulate by thousands instead of

hundreds. To an extraordinary, probably a mischievous degree, men who read books formerly read
periodicals now. The vitality of the national intelligence has been incalculably enhanced; it is more
susceptible to impressions, and the avenues through
which impressions reach it have been indefinitely
multiplied. The staff of writers, too, is beyond comparison more numerous; they write better, usually
in a higher tone, nearly always with more knowledge; on the whole, we think more decorously, more
moderately, more fairly, and with that stronger sense
of responsibility which springs out of the conscious-
ness of power. In point of mere style the improvement is extraordinary; it is rare to meet with bad
and clumsy writing now, and it is not rare to encounter compositions of singular terseness, vigour, and
even racy eloquence.

It is impossible for any one conversant with the
motive agencies of the time not to recognise the
extent to which the Press now performs—some
might say " usurps"—many of the functions both of
Parliament and the Executive Government : in fact,
does their legislative and administrative work for
them, or shows them how it should be done. Measures have to be prepared out of doors, as well
as the mind of the people to be prepared for them.
The Administration scarcely ever detects an abuse
or forestalls a grievance, or rectifies either, till forced
by the urgent and reiterated comments of the Press,
and the menacing public feeling which these excite.
It may not be as much to blame for this seeming
abnegation of its functions as at first appears; for it
is busy, feeble, and hampered, and has little leisure,

little energy, little taste for works of supererogation. But the fact is so.   The most discreditable instances of mismanagement and cruelty connected with the administration of the Poor-laws have lasted for years, undisturbed by official vigilance, and might have been perpetuated for many years more, had it not been for the restless investigations and the ceaseless outcries of the Press.   The same may be said in reference to the Army and Navy.   The journals of the day may not always have been wise, nor always quite well informed, in the matters they have dragged to light in these two services; but without them these matters never would have come to light at all.   Whom do stupid and oppressive magistrates, local tyrants, jobbing or malfeasant officials, dread most?   Not the House of Commons, not the Home Secretary, nor their immediate chiefs; but the newspapers, whose omnipresent watchfulness nothing escapes, and whose audacity no influence or rank can daunt.   Again, what great reform, what signal improvement, what vast social blessing, ever originated *within* the office or department most concerned, was *volunteered*, or really inaugurated, or spontaneously conceived, within its walls?   Ministers are almost never initiators— scarcely, perhaps, can be.   In reference even to minor evils the case is similar.   If we want to force policemen to do their duty and protect our peace and property, if we want convicts to be kept in gaol or supervised when they come out, we do not apply to the Home Secretary (and get snubbed); we "write to the *Times*" (and are listened to).   It is the same with legislation.   The House of Com-

mons does not *open* questions, seldom even really
originates measures. In fine, what new law is ever
passed, what old law is ever repealed, what beneficent line of policy is ever entered upon, what grave
or pressing evil is ever officially dealt with, what
legislation, in a word, is ever done, till the outside
public, acting through the Press and roused to action
by it, has at once *forced* Parliament to take up the
question and *enabled* Parliament to settle it ?

Not only has the writer far greater true power
than the speaker and the member of moulding public
opinion, and directly affecting both legislative and
administrative action ; not only can he do more
good and prevent more evil—and the power wielded
by a vigorous and well-informed pen, addressing day
after day an audience of from 20,000 to 200,000
readers, a great proportion of whom belong to the
governing and legislating classes, cannot easily be
measured ; but this power is within the reach of
many more aspirants, and it is far easier of attainment. For one effective speaker you may find
twenty effective writers. The writer, too, needs
nothing but education, talent, and knowledge. He
is called upon for no preliminary expenditure. He
need go through no dirty or degrading work. There
are no dragons standing on the threshold of his
arena to drive all poor and all fastidious men away.
He can begin his task without the *exequatur* of a
returning-officer, or the sweet voices of a hard-to-
please constituency. Pen and ink, and access to
some one of the thousand organs of opinion, are all
he wants ; and when he begins, he has the inestimable advantage of being a free man instead of a

pledged and fettered one.   The journalist can expose his whole case, and make the most of his
arguments and facts.   He needs neither to trim, nor
flatter, nor disguise.   The member of Parliament
must perpetually compromise and emasculate not
only his measures but his pleas ; sacrifice much
to carry a little ; give up one point to buy off this
opposition ; modify another to conciliate that ally ;
not unfrequently mask or surrender his brightest
reasons and most forcible representations, in order to
avoid offending colleagues whose support is indispensable ; nay, even sometimes, though a man of
the most superior intellect and established fame,
sacrifice wide-reaching views and philosophic principles, or place them in abeyance, in obedience to
the harsh, low exigencies of party strife.   In endeavouring to get things done, you are forced incessantly to bend, to swerve, to bargain, to compromise,
if not to truckle.   In showing what things ought to
be done, and why, you can resume your manly
attitude and your outspoken truth.

Even if Parliament were more attractive and
more rewarding than we have seen it is to those
young men of talent and education (apart from rank
or wealth) who, fired with the noble ambition of
statesmanship, wish to embrace politics as a profession, it is to them far less accessible than formerly.
In fact, they are precisely the class to whom it is
not accessible.   In other times, men of this sort had
made themselves known at college or in society, or
perhaps by their writings, to the Ministers or chiefs
of party, who were always on the look-out for rising
ability wherewith to recruit their respective ranks ;

they had a quick eye for serviceable genius, and were at once eager to enlist it and able to reward it. A generation ago, it is scarcely too much to say, that any young man of energy and talent, desirous to enter the House of Commons and likely to succeed there, was certain of a seat. He was brought in by Whigs or Tories for a nominee borough, and when he had once made himself known, he could command the suffrages of larger constituencies if he wished. Now, he has no such means of access. He is unknown, and can scarcely make himself known, to popular city constituencies, and counties are both out of his reach and out of his line. Middle-class electors don't go to college and make friends there; they do not read books or pamphlets extensively; and moreover, four-fifths of the political writing of the day is anonymous. Nor are they, as of old, ready to accept the recommendation of Ministers and leaders in favour of a young genius of whom they have never heard before. *Their* "world knows nothing of its greatest men"—not, at least, till they have become great; and how are they to do this if the opportunity is never given them? The sort of men whom large boroughs prefer and select —and all small boroughs would seem to be dead or doomed—are either eminent and established political leaders, or young nobles who have accepted popular or locally-prevalent opinions, or favourite demagogues and agitators who share or reflect their extreme doctrines, or, still oftener and increasingly, local celebrities, fellow-townsmen who have made themselves respected or conspicuous by a useful or successful life, or prominent and influential by mere overshadowing wealth, and who, therefore, *ex vi termini*, are pretty sure to be well advanced in years. For the unknown man, for the moderate man, for the thoughtful and conscientious man, who can neither swallow shibboleths nor purchase votes, there would seem to be no place reserved, no avenue left open.

But this is not all, nor the worst. To the men we are imagining, and whom few will deny to be the most desirable and promising elements of future statesmanship—the men of clear intellects, strong convictions, high purposes, and honest minds, who *must* think for themselves, and think in detail and not in the lump, who know facts too thoroughly, and have mastered principles too profoundly, to be either fanatical or extreme, and who have recognised how shallow and unsound are many of the schemes which most tickle the popular fancy—to such men the circumstances that stand at the very threshold of political life are singularly repellent. The conditions of candidature, the indispensable means to success, revolt them. However philosophical and practical they may be, the finest and fairest and most far-seeing minds are necessarily in a slight degree fastidious, and the natures who will make the strongest and grandest statesmen are necessarily, in not a slight degree, inflexible. They will resent the dictation, they will despise the superficiality, they will be disgusted at the virulence and unfairness, which meet them at the outset before they can even be accepted as candidates, and accompany and irritate them at every further step they take. It will be eminently difficult for them, and will be felt as painfully degrading, to have as it

were to accept and re-echo the coarse, and therefore
false, shapes which their well-digested Liberal or
Conservative views assume, in the minds and
clamorous dogmatism of the grocers and publicans
whose suffrages they solicit, and who for the
moment can make or mar their prospects. They
shrink from the notion of becoming almost the delegates—and delegation is more and more growing
the favourite conception of representation among
popular constituencies—of electors who cannot even
for a moment rise to the comprehension of the
deeper, loftier, subtler, remoter issues involved in
all great political questions. Their sincerity will be
outraged, and their consciences, if either strong or
tender, will be stained, by having to suppress or
disguise or modify that portion or that *nuance* of
their doctrines, perhaps to them the most cherished
and the most believed of all, which the electors would
neither understand nor like. They cannot " stoop
to conquer;" they feel it as something incongruous
and unfit for wisdom and knowledge to stand cap
in hand before ignorance and folly ; their dignity
recoils from the mere clap-trap oratory of the plat-
form or the committee-room. Yet all these things
they must submit to if they are to win.

These have at all times been to some extent the
conditions of successful candidature in popular constituencies, and now all constituencies may be called
popular, and the onerousness and severity of these
conditions are increasing year by year. But with
the new Reform Bill another concomitant of election
contests will creep in, almost more evil and intolerable than the old ones, the first indications of which

have become already unmistakably apparent. The size and unwieldiness of the new constituencies, and the crowds of candidates, while they make canvassing more difficult, and are likely to alter the *forms* of electoral corruption, have an inevitable tendency to throw the business into the hands of wire-pullers and professional electioneerers, usually the narrowest, most undesirable, and most unscrupulous of politicians —men who make the canvassing, organisation, and management of voters their vocation ; who will *contract* for the support of classes, of sections, and of cliques ; who will, by " caucuses " and committees, as it were, discount and prefigure the election ; who must be conciliated and reckoned with as distinct poten- tates and influences probably weightier than any other, and dependence on whom may be made, and will be felt to be, especially humiliating to the man of unsoiled patriotism and unselfish ambition. Be- longing to no interest, refusing to lend himself to any faction, too eclectic, because too reflective and too just, to go the whole hog with any party; too honest to swell a cry, too independent to sink into a dele- gate, too proud to canvass and too poor to bribe;— the candidate we are describing—the wanted embryo statesman—will be nowhere at the poll, if even he be suffered to become a candidate at all. Why, then, should first-rate intellects and first-rate natures be eager to enter the Great Council of the Nation, when they must soil themselves in order to get entrance, and find themselves shorn of half their freedom and half their strength when they have entered ?

There is yet another reason—not indeed as appa- rent just at this crisis as it sometimes has been, and may again become, yet not to be ignored,—which may make a Parliamentary career a less grand and worthy one than it once was :—we mean the tendency, as civilisation advances, and its great political achievements are gained, of parties to dwarf and degenerate into factions.   This danger merits a few moments' reflection.

It has passed into an axiom that government by party has been the making and the saving of England, has imparted to our constitutional and parliamentary life both its vigour and its dignity, and has made our administration at once so popular and so powerful.   Party, we are told, is the healthy and grand form of action of the political will of the nation; the country is safe and will continue to be great so long as one party or the other governs in turn, because each represents one of two powerful, pervading, indestructible elements of the national character which successively come uppermost, as being for the time most in harmony with the changing phase of the popular feeling.   We may accept the axiom and the faith without much caring to question or to qualify; but they are true only so long as parties are the embodiments of principles— of those distinct forms of sentiment and opinion which in the main divide the national mind between them.   While the great constitutional battles of the country were still unwon; while political privileges had to be conquered from the Crown, or popular rights to be protected against the nobles; while religious liberty and the claims of the individual conscience were yet unrecognised or unsecured by law, the divisions of Parliamentary array corresponded to natural and enduring divisions of class interest or feeling, and parties shared in the grandeur and the clear distinctiveness of the causes which commanded their allegiance and constituted their cement and bond of union. So long, again, as the two parties which alternated in power represented *bonâ fide*, and were conterminous with those two prevailing sets of views and dispositions, one or other of which is so strong and so marked in what we may term the political classes of the community, *viz.*, the love of progress and the dread of innovation, the passion for, or the inclination to prefer, the old or the new—the predominating reverence for the established and the past, or the sanguine aspiration after the possible and the untried—in a word, the Conservative and the reforming temper of mind— so long parties, whatever might be the momentary matter under controversy, had distinct and intelligible banners, characteristics, *raisons d'être* in short ; and no honest man who thought or felt with any tolerable degree of clearness could be in doubt as to which he belonged to, or in which ranks he ought to enrol himself.

But no one can say that either of these descriptions corresponds to the state of things at present. The greater battles of human rights and social emancipations have been won ; our condition is full of grievances and evils, but hardly of wrongs ; there is an immense deal to be practically done, but not a great deal to be theoretically settled. Then, again, both parties are now alike disciples of progress—lip disciples, at least ; neither talks of " standing in the old ways ;" the only difference between

them is how fast and how far they shall move in the
new ones. All faces are set, or profess to be set, in
the same direction; the controversy has become
simply one about the vehicle, the road, and the pace,
and threatens even to become one merely about the
driver. If the age does not really need administrators rather than statesmen, at all events it is
conscious of wanting the first, and is not conscious
of wanting the second; in fine, there is a great work
to be done, but hardly great campaigns to be fought
or great principles to be established. There is
wherewithal in plenty to make *factions* out of—not
wherewithal to create or to continue *parties*. So at
least it would seem upon the face of matters; and if
it should turn out to be really so, parliamentary
politics will become very small and the reverse of
ennobling, and parliamentary conflicts will degenerate
from battles into intrigues. Public men will combine themselves, as they have done in the United
States, into artificial and temporary associations, in
the lack of natural and enduring ties, and the reign
of petty and fluctuating factions will have set in.
Each successive question will give origin to new
political combinations with uncouth names; or politics will become a mere individual strife and
scramble for power and office—not necessarily a
wholly low and selfish ambition, because, as we have
said, there is yet a vast amount of beneficial and
noble work to be wrought out, which can only
be accomplished by administrative and legislative
action; but still, and in either case, the largeness
and grandeur of the old party warfare will be over.
At the best public men will be fellow-labourers in

the service of the State, not rulers of its destiny. At the worst, they will be competitors, not for the glory of standing at the helm, but for the work and the pay of stoking up the boiler fires.

There may not be so much mischief or peril in this change, if only our politicians will recognise it and adapt their action to it; but old men, experienced men, hackneyed parliamentary campaigners, it is to be feared, will be slow to do this. And there will be great evil and danger if these men go on in the old beaten track and the old inveterate habits; if they think it necessary to fight still with men on opposite benches, because they have fought with them from their youth up; if the Opposition commit themselves to their habitual tactics and their native function of thwarting the Ministry *quand même*;—if public men *will* fight still, they will have to fight over small questions or over intricate details, and conflict of either sort is deteriorating to the intelligence and the temper. There is something ennobling in doing battle for a great principle or a noble cause. There is something narrowing and lowering in doing battle for little measures or machinery, and trying to represent them to ourselves as great.

We do not mean to intimate for one moment that public life may not still remain a worthy and dignified career, attractive to honourable men, and offering the highest sphere for the exercise of genuine patriotism ; only that men must look at it from a somewhat different point of view, and set about its tasks in a different fashion. Indeed, the consideration which might make modest and conscientious men hesitate to enter it, is not that its dignity or its rewards are so inadequate, but that its field is so wide and its obligations so vast and so imperative. Half the functions of statesmen are still unperformed, half the possibilities of national prosperity are still undeveloped. Commercial enterprise, it is true, is quite unshackled, industrial energy is absolutely gigantic in its aims and its achievements; but a sterner legislation and a healthier morality want introducing into both. We are great, but we are not sound. Three-fourths of the masses are neither socially, nor physically, nor morally what they might be, and what in a Christian nation they ought to be made. Nay, more, one-half of these cannot help themselves in the matter. A large proportion of the poor in towns live in dwellings and in scenes which render virtue, comfort, and self-respect almost unattainable. A large proportion of the poor in the country districts can, by no exertion of their own, either rise out of their indigent condition, or live contentedly and hopefully in it. Neither of these things need to be, or should be. The great problems at issue between capital and labour are as yet unsolved, and will sap the strength and prosperity of England if no solution can be found. The whole science of social life needs revision in the light of a juster philosophy and a purer faith. We are lapsing yearly further and further from simplicity and sense; we are wading deeper into heavy luxury, which brings no enjoyment, and is inspired and sanctioned by no æsthetic taste. In plain truth, and by nearly unanimous admission, the life of no class in the community is either dignified or enjoyable. In too many respects the existence of Englishmen is an existence which has missed its aim. Yet we toil hard enough and spend freely enough to succeed, if only we were not sailing on a wrong tack. If we fail, as we certainly do, in being happy and noble and truly great, it is not from want of taking pains, but from want of knowing how. "*Vitam perdidi operosè nihil agendo*" were the dying words of the great and good Grotius. What should be those of the average Briton of this nineteenth century, if he thought as frankly and spoke as sincerely as Grotius?

X.

THE PRICE WE PAY FOR SELF-GOVERNMENT.

WE have so long been accustomed to Parliamentary Government, to regard it as an indisputable and exceptional blessing, to be proud of it and proud of ourselves for having it, and to look down with a kind of Pharisaic compassion and contempt upon all nations which have it not,—that it will actually startle most of us to be asked to consider whether it has not accompanying evils to which we have been resolutely blind, and whether we do not pay a price for it of which we have never dreamed; and it sounds like disloyal heresy and lese-patriotism to suggest a doubt whether it is really so great a good after all, and a suspicion that it may be fast growing into a mischief. Yet something very like this is becoming the dim sentiment of numbers, and the half-confessed belief of a few; and both the vague thought, and the definite conviction, can find much justification in a close observation of our political progress and position. That we shall ever abandon our cherished system of government by party and legislation by a popular assembly, it is of course idle to fancy, and would be a grave error probably to desire; but it is something to take an impartial and searching view of its real working: and perhaps when once the country has fairly realised its mischiefs and its dangers, it may not be indisposed to listen to suggestions designed to mitigate the one and to avert the other. Therefore, let us sit down for a few moments and count the cost.

What Parliament was to us in the days of our forefathers, what it has been to us throughout our history, as a security for our liberties, as an instrument of our progress, as an education of our patriotism, it is impossible to estimate too highly; and the estimate may well be held to explain and to warrant the reverential worship with which we are habituated to regard it. When popular rights were inchoate or undefined, and our dearest privileges and possessions were in danger, now from the encroachments of the Sovereign, and now from the oppression of the nobles, Parliament was a notable and grand device for consolidating and extending them, and for enabling the people to protect themselves against both forms of power by alliances with each in turn. It enabled them to make themselves heard without violence, and recognised as an influence that must be counted with and conciliated, without driving it to the necessity of asserting itself by riots or rebellion; it offered an organisation which at once taught them to feel their strength, and to achieve great aims by reason of that strength; it fostered and concentrated public spirit and public opinion, if it did not create them; it first won our freedom, and then secured it;—and to that freedom we owe our developed energies and our historic grandeur. Parliament may be said to have been the condition of our safety and our greatness. As a preservative against *misgovernment*, it has been invaluable. It is as an instrument of *self-government* that it fails. For that it was not designed : that it does not do, scarcely perhaps could do, well. The work for which it was fitted it has done thoroughly and splendidly ; and we owe it all gratitude and reverence for the achievement. We have now set it to a task for which it is not fitted, and there is some risk that it may be discredited by undertaking inappropriate functions.

The true indictment against Parliamentary Government may be summed up in very few words : and in using this term, Parliamentary Government, we must be understood to mean the form which it has assumed in this country,—a form of which party struggle for Parliamentary supremacy, and consequent administrative command, constitutes the main feature and almost the essential element. Nominally, it is government by an elected popular assembly ; virtually, it is (as it was called, we believe, by Mr Bagehot in his excellent and original work on the " English Constitution ") government by a public meeting, modified by sundry empirical contrivances which experience and ingenuity have devised to mitigate the difficulties and perils of such a machine. Practically, it subordinates and sacrifices the *primary* to the *secondary*—the main to the incidental—aids of a polity. Admirable, to a certain point, for educating the nation, and diffusing throughout the community that vigilant interest in politics which constitutes so essential a part of national life, it is, for the immediate purposes probably of wise legislation, assuredly of good ad-

ministration, about the clumsiest and most inefficient contrivance extant. Everything is done by
amateurs, and most things by novices. The entire
system of our government is pervaded and saturated
with the *vestry* taint and tone. We are content to
administer ill, in order that we may learn to· administer. We constantly discard or displace our
experienced men, in order that as many men as
possible may gain experience. We quicken our
skill and gain our knowledge by experimenting, not
in corpore vili, but on the sacred person of our
country. We are constantly obliged by the force
of party ties and the exigencies of party obligations
to allot high offices to incapable or unpractised
hands, though the gravest interests may be compro-
mised thereby. We compel ourselves to select our
men of action exclusively from among our men of
speech. We judge of a man's claim to· a post demanding especially sober wisdom, thorough knowledge, and sagacious deeds, by his position in the
front ranks of an assembly where fluent words,
plausible statements, and shallow but incisive arguments, confer distinction and bear sway.

This last remark contains, in fact, the clue to the
whole matter. For government, for legislation, for
administration, we need statesmen ; and the House
of Commons is not a school either to train statesmen
or to mend statesmanship. It stimulates oratory, it
enthrones oratory, it makes oratory the indispensable
condition of high office—where rank does not pre-
sume eloquence or atone for stammering or silence ;
it places orators in posts where oratory is about
the last thing needed ; and, moreover, the peculiar

character of the oratory which is most successful in a popular assembly, is often the most questionable indication of the peculiar qualifications required in the ruler and administrator.

"A politician," it was said forty years ago,* "must often talk and act before he has thought and read. He may be very ill-informed respecting a question ; all his notions about it may be vague and inaccurate, but speak he must ; and if he be a man of ability, of tact, and of intrepidity, he soon finds that, even under such circumstances, it is possible to speak successfully. He finds that he may blunder without much chance of being detected, that he may reason sophistically, and escape unrefuted. He finds that, even on knotty questions of trade and legislation, he can, without reading ten pages or thinking ten minutes, draw forth loud plaudits, and sit down with the credit of having made an excellent speech. . . . It would be as idle in an orator to waste deep meditation and long research on his speeches, as it would be in the manager of a theatre to adorn all the crowd of courtiers and ladies who cross over the stage in a procession with real pearls and diamonds. It is not by accuracy or profundity that men become the masters of great assemblies ; and why be at the charge of providing logic of the best quality when a very inferior article will be equally acceptable ? Why go as deep into a question as Burke, only to be, like Burke, coughed down, or left speaking to green benches and red boxes ? This has long appeared to us to be the most serious of the evils which are to be set off against the many blessings of popular government. It is a fine and true saying of Bacon, that 'reading makes a full man, talking a ready man, and writing an exact man.' The tendency of institutions like those of England is to encourage readiness in public men, at the expense both of fulness and of exactness. The keenest and most vigorous minds of every generation, minds often admirably fitted for the investigation of truth, are habitually employed in producing arguments such as no man of sense would ever put into a treatise intended for publication, arguments which are just good enough to be used once, when aided by fluent delivery and pointed language. The habit of

---

* Macaulay's Review of Gladstone's " Church and State."

discussing questions in this way necessarily reacts on the intellects of our ablest men, particularly of those who are introduced into Parliament at a very early age, before their minds have expanded to full maturity.   The talent for debate is developed in such men to a degree which, to the multitude, seems as marvellous as the performance of an Italian *improvisatore.*   But they are fortunate indeed if they retain unimpaired the faculties required for close reasoning or for enlarged speculation.   Indeed, we should sooner expect a great original work on political science— such a work, for example, as the ' Wealth of Nations '—from an apothecary in a county town, or from a minister in the Hebrides, than from a statesman who, ever since he was one-and-twenty, had been a distinguished debater in the House of Commons."

In a Ministry which is really to do its work, thoroughly to discharge the function of *ruling*, we require certain elements of intellectual and moral competence, as well as certain favouring conditions to which our present system of government by party is hostile and all but fatal.   For, be it observed, the tasks that lie before a British Cabinet in our times are no longer the comparatively simple ones they once were.   Society has grown wonderfully complex, its relations deplorably involved, its constitution horribly deranged and diseased, its requirements proportionally numerous, intricate, and urgent, while at the same time the power, the means, of meeting these requirements are decidedly reduced.   We have to do harder work, and incomparably more work, with feebler instruments and more fettered hands.   We have not only to keep things going, but to set them straight.   We have not only to keep the peace at home, to wage necessary wars, and to maintain the national honour, but to solve a number of the knottiest problems in social, economic, and administrative science.   We have to govern and legislate

for, as well as to defend, an empire singularly varied
as well as singularly wide—an empire which includes
India and Ireland, Canada and New Zealand, the
Hudson's Bay territory and Hong-Kong. We have
to administer the affairs, and deal with the sufferings,
and redress the wrongs of a crowded community,
where wealth is at once greater and more unequally
distributed than in any other, where enterprise is
wonderfully daring, interests wonderfully complicated,
passions wonderfully strong, and freedom wonderfully
unrestrained. In a word, we have duties to perform
needing the greatest intellectual gifts and the most
thoroughly scientific training. We want the most
special qualifications assigned to the precise post
where they are most signally and distinctively required—the right men in the right places, in short.
Yet the exigencies of our parliamentary and party
system absolutely preclude our obtaining these things.
We need profound thinkers and consummate actors ;
and, as we have seen, our system gives us clever
talkers and subtle arguers. We want the ablest law
adviser the entire profession can produce, and we are
forced to confine our choice, not only to those who are
in Parliament, but to those whose seats are secure.
We need a Secretary for War of first-rate experience and talent, and of inflexible volition ; and we
are reduced, or find it " advisable under the circumstances," to nominate a young nobleman of somewhat incongruous antecedents, but of powerful
connexions and great Parliamentary influence, or a
statesman of acknowledged and unusual capacity,
but utterly misplaced in such a post. We are in a
position which renders it most important to appoint

as Home Secretary or Minister for Foreign Affairs a man of known and tried fitness and capacity; but before we can do this, we must pause to consider whether this or that capricious and perhaps insignificant constituency will confirm our choice.

But passing over the mode in which Parliamentary Government limits and perverts our choice of the most suitable *individual* statesmen, we have a yet more serious indictment to bring against it. One of the chief needs of the day is a *strong* Ministry,—strong, not only in talent, but in position; strong, not only in definite purpose, but in resolute volition; strong enough to have no anxiety about its own existence, and to be driven to no unworthy or damaging compliances in order to secure it. No man can do first-rate work in first-rate style who lives from hand to mouth, and is always fighting for his life. No Cabinet can legislate wisely or govern firmly which has to legislate and govern with a view to its own security, instead of with a single eye towards the country's wants. It is not only humiliating, it is evil—and evil in a degree which we never adequately estimate—when a Government has to decline grappling with a great question or introducing a courageous measure, because it doubts its own power to grasp the one or carry the other in unmutilated and efficient integrity. It is almost as great an evil when Ministers are forced to curtail or emasculate a well-considered and consistent scheme of regeneration or control, in order to meet blind prejudice, or conciliate shallow sentiment, or buy off interested opposition, which they are not strong enough to put down or dis-

regard. It is miserable to see legislation thus
spoiled, reform thus paralysed, government thus
dishonoured; yet it is, as we all know, the commonest, as well as the saddest, of spectacles; and it
is one for which our system of Parliamentary and
party conflict is clearly responsible. Every Ministry
has its rival and successor ever in its front, strict
to mark, severe to punish, vigilant to detect each
error, and skilled to represent as an error, and to
magnify into a sin, any step or measure of which
the public mind is too uneducated to discern the
real bearing, or too impatient to wait for the result
which would vindicate its wisdom. Whatever the
Government in office may propose, it is all but
certain the Government in expectancy will object
to or pick holes in, and will resist by all the strata-
gems and weapons deemed permissible in party
warfare; and it is scarcely possible, therefore, that
a Cabinet should not frame its schemes rather with
a view to the minimum of opposition than to the
maximum of good; that it should not think more of
what will pass than of what is intrinsically desirable;
that, to borrow a ship-builder's phrase, it should not
seek first and chiefly in its constructions to discover
" the curve of least resistance." Nor is there anything necessarily selfish or condemnable in this
tendency, though its sagacity may be short-sighted ;
for Ministers, like actors, " must please to live," and
the maintenance of their position is the first condition of their administrative usefulness. Popular
favour is proverbially fickle, and the existence as
well as the power of Cabinets now-a-days depends
on popular favour. As long as Parliamentary

Government is carried on by the competition of two not very unevenly-balanced parties for the helm of state and the dignity and emoluments of office—which is the very essence of our system,—so long must each successive Cabinet be deficient in that strength (and notably in *security*—that is, conscious-ness of strength) which is the indispensable pre-requisite of the highest wisdom, the calmest courage, or the most stainless integrity ;—so long will it not dare to be thorough and foreseeing in its legislation, or inflexibly righteous in its administrative appoint-ments.

It is but another phase of the same argument to say, that something of *permanence* is necessary to good government, and that now-a-days our system of party rivalship forbids permanence. This evil would appear to be on the increase. Formerly we had Ministries which lasted for half a generation. In our times they seldom last for half a decade. Pitt was in office, with an interval of only two or three years, from 1784 till his death in 1806. Lord Liverpool was in office from 1811 till 1827. The party of which these men were leaders held the reins of power, with a very brief exception, for six-and-forty years. We see nothing of this sort now ; probably never shall see it again. Ministries now succeed each other like dissolving views. No ad-ministration is long enough in power to plant and build ; to look to the future, and let the future be its judge ; to consider the next generation, and trust to that generation to vindicate its sagacity ; to sow seed for any but the most immediate harvest ; yet no good or great crop ripens instantaneously ; to

lay deep and secure foundations—yet no noble or
enduring edifice can be raised without them. No
administration, none at least that is not almost prophetic in its insight, and almost martyr-like in virtue
—none that knows it must be short-lived—will
have courage to begin great works which need years
to mature ; to incur present outlay in order to secure
future economy ; in a word, to introduce measures
or inaugurate a system of which the effect will only
be seen under, and the recompense reaped by, their
successors and possibly their rivals. We need not
illustrate this obvious truth in any detail. Examples
of what we mean will occur to every mind. One
of the most urgent needs of the hour is a complete
and systematic reorganisation of the municipal
government of the metropolitan districts. Yet the
task is so difficult, would prove so laborious, would
encounter such powerful opposition, would arouse
such vehement hostility, would give such perilous
advantage to party antagonists, that a Ministry
which only looks to a brief tenure of office may
well hesitate to make it briefer still by undertaking
the herculean and unthankful toil. The railway
system offers another case in point. To deal with
it successfully, courageously, and on principle, would
cover any Ministry with glory. But the attempt
would be hazardous in the extreme, and failure
would be fatal as well as ignominious. Why
should "the insect of an hour" cut short the thread
of its existence by an enterprise beyond its strength?
To deal systematically and thoroughly with the giant
evil of pauperism, now advancing upon us with por-
tentous strides, would bring those who undertook it

P

face to face with the vast opposing army of vestryism, strong in its ignorance and its inertia, strong in its identification with the narrowest prejudices and the harshest feelings of the half-educated middle ranks, strong too in its influence over both the borough and the county representation. To handle the matter boldly and effectually would need both the assertion of a broad principle—to which vestryism is intrinsically unequal, and a large immediate outlay—which it always hates; while the results, both in saving money and in curing a social gangrene, would require time to realise, and faith and intellect to conceive. The hostility, which might wreck the scheme, would have to be encountered by one Government; the beneficent harvest of success, which would justify the sagacity and repay the expenditure of the undertakers, would be reaped under subsequent Governments, composed, in all likelihood, of the very men who had made political capital by opposing the unpopular adventure. A similar difficulty will be felt in dealing with crime and disorder. To exterminate that enormous system of professional and organised depredation and ruffianism which is the curse and the obloquy of a community like ours, it must be grappled with scientifically and on principle. To do this would eventually save millions, but would involve an immediate outlay of some hundreds of thousands. It would, as a first consequence, considerably augment the rates, and therefore exasperate the ratepayers. It would require the unflinching application of rules of stern and rigid justice, such as the maudlin and foolish sentimentality of our humanitarian age would be perpetually interfering to set aside. The endeavour would, therefore, meet with inevitable opposition, both from prejudice and softness and stinginess, of which party warfare would not be slow to take advantage, and might not improbably so work upon as to secure a party victory. In fact, no Ministry which has not a sufficiently secure tenure of office to be able to wait for results, and appeal to the *ultimate* operation of its measures, can ever have what the French call "the courage of its convictions," or be bold enough to risk life and reputation on slowly-ripening issues.

But this does not exhaust all the mischief of those short-lived Governments which are the product of party politics. We suffer greatly from the quick succession of individuals at the head of the more important departments of State. As soon as a Minister has mastered his business, formed his plans, and commenced his improvements, he is turned out—possibly upon some entirely side question—and a rival succeeds him, with new schemes and a wholly different set of ideas, and bent upon showing that his predecessor has been on a wrong tack. We need go no further than the Admiralty for an illustration. It is scarcely possible to over-calculate the millions that have been sacrificed in that department by the alternation of competing systems and hostile chiefs. Probably the permanence of the least able man who has ever presided there would have been cheaper and not less efficient than the rapid succession of the most able. It is not so much this party or that party which is extravagant and wasteful, as party government itself. In public as in domestic life, nothing is so costly as perpetual change. Yet perpetual changes are inevitable wherever party is the ruling system. It not only involves a change of men with every change of popular sentiment or political caprice :—it often involves such change where no shadow of dissatisfaction or dissent exists. Men are constantly turned out of posts which they are managing admirably, and where their policy meets with universal approval, simply because some one of their colleagues has disgusted the public or got into a scrape, or because the Cabinet has been defeated upon an entirely unconnected question, and because it is a maxim of party honour and etiquette for all members of a Government to stand by one another. A Foreign Secretary, who has won golden opinions from all classes and all sections, and who has by universal admission conducted our external relations with unexampled good sense and success, is forced to resign the helm because his party take unfashionable views on the subject of the Irish Church. The head of the Home Office may be a man peculiarly adapted for his place, and may be discharging all his difficult and delicate functions with admirable tact, yet may be lost to his country because he cannot agree with his colleagues on a Colonial issue, which happens for the moment to have assumed an unnatural prominence. One of the very best Indian Ministers we have ever had, found himself under the necessity of abandoning his work, much as he liked it and well as he was doing it, because he was not prepared to join the rest of the Ministry in conceding household suffrage pure and simple. Or a first-rate financier, whom the nation would wish to see established permanently at the Exchequer, is obliged to

give way to an incompetent successor, because the
Foreign Secretary has made a blunder about a Con-
spiracy Bill or a Chinese war, and the Cabinet feels
called upon to resign in consequence.

And this brings us to another feature of the case,
and opens a wider question. Government by party
constantly prevents the country from securing or retaining the services of its ablest statesmen. The
best men, the most consummate and experienced
politicians in their several departments, can never
join to form an administration, because they belong
to opposite camps, and must, therefore, according to
the recognised creed and the established practice, be
always busy in decrying each others' merits and
thwarting each others' work. They may agree as
individuals and in their *specialités*, but they differ as
party men, and must, therefore, not co-operate, but
fight. This comes of our theory of government by
party, and is one of the heaviest items in the price
we pay for it. It forces us to take our Ministers *in
the lump*, instead of selecting them in detail. We
determine that Cabinets ought to agree among
themselves on all the points of their policy, and we
assume that they do,—knowing very well all the
time that they do not and cannot, and only gain the
appearance of doing so at a serious cost. Yet still
we insist upon the theory, though suffering from it
day by day. It is scarcely too much to say that, as
a rule, nearly half our great offices might be filled far
more satisfactorily to the country than they habitually are, were we able to select their occupants from
both sides indiscriminately.

Government by party, again, involves another

mischief which is not the less serious from being more subtle and less manifest than several of those we have named. Being based on the theory that the administration of the country must be carried on by men who, belonging to the same camp and section, may be held to agree in their general principles of policy, it proceeds to assume further that they must agree on all essential views, whatever department these may relate to, or that if they do not agree, they must act and speak as if they did ; that each Minister must stand by his colleagues, and that the proceedings and decisions of each must be taken to be the acts of the whole Cabinet. Now this system entails a double evil—the evil of actual compromise, and the evil of apparent insincerity. Four statesmen sit in the same Cabinet, each a consummate master in his own line, but an amateur only, though a deeply-interested amateur, in all the other lines. Each knows that he will have to defend the policy of his colleague in Parliament, and he therefore naturally endeavours by discussions in conclave so to modify it as to render it such as he can conscientiously defend. The colleague, again, recognising this necessity, feels also the justice of conceding all he can, and probably more than he ought,—and requires a corresponding concession in his turn. Harmony is thus sought and obtained through the channel of compromise; and compromise in such cases means the spoiling of the original conception or the scientific scheme. The financier modifies and mars some portion of his well-devised and self-consistent plan to humour the crotchets of the Indian Secretary or the First Lord, and ensures vulnerability and perhaps risks failure by the concession. The Foreign Secretary, respecting the scruples and needing the eloquence of the Chancellor of the Exchequer, suppresses a despatch or alters his instructions, and thus introduces perplexity and an appearance of vacillation or timidity into a previously clear and courageous policy. The Home and Colonial Ministers follow suit, requiring consideration for their own crotchets, and therefore yielding it to those of others. The consequence is, that every one of these Ministers has succeeded in damaging the policy of the others, and rendering it comparatively weak and assailable; they have all spoiled their own judicious and masterly plans, and it is no consolation to the country, though it may be so to themselves, that they have spoiled those of their colleagues likewise. The wisdom of the Cabinet has been sacrificed to its union—or rather to the shadow and simulacrum of that union. In order to obtain a creed which they could all repeat in unison, they have to put up with a creed which none of them thoroughly believes. In order to obtain a policy in which they could all unite, they have to adopt a policy which none of them thoroughly approves. The first evil, therefore, of the constitutional theory we are impugning is, that each department is conducted on less sound principles, and in a less judicious fashion, than need be the case. The second evil is, that when Parliament and the Ministry differ upon any important question, the whole Cabinet resigns instead of one single Minister retiring;—an honest and sagacious Government is ousted, in order to get rid of a blundering Indian

Secretary or an incapable President of the Council :
we burn down a house to roast a potato. The
third evil is, that, as the real views of leading
statesmen are usually well known before they enter
the Administration, and as their differences with
their colleagues are certain to leak out afterwards,
it is constantly found that they have been defending in the House a line of action which they
had opposed in the Cabinet,—had, in fact, been acting and speaking (possibly for years) against their
own convictions ; a proceeding which, though
defensible enough, and even necessitated by the
system in question, yet, to the broad instinctive
moral sense of the nation, savours of double-dealing
and dishonesty, and gives a rude shock to public
confidence in public men. In fine, government by
party in its present form assumes what can never be
quite true, and necessitates what is not strictly
righteous.

The evils arising from the spirit and the practices
of party are even yet far from being exhausted.
Not only are they costly in actual expenditure,
costly in mistaken steps, costlier still in retarding
progress towards a better day, but they are fraught
with actual peril—peril to our national position, our
national strength, sometimes even to our national
honour. In the long death-struggle with Napoleon,
in which we spent the first fifteen years of the century, we caught a glimpse of what might be done in
this direction, when, under the brilliant leadership of
Fox, and inspired by his implacable hostility, the
Whig party, weak in numbers and popularity, but
strong in talents and hereditary possessions and

prestige, did all that faction could do to hamper the action of Government, to damage and discredit our cause both with foreign powers and with our own people, to crush zeal, to spread despondency, to praise our enemy and extenuate his misdeeds, to stint and grudge the resources of the country, and even to starve, cripple, and depreciate the gallant armies who were fighting an up-hill battle in a distant land. It is painful even now to read the speeches of the great Liberal orators in those evil days, though the perusal might bring us some warnings not quite untimely. We should scarcely, we fancy, go as far now; though at the commencement of the Crimean war a faint echo of the old unpatriotic voices might be heard. The danger in future wars would be, not that we should stint men and money for the conflict—popular sense and enthusiasm would effectually prevent that; but that the Ministry of the day, in the presence of ruthless party antagonists, unscrupulous to misrepresent and vigilant to seize advantages, might be shorn of that daring confidence and enterprise which are essential to victory, might be more anxious to avoid damaging errors than to achieve signal triumphs, and might in critical moments prefer a course of action which could be easily defended in Parliament, to one which, while more open to criticism, would be more really likely to secure success. They would be always casting a side-view to the reflex action of events upon their own position, instead of struggling with a concentred purpose and a single eye. They would be like the French generals in the early revolutionary battles, ever fighting with suspicious

and half-hostile commissioners from the National
Assembly at their side, fettering every movement,
watching every error, and ready to condemn without mercy on every, even unavoidable, reverse.
Another danger, and a no less serious one, which
the spirit of party and the system of Parliamentary
Government would bring upon us, were we again
engaged in a desperate struggle with a powerful foe,
is, that every weak point in our armour, every vacillation or division in our councils, would be infallibly
drawn out and recklessly exposed in the heat of
debate; while each attack made by the Opposition
on the Ministry would be regarded by the enemy as
a diversion in his favour, and would even sometimes
actually operate as such ; would encourage him to
prolong the contest, and to drive a harder bargain
when the period of negotiation came.   In fine, till
the patriotism of our public men is both more careful, more deep, and more self-denying than it has
shown itself as yet, the existence of parties in the
British Parliament will always be felt by a foreign
potentate at war with us as an ally in the camp of
his antagonist.

Even in our domestic affairs, moreover, the spirit
of party is inherently dangerous, from its tendency
to choose as its battle-field questions whose perilous
elements ought most especially to mark them out as
sacred from such treatment.   If there are two
subjects which on every ground should be kept
scrupulously apart from needless controversy, and
which all parties might be expected to feel were too
hazardous for wanton handling, they are India and
Ireland.   The politics of both are strangely com-

plicated; our hold over both is precarious; in both
countries we are face to face with fellow-subjects of
alien races and discrepant creeds; in both cases the
national peculiarities imperatively demand a treatment at once tender, considerate, calm, uniform,
inflexible, and instructed; in both cases it is scarcely
too much to say, that our dominion as well as our
tranquillity is every hour at stake. We appear to
have felt this as regards India; though perhaps the
immunity which that great dependency has hitherto
enjoyed from being made the scene or subject of
party strife, may be more owing to languid interest
and scanty knowledge than to wise and deliberate
abstention. But Ireland, with a fatal and a strange
perversity, has for generations back been constantly
selected by both parties as their favourite arena for
conflict. They have consistently chosen the especial
powder magazine of the empire as the spot on which
to play with fire, and to let off their squibs and
crackers. Whig and Tory seem to have known,
just as well as America and France, that Ireland
was our vulnerable point, and to have used the
knowledge just as unscrupulously. If " political
capital" is wanted, it is sought by some proposal for
flattering the hopes or relieving the grievances of
Ireland. If a Ministry is to be upset, it is always
their Irish policy that is assailed. If their position
is to be made untenable, the object is effected by
dangling before the eyes of Ireland some mad boon
that neither Government nor Opposition could ever
seriously dream of bestowing. If a particularly
obnoxious statesman is to be struck at, it is through
the side of Ireland he can best be stabbed. If a

disorganised party is to be re-united, or a grand *coup* to be struck for popularity, the Irish Church or the Irish land offers the readiest means. If the two sides are nearly balanced, and a death-struggle for office is preparing, the ground preferred for the conflict is some piece of policy which will catch the Irish votes ; and the bidding between the competitors grows reckless, till they lose sight alike of the true value of the prize and the probability of being able to realise the promised payment. The peril of this course of proceeding is so manifest and so grave, that the faintest lingering sense of patriotism should prevent it ; yet it is precisely the one most persistently pursued, and is likely to land us in difficulties, discoverable enough, one would fancy, but kept curiously and resolutely out of sight.

I have already pointed out the steady, systematic, and unrelenting opposition offered by the Roman Catholic priests and bishops to the three measures most indispensable to the amelioration of the material and social condition of the Irish people—emigration, consolidation of farms, and mixed education—to say nothing of their encouragement of those early and improvident marriages to which so much of the past wretchedness of Ireland must be attributed. We need not go back over this ground. What we are now concerned with is, their operation on the representation of the country, by means of their influence over the lowest and most numerous class of electors. Hitherto the struggle has been carried on with some degree of equality between the landlords and the priests ; but the latter are gaining ground, and bid fair soon to be supreme. In this Parliament already are thirty-six Roman Catholics against thirty in the last. Thus one-third of the Irish members are Catholics, while nearly two-thirds are pledged to the support of the most extreme popular views. The Romanists hope before long virtually to return all the members for at least three out of the four provinces of Ireland; to return them pledged to act " in conformity with the interests of their Church "—*i.e.,* with instructions from Rome; and to render their seats dependent on the faithfulness with which they redeem this pledge. There is every prospect of their succeeding in this scheme. We shall then have a compact band of seventy or seventy-five members in the Imperial Parliament acting together on all critical questions and party divisions, *and acting in obedience to orders issued by a foreign potentate,*—orders issued, be it remembered, with no reference to British, nor even, properly speaking, to Irish interests, but solely to ecclesiastical, Catholic, and Papal ones. Now, as we all know, party strife runs high in this country, party struggles are fierce and passionate, and party morality, when both sides are heated with conflict, not always as scrupulous or far-sighted as might be wished. The strength of the two parties is often—usually, indeed—so nearly matched, that a band of seventy auxiliaries can turn the scale, and give the victory to whichever side it may choose to strengthen by its compact and disciplined weight. It will constantly, therefore —nay, habitually—be in the power of this faithful phalanx, holding its existence at the will of the Catholic priesthood of Ireland, and pledged to act as they direct, to dictate the most important decisions of the Imperial Legislature, sometimes to determine the fate of British Ministries—always to modify, often to guide, unceasingly to tone and colour, British policy. Rarely, indeed, can seventy votes be reckoned as insignificant in a political question or a party struggle; rarely, we fear, can the virtue or prudence of statesmen be relied upon not to purchase such votes at the demanded price.

Now, in what relation does the Foreign Potentate who, through the medium of the ultramontane priesthood of Ireland, commands this faithful and advantageously-placed phalanx, stand towards this country? Obviously, in a relation of direct, absolute, implacable, inevitable hostility — an hostility which is not transient, accidental, or appeasable, but radical and essential. Not only in Ireland, but all over the world, are England and the Pope of Rome at variance. No concessions we *can* or ought to make in our Irish policy could patch up even the hollowest peace between us. We look at all subjects from an opposite point of view. We treat all questions on opposite principles. Wherever we come into contact, we cannot help coming into antagonism and collision. England is the champion of religious and intellectual freedom : the Pope is by virtue of his position its bitterest and its eternal foe. England leads the vanguard of progress; the Pope is the chief and the embodiment of stagnation and reaction. England sympathises with the aspirations and struggles of political liberty in every land : to the Pope they

are Anathema Maranatha—except in the rare cases
where the insurgents are Catholics and the authorities Protestant.   England rejoices when Spain
chases away a bigoted and profligate, but nevertheless "Most Christian" oppressor.   The Pope
blesses and decorates her, and receives her to his
paternal arms.   She may be a tyrant and a sinner,
but at least she is a devoted servant of the Church.
Worst of all, England is warmly attached to the
Italian cause, longs to see Italy absorb Rome and
relieve the Holy Father of all temporal authority,
and has expressed these sentiments without reti-
cence ; and to the Pope, naturally enough, such
sentiments constitute the unpardonable sin, "for
which there can be no forgiveness, neither in this
world, neither in that which is to come."   England
can never abjure her progressive and liberal
sympathies, and the Pope can never pardon them.
The case, therefore, is as plain as the noonday, and
no one will say that the danger is either to be
ignored or despised.   The Catholics of Ireland will
be able to return seventy members, tied hand and
foot by pledges, if not by inherent zeal, to act
according to the instructions of a foreign power ;
those seventy members will be able to hold the
balance and decide the issue in all great political
and party conflicts ; and the foreign power whose
instructions they will obey is the one sovereign in
all the world whose hostility to this country is intrinsic and incurable.

But Ireland is not the only subject on which party
spirit acts with the same reckless disregard of consequences. Indeed, it is difficult to name the political

question on which it does not so act.   Two illustrations only need be specified; and these two are so
notorious that they present themselves to the mind
at once.   Electoral Reform has long been one
favourite ground for party fights.   In the heat of
conflict, in the very wanton ferocity of mutual animosity, in the keen competition for the conquest or
the retention of office, Whig has bid against Tory,
and Tory against Whig, for Radical support or
popular enthusiasm; and orators, and even statesmen, who might have kept cooler heads and sounder
hearts, have given utterance to sentiments and pro-
claimed doctrines so wide and wild as to cover and
entail practical conclusions which they never meant
to sanction; till, among them, they have ended in
handing over constitutional preponderance, and the
possibility at least of actual supremacy, to the lowest
and least educated classes in the community, and
made Great Britain a virtual and contingent, if not
yet a realised democracy.   And now the same party
strife, the same inconsiderate rivalry, threatens to
land us in a further danger, and to relieve from the
burdens of the State the classes whom they have
already invested with its government—to exempt
from taxation those whom they have just endowed
with power.   For such indisputably would be the
effect of that substitution of direct for indirect imposts which at least one member of the Cabinet is
pledged to bring about, and for which others have
shown an ominous inclination.   What patriotism
does, it should do at all events with his eyes open.
What party warfare does, it does always with his
eyes shut—thinking only of immediate victory, never

of remote issues—seeing nothing but the hereditary
foe in front, and never dreaming of the time, drawing
nearer with each fresh error and each added year,
when the alliance of that foe will be sought in des-
peration to help against the new rival to whom their
senseless contests have given the mastery over both.
It is the fashion to treat these distant dangers as
the exaggerated and distorted visions of alarmists,
or as too far off to claim the attention of men who
have only a life-tenure of this earth. We hear it
said on every side that property, rank, education,
and refinement, will always command due respect,
will always wield vast influence, will always practically be able to keep the government in their
hands ; and if it were not for the inveterate habits
and the inevitable operations of party strife, the saying would be true and reassuring. But those who
lay this flattering unction to their souls, and cradle
themselves in the comforting consideration, lose
sight of one main feature of the case—which is, that
these four grand elements of political preponderance
and strength are not found fighting side by side
against a common danger and a common rival, but
are split into hostile camps and arranged against
each other—the rich, the noble, and cultivated
Liberals contending with the rich, the noble, and
cultivated Conservatives for the alliance and the
leadership of the masses, who have their own
objects and their own ideas, and amid the disunion
and consequent weakness of the other combatants,
will be able to dictate terms and bear away the
prize.

The last indictment we have to bring against our

system of Party Government will appear, to earnest minds, perhaps the heaviest of all. We speak of its ceaseless and inevitable operation in retarding real progress, in postponing year after year the most urgent social and administrative reforms to mere struggles for the mastery. The strife for power is naturally more exciting to ordinary natures than the dry hard work of legislation or inquiry. The exigencies of Parliamentary conflict need things to fight over, not things to do. Now, practical measures, however important or comprehensive, do not supply this want; it is often not easy to differ about them materially, or to wrangle over anything save their details, which are wearisome to the controversialists and not interesting to the country. Nay, the Opposition are not anxious, as a rule, to see the Ministry take them up, lest they should gain credit by their mode of dealing with them. Even the sorest social grievances are no favourites with the spirit of party, if they are so undeniable and grave that they cannot be ignored by either side, or transmuted into weapons or occasions of reproach and assault by intertwining with them some vulgar prejudice or popular passion. Party conflict must have a party " cry," and measures of administrative progress and reform do not usually furnish materials for a cry. They must therefore be thrust into the background, and other questions more available for the purpose must be brought forward or manufactured.

Few periods of our history afford an ampler illustration of this evil than the present and the very recent past. Rarely has so great a burden of responsibility lain at the door of statesmen who, ses-

sion after session, insist on struggling with each
other, in place of labouring in unison; in mending
their tools, instead of working with the tools they
had; in seizing the helm of State, instead of aiding
those who held it to manœuvre skilfully and to steer
for the right haven. Some allowance must no doubt
be made for the inveterate conviction which Parliamentary conflict seems to ingrain into the minds of
nearly all who enter it, that their adversaries *cannot*
legislate wisely or govern well, and that the only
hope and safety for the nation lies in a transfer of
power to the right hands. Still more, perhaps, may
be conceded to those who, after sincere and patient
effort in the cause of practical improvement, have
been forced to feel that no great progress could be
made till increased popular influence gave increased
power to statesmen, who were pleading the people's
cause, to overpower the obstacles which privilege
and tradition placed in their way. But neither plea
can avail much to politicians who, professing to be
par excellence the people's friends, and to seek power
only in order to promote the people's welfare, wasted
two or three sessions in profitless disputes over the
extension of the franchise, and at least one more in
fierce controversies over the Irish Church, when it
could scarcely be pleaded that the opening of either
question was essential to those objects of progress
and improvement which all sides declared they had in
view; when the old House of Commons was not only
able to carry, but was powerless to refuse, any beneficent measure on which the nation had really set its
heart; when no reason whatever could be assigned
for believing that the recent exacerbation or the

standing nucleus of Irish disloyalty would be cured by surrendering the Irish Establishment; and when, at the same time, such a multitude of grave and painful questions, affecting the daily life and the deepest interests of the most numerous and helpless classes of the community, were clamouring for solution. Let us consider for one moment what these questions are which have been obliged to stand over for some years, till ignorant ratepayers had been placed upon the voting-list, and till the Irish Church controversy, with all its uncalculated perplexities and unforeseen ramifications and entailed elaborate enactments, had been laid to rest;—and then pronounce whether what has been dragged to the front, or what has been pretermitted and thrust into the background, had the prior claim to the attention of benevolent and earnest statesmen.

First on the list comes the whole subject of the condition of our agricultural population,—a subject especially large, as affecting the most numerous section of the labouring poor,—especially urgent, inasmuch as they are of all classes the most helpless, and as their condition is perhaps the greatest blot upon our social state, and a matter both for grief and shame,—especially difficult, since few of us can tell at which end to begin, or what agencies to call to our aid. It is enough to remember that, as a rule, *it is simply impossible* the average English peasant should live as Christians ought to live, should feed as men must feed who are to work efficiently, should clothe and educate his children as our fellow-citizens ought to be clad and trained, should make any provision for old age by which he can escape parish charity and the workhouse, and end his days in comfort when he can no longer toil,—it is enough to remember all this, which no one attempts to deny, and not recognise a question far otherwise grave and pressing than the franchise. It is sinful to postpone matters like this : it is merely hopeless to attempt to deal with them while every one is passionately busy and resolutely blinded with the heat and dust of party strife. Next to this, and closely connected with it, though embracing many other classes, is the Reform of our Poor-law Administration—the Law of Settlement, the Equalisation of Rates, the systematic Classification of the Paupers, so that, while the able-bodied and the idle should be sternly handled, the aged and infirm may be dealt with tenderly, and the young severed from corrupting influences and companionship, and trained up to be something better than hereditary and incurable paupers; and, lastly, some more efficient control, which shall, in cities, at least, take the administration of the rates out of perhaps the unfittest hands to which any fragment of government was ever yet committed. One might have expected that the perpetually recurring floods of unmanageable distress, such as we saw last winter, and are seeing again now at the east end of the metropolis, and the frequent individual instances of deaths from starvation, and diseases sure to end in death, scandalising and shocking us at our own doors, and in the midst of the wealthiest capital in the world— scenes that could scarcely occur, or at least would not be long endured, under any system of administration less strangely anomalous than Parliamentary

Government entails upon us—would have induced all political combatants to stay their strife, and rush in rivalry to aid the suffering and to stave off the calamity in future.

Passing over the wide subject of Education, which *has* excited considerable attention even in the midst and in spite of our party conflicts, and which is at least as large and urgent as it is difficult, what have we done towards improving the dwellings of our metropolitan and other city poor, and providing new dwellings for those whom our public works turn out of their homes by thousands?   Here, again, the distress and the scenes of brutality, infamy, and filth, lie close around us, and might be witnessed for ourselves any day at the cost of a couple of miles' walk; there is no doubt about the facts—the shocking and·disgusting details have been published till we have been nauseated by them; there is no more doubt about the danger than about the shame,—for when cholera or other epidemics threaten us, we wake up in a panic, and talk wildly of "doing something;" there is no question as to the social and moral evil generated by this state of things, and no ignorance as to the vast numbers concerned in it; yet statesmen and philanthropists, sitting in the midst, shut their eyes to it, fold their arms over it, put it off till a more convenient season, and let hundreds of thousands go to their premature graves with the wrong unremedied, while they grow frantic over the figure of the franchise, or an ecclesiastical grievance over the water. But besides these subjects, there are many others affecting the general community, which can no longer be neglected with impunity.   We need a Minister of Justice and public prosecutors, so that scandalous crimes and gigantic frauds shall not, day after day, escape exposure and punishment, because the prosecution of them is left to the option of private sufferers, who either shrink from the toil and expense, or prefer to save and spare themselves by compounding with the offender, rather than do their duty to the nation by resolutely exacting penalties for the offence. We need to have justice, in small things as well as great, made easy, prompt, accessible, and cheap, so that the injured party shall not dread the process of atonement and retaliation far more than the endurance of the wrong, and that witnesses and jurymen shall not be made to hate and evade their duties, and find it almost more annoying and vexatious to have seen a robbery or an assault, and to be called upon to judge it, than to be either the victim or the criminal. Then we have the vast problem of the criminal classes to solve,—to discover how to baffle them and cripple their powers of mischief, how to neutralise their gradual growth in numbers and in daring; how, in a word, to protect the community from the army of malefactors, scarcely fewer than the Queen's army, which is for ever encamped in the midst of us, making war upon us, feeding on the produce of our industry or the accumulations of our wealth, menacing our peace and destroying our security. What other civilised state in Europe, what other Government than a Parliamentary one, would endure, decade after decade, the existence in the very heart of society, and of the metropolis, and the great cities of the empire, of 150,000 known ruffians and rascals who live by crime, and make a good living out

of it ; who keep us in a state of perpetual uneasiness
and frequent panic ; who disgrace our civilisation by
their occasional outbursts of defiant turbulence ; yet
whom we insist upon dealing with as tenderly as if our
first object were to avoid any possibility of trampling
on their rights or materially interfering with their
vocation,—giving them merely a casual rap on the
knuckles when we catch them in the act, and then
turning them loose again to follow their trade a trifle
more cautiously and skilfully than before ? Those
who have studied the subject most closely, entertain
little doubt that it is in our power almost wholly to
extinguish habitual and professional crime by cutting
off its feeders, locking up all its practisers peremp-
torily and permanently, and stopping the earths of
its encouragers and capitalists—in a word, by merely
resolving that it shall no longer flourish unopposed,
by making it too perilous and difficult and unpleasant
a business to be carried on for gain. Yet in spite of
all, we have gone on, year after year, session after
session, simply growling at the nuisance, simply
nibbling at the evil, simply applying poultices and
palliatives to the eating cancer, and devoting our best
energies and our warmest interest to the compound
householder of London and the Fenian cottier of
Tipperary.

We have already incidentally mentioned two other
great questions, both very complicated, very extensive, and very urgent,—the government of the
metropolis, and the reform of our Railway Management and Legislation,—with which it is impossible
to deal comprehensively or satisfactorily while parties
are struggling for power, and contending on barren

battle-fields.   The municipal administration of this
overgrown congeries of cities which we call the
Capital of the Empire, is notoriously inefficient, imbecile, and absurd,—without system and without
grasp.   Its police is feeble and inadequate, its public
works are administered by an improvised makeshift
of a board, and everything else is managed by
vestries.   In short, the affairs of a town population
of three millions of souls are more clumsily provided
for, and more disgracefully transacted, than those of
any decent provincial city, yet no Government has
either time or strength to grapple with the problem.
Our railways have cost four hundred millions when
they ought only to have cost three ; half of them
are insolvent, many are in abeyance, some in
Chancery ; thousands of shareholders have been
ruined, and the incomes of others are indefinitely
suspended, in consequence of proceedings so nearly
insane as to look like fraud, and so manifestly
illegal as to invite the penalties of the law ; the nation
is heavily taxed, and at the same time inadequately
served ; the entire subject calls clamorously for the
most searching investigation and the most energetic
handling ; yet the attention of the public, and the
·powers of the Administration, are so engaged with
more exciting topics that nothing can be done ;
there is no leisure, no strength, and apparently no
capacity or daring, in any set of statesmen to take
the thing in hand.   These grave and pressing
questions have already been pushed aside for three
sessions, and are most of them still pushed into the
background, in order that we might force on an
electoral scheme which has done so little to change

the face of England, and an ecclesiastical one which
has done even less to change the temper or the tone
of Ireland.   Is there no guilt and no folly in all
this ?

In closing this sketch of the heavy price we pay
for the blessing of Parliamentary Government,* if it
be a good—of the manifold mischiefs it entails upon
us, if it be an evil and a blunder—one grave consideration may be just alluded to.   Whether its
drawbacks and intrinsic defects are to be cured or
to be aggravated by our recent changes, it would be

---

* Many other clauses might be added to this indictment. One
has been thus sketched by a most competent hand :—" If any
one wants to know how this extraordinary waste of national property (the surrender to the colonists of the waste lands of the
empire) took place, the answer is to be read in the Parliamentary annals of the last thirty years.   The cause was the same
with that which has defeated so many schemes of general improvement, and prevented so many more from being even introduced : the same cause which keeps us without decent municipal government, and without some of those legal improvements
which have passed into the jurisprudence of civilised countries in
general ; the same cause which has contributed to reduce Ireland
to its present condition by making it the battle-field of factions—
party government, namely, in a state of things where neither
party could afford to give fair battle to the other.   Our colonists
always had clever agents at hand, able to watch the turn of the
tide.   The advocates of ' colonial rights ' could always make it
worth the while of the outs to help them in any dispute which
they might have with the ins.   Ministers rarely thought any colonial question, unless it happened to be a personal one, worth the
risk of a division.   The Colonial Legislature, therefore, got everything they asked for, and even more.   No advocate was retained
to defend the interests, not of the Crown, but of the nation.   And
in this way the greatest estate in the world passed from the hands
of our people, the people of this empire in general, into those of
small separate fractions of that people."—*Letter to " Pall Mall
Gazette," by Anglo-Colonus.*

rash to predict. But one thing is certain. Whatever be its failings and incompetencies, they can no longer be attributed to a restricted suffrage or an imperfect representation of the people's will. If they continue and augment, it must be because they are inherent in its essence,—because, for a great empire and a complicated social State, government by a popular assembly or a " public meeting," is a system essentially at fault.

XI.

VESTRYISM.

W E are in this country so accustomed to live in the habits and institutions of the past, that it is only when startled by some unexpected catastrophe, or some strange and sudden incongruity, that we wake to the perception how far that past differs from the present alike in its conditions and its wants. Nay, more, we constantly retain the ideas out of which those habits and institutions sprang long after those ideas have ceased to possess any clear or real vitality—sometimes even after the truth they once contained has passed out of them altogether. The national mind, both intellectually and politically, is so singularly *unenterprising*, that beliefs die out and laws become obsolete generations before they are ostensibly renounced or repealed. We almost instinctively refuse to *recognise* the changes which yet all feel in our secret souls to have passed over us ; we shrink, with a curious want of faith and courage as well as candour, from avowing, by any overt action, the new wants and convictions of the age, from announcing them as the principles which are to guide our future conduct, or from embodying them in legislative measures ; preferring invariably clumsy modifications to thorough reorganisation, giving to inefficient managers assessors instead of successors, and, as the needs of our modern civilisation grow more urgent and imperious, adding here, and patching or enlarging there, but seldom creating, and almost never destroying even the useless, the noxious, or the altogether dead. This temper or habit—originating partly in laziness, partly in languid convictions, partly in want of comprehensiveness of mental grasp, partly, no doubt, in reverence for the ancient and the moss-grown—has its beauty and its safety; but it may easily be carried too far and last too long. The evil resulting from it is, that our reforms lag far behind our needs; we outgrow our garments and our dwellings faster than we enlarge them; we seldom revise systematically, and we never recur to first principles.

Now, there is one habit and one idea which together have done more to determine and colour our entire social and administrative system than perhaps any other influence; namely, the habit of the community doing everything for itself, and the idea that the Government has not capacity enough to do anything well, nor public virtue enough to do anything conscientiously or disinterestedly. The former is an hereditary practice, which has come down to us from the earliest times; the latter is a notion which, twenty or thirty years ago, had almost passed into a proverb. And between the two, we find ourselves in the midst of the most complex and artificial social condition, struggling to get on with the same administrative machinery and *personnel* which were devised to meet the wants of a very simple and monotonous civilisation, and were perhaps not inadequate to its requirements. With thirty millions of population; with the widest and most gigantic commerce the world has ever seen; with the most productive and intricate industrial establishments; with connexions, engagements, settlements, possessions in every quarter of the world; with the most overgrown metropolis of ancient or modern times; with perhaps deeper cankers and more insidious dangers than have menaced any nation since the Roman Empire; —we still retain, for the most part, the identical institutions which sufficed for our Saxon ancestors, with their scanty and scattered numbers, their limited and insular interests, their simple habits, their monotonous occupations, and their few wants. We live, or try to live, in their parochial and municipal systems. Unlike the Irish and the French, who call on the Government to do everything for them, we warn the Government against any intermeddling with what we regard as our own affairs. We like, as a community, or rather as a collection of communities, to do our own business, to govern ourselves, to judge ourselves, to levy and expend our own rates, to deal with our own paupers, to make our own roads, to undertake our own public works. It is curious how obstinately we cling to this old notion, and how grievously we suffer from it, and how slightly experience and suffering have yet shaken its hold upon the national mind. We habitually *mistrust* the Government, both as to its intelligence and its moral sense. Dread of its oppression, conviction of its selfishness, suspicion of its incapacity, rooted notions of its incurable jobbing propensities, are traceable everywhere throughout our administrative system;

while the hereditary reasons which lie at the root of these sentiments, and the half-truth that still lingers in them, are not difficult to recognise; and relics of the feudal ages which have survived to this industrial age, complete the explanation of the singular anomalies we see around us.

Look, first, at the *Administration of Justice.* It would seem that if ever a community required the most perfect, efficient, and scientific system that experience and sagacity could devise, it would be such a complicated, crowded, and wealthy community as ours. We should have expected to see the wisest heads and the strongest arms enlisted in the cause —a cause, after all, of the very first magnitude and the most imperious urgency to a nation like Great Britain. It might be supposed that here, at least, no niggard economy, no antiquated prejudices, no clumsy or out-of-date institutions,—above all, no wholly obsolete ideas, would be suffered to interfere with the most skilful contrivances for protecting property and person, for detecting and preventing crime, and for punishing with deterring severity and terrifying promptitude all who attempt to prey upon society. Yet what is the main sentiment which we find pervading our whole judicial proceedings from first to last? Not the protection of the community against the criminal, but the protection of the subject against the Crown. We do not seek to guard the citizen against the robber or the rough, which is the want of our times—but to guard him against possible wrong at the hands of a feudal oppressor, which was the danger of bygone baronial ages. First comes Trial by Jury, an institution of inestimable service in its day, and not without its value even now, but which we are proud of and fond of to an inordinate degree, and insist upon retaining and applying in wholly unsuitable places and conditions. It was once the palladium of personal liberty; it has become in too many instances the shield and the safety of the malefactor; yet still we cling to it with undistinguishing veneration. We are not in the least shaken in our allegiance to it, even when accident reveals its occasional injustice to the innocent accused, as well as its habitual complicity in the escape of the notorious ruffian. Every year, verdict after verdict, even in comparatively simple cases, excites the amazement of the public and the half-expressed and contemptuous surprise of the judge, and makes manifest the incompetency of the hands to which we commit such grave and solemn, and often such intricate and perplexing issues. Only a year or two ago, in the metropolis, we were startled by two instances in which a petty jury found the accused guilty when the grand jury had ignored the bills, as not showing even a *primâ facie* probability against them, and where they had been put upon their trial by mistake. Yet no one appears to draw from incidents like these the legitimate and irresistible conclusion, that the jury system habitually withdraws the decision from competent to place it in incompetent hands. It is sometimes defended on the ground that it gradually educates these incompetent judges in their amateur functions, and associates the mass of the citizens with the daily administration of the law. Perhaps it may do this to some extent; but how few are thus trained, and at what a cost to the community and the accused is this imperfect training given? Few thoughtful persons, and no innocent ones, would not rather have their case tried before a judge unfettered and unassisted by his twelve chance assessors; yet only in the Divorce Court are parties allowed to make their choice.*

* 11,997. In the majority of cases, do you think that trial before a jury or before a judge is to be preferred?—That is a very large question indeed. I think, if I wanted the truth to be ascertained in the particular case, I should prefer an intelligent man who had been in the habit of exercising his faculties all his life on such questions, to twelve men who had not been in the habit of exercising theirs, who might not be so intelligent men, who certainly have not been in the habit of exercising them together,—farmers and others, who are very much fatigued from being taken and shut up in a hot court. If I wanted nothing but the truth in the particular case, I should prefer the verdict of the judge; and it seems to me impossible to doubt that he is the preferable tribunal. When I was first made a judge myself, I was very strong in favour of trials being before a judge; but I am afraid that the jury is a crutch that I have been leaning on for so long a time that I have now got used to it, and I don't think I am as good a judge of the question now as I was thirteen years ago. Moreover, there is no doubt that trial by a jury popularises the law. I remember a case before the House of Lords in which I was contending for a particular construction of a covenant, and my brother Willes was contending the other way, and the question put to me was, How was it possible that people should enter into so stringent a covenant as you contend for? I said, " My Lords, they will trust to that true court of equity, a jury, which, disregarding men's bargains and the law, will decide what is right in spite of all you say to them." And it is so; I don't say that they do not regard the law, for I believe they do; but every man must feel that, although he may have the law on his side, he is in some peril if the justice of the case is not with him also. I think it would be difficult to discriminate between civil and criminal cases; and in criminal cases I think it is better that the judge should not be the man to find the prisoner guilty.

R

But it is not in the matter of trial by jury only
that we habitually suffer antiquated notions and
associations to override modern interests. Nearly
every detail, whether of action or omission, in
our justiciary arrangements, seems contrived to
favour the escape of the criminal. It would almost
appear as if the English public sympathised with
crime as much as we often accuse the Irish public
of doing. We have *no public prosecutor*—no official,
independent of the injured or outraged individual,

But it is a very large question; and I feel some hesitation in
offering an opinion about it.

11,998. *Mr Clark.*—What do you mean by saying that it is
difficult to distinguish between civil and criminal cases?—I mean
that is difficult to say that the one should be tried differently
from the other.

11,999. *Mr Shand.*—You have had no cause from your great
experience to be dissatisfied with jury trials?—No. There are
cases in which juries go wrong: for instance, in an action against
a railway company—they generally go wrong there; in actions
for discharging a servant, they generally go wrong; in actions by
a tradesman against a gentleman in questions of whether articles
supplied were necessary to an infant or wife, they are sure to go
wrong; in actions as to malicious prosecution, they are always
wrong. You may say to them, " The question is not whether the
man is innocent, but whether there is absence of reasonable
cause and malice," but in vain. They find for the innocent
man.

12,000. *Mr Justice Willes.*—And cases of running down?—
There they generally find for the plaintiff; so much so, that a
man who has run down another, if he is wise, will bring the action
first. I have been in cases myself where each party has brought
an action, and each plaintiff has recovered. I remember one
case particularly, in which the question was, whether the man
that recovered was free from blame, and there was blame in the
other; and each recovered in the action where he was plaintiff.—
*The Hon. Baron Bramwell's Evidence before the Scotch Law Courts
Commission.*

whose duty it is to take cognisance of the offence, and bring the offender to punishment. Theoretically and practically the relations between a robber or a murderer and his victim are those of adverse parties in a civil suit. It usually lies with the sufferer to determine whether he will be at the cost, and trouble, and nuisance of prosecuting his assailant, or his thief, or his fraudulent debtor, or his systematic swindler; and we are careful to enlist every consideration, except passion and public spirit, on the merciful, immoral, unpatriotic side. It is made as expensive and vexatious as possible to pursue a malefactor, whether he be cheat, burglar, or garrotter: the police courts are disgusting places; the witnesses are surrounded with inconveniences and annoyances. Of late years the felon has had counsel allowed him, and the cross-examination and bullying to which this counsel subjects the prosecutor, is an addition to the injury already suffered at the hands of his client, to which few men who are not very resolute or very angry will readily expose themselves. Then the same lingering ancestral feeling shows itself in our police arrangements. It is scarcely more than a generation since the old parish constable—the amateur policeman, chosen like a churchwarden, and trained as little for his functions —was superseded by the uniformed guardian of the public peace; and many of us can remember the jealousy and opposition with which this best of Sir Robert Peel's reforms was met. Much of this half-avowed sentiment survives even now; we refuse to arm our police force, or to organise them in sufficient numbers for their safety or our own, or to afford

them any adequate or exceptional protection. The
average Englishman still looks upon them less as
protectors and allies than as possible bullies and
intermeddlers ; and we surrender ourselves to the
tender mercies of the ruffian and the rogue, because
our ancestors were oppressed by the Crown or the
baron and their " myrmidons," and because we have
not yet shaken our slow intellects free from the
inherited suspicion.

The unpaid magistracy is another relic of past days,
which is unsuitable to the vastly enlarged requirements of the present.   It is also a characteristic
specimen of our national preference for amateur
over scientific work.   The nobleman, the squire, and
the clergyman, formerly the most influential and the
best educated — perhaps the only educated — men
in their respective neighbourhoods, were naturally
entrusted with the administration of justice in the
simple old times.   Often they represented, in fact,
the surviving elements of baronial courts and feudal
jurisdictions.   They constitute a valuable element
in many places and in many respects still, and in the
remoter rural districts they meet the requirements
and do the work of the community with great diligence and conscientiousness, and on the whole with
very passable completeness.   But the gentlemen who
thus discharge the gravest and sometimes most
difficult functions of the Judge are nearly all untrained
men.   If lawyers, they are so only as having been
nominally called to the bar, or having attended a
circuit or two as spectators ; they trust to their common sense and their natural feelings, and depend
upon their clerk for the announcement and interpre-

tation of the law. On the whole, they fall into
fewer errors, and give fewer questionable decisions
than could be expected, and are usually pretty well
in harmony with the sense of justice of the population round them ; and it is only in rare cases, as, for
instance, where the Lord Mayor—a respected civic
dignitary, but no lawyer—had to sit in judgment
day after day in the complicated and very difficult
charge against Overend and Gurney, that the full
inadequacy and anomaly of our magisterial arrangements are brought into clear light. In many cities
and boroughs they have been mitigated, under the
pressure of necessity, by the appointment of stipen-
diary magistrates, and the nomination of trained
lawyers as chairmen of quarter sessions.

The same characteristics pervade all our proceedings in regard to *Education*—one of the first necessities of a people, if it be not one of the first duties
of the State. It has been habitually left altogether
to the promptings of individual zeal or the efforts of
individual benevolence. It has been conducted on
what is termed the voluntary system—that is, it has
been consigned to chance. Four-fifths of our muni-
ficent and mismanaged educational endowments are
the gifts or bequests of private benefactors. The
State has seldom been a donor—more seldom still
has exerted itself to watch and carry out the intentions of other donors. The primary instruction of
the masses, where secured at all, is secured by the
extraordinary and meritorious but often misdirected
efforts of manifold religious bodies, anxious rather
to inculcate special doctrines than to cultivate or enlarge the general intelligence. Higher instruction

the nation has had to pick up and pay for as it can. Any man or woman may open a school and set up as a teacher without Government aid or Government interference. The State never troubles itself to control schools when established, nor to create them where they do not exist ; and it is only within the present generation that it has given subsidiary aid in return for the right of supervision and report. The result is what we all see and lament—a population perhaps the least instructed of the great nations of Europe ; vast masses growing up in our crowded cities in absolute heathenism and the darkest ignorance, disgracing our civilisation, menacing our peace, preying on our wealth, and burdening and saddening the conscience of every man alive to the full bearings of the sin of negligence ; and with the education of our middle classes (such as it is) deeply tinctured, and not a little spoiled and narrowed, by the harsh spirit of sectarianism.

Then turn to our whole system of *Municipal Administration*, with its inextricable confusion, and its astounding and costly inefficiency—imbued throughout with the " vestry" spirit—guided everywhere by the " vestry" mind. Men elected by household suffrage, often practically by the lowest householders under the influence of the corruptest motives, for the most part immersed in their own private businesses, usually half-educated and always quite untrained in· administrative functions, are entrusted with the management of large funds and the direction of the most important social and civic undertakings, such as police, lighting, paving, draining, scavenging, &c., and discharge them—as we sec. Grocers and publicans and speculative builders, or the nominees of less enlightened classes still, determine what rates shall be levied and how they shall be expended; appoint amateur surveyors of roads, perfunctory inspectors of nuisances, commissioners or boards of public works; employing fragments of their time, and the spare portions of "what they are pleased to call their mind," on objects which might well task the full powers of the best professional capacities. In this enormous overgrown metropolis the evils of this inappropriate system are even more salient than elsewhere, and, while more manifest and more monstrous, are more difficult to deal with; and we are virtually managing and governing the greatest city, or congeries of cities, in the world, through the antiquated machinery of a dozen vestries, aided by half-a-dozen boards improvised for special service, but often, like the vestries themselves, consisting of untrained functionaries. Yet so deeply is the notion of vestry rule ingrained in the middle-class English mind, that, keenly as we all feel the discredit and discomfort of this state of things, it seems as if no Government could summon up the combined strength, courage, and capacity to grapple with the mischief and apply a remedy.

The *local taxation* of the kingdom amounts to £20,000,000—more than one-fourth of the entire revenue collected for imperial purposes. Of this sum the contribution of England and Wales exceeds £16,000,000, the whole of which is levied and expended by vestries and their nominees, by amateur and untrained functionaries. But let us confine our attention to one branch of the management of these enormous funds—equal to the whole expenditure of more than one Continental State. A generation ago, in 1833, when the population of the country was only fourteen millions, the Poor-rates—*i.e.*, the sum actually expended in the relief of the poor— had reached £6,800,000, and the number of recipients considerably exceeded a million : every tenth man, in fact, was a pauper. The management of this vast sum and this consuming army was entirely in the hands of parish officers and parish vestries, men elected by the rate-payers, overseers appointed from year to year, principally by farmers in the country and by tradesmen in towns. Now, the task of administering legal charity is perhaps of all others the one demanding the very maximum of sagacity and firmness, the acutest and profoundest intelligence to discover sound principles of action, and the most unflinching severity and constancy in adhering to the rules deduced from those principles. Yet that task was habitually confided to the narrowest minds of the community,—to men utterly incapable from want of education of grasping a great principle or looking to remote consequences. The result was what might have been anticipated—was worse even than could have been anticipated. There was no uniformity of system whatever ; each guardian, and sometimes each overseer, did what was right in his own eyes : some were brutal and stingy ; others were lax and lavish ; and one officer constantly reversed the entire practice of his successor. Every conceivable mistake was committed, and every conceivable abuse crept in. Wages were reduced, and were systematically made up out of the rates, till farmers cultivated often a fourth of their lands out of the public purse. The increase of an already redundant population was stimulated by relieving married men far more liberally than single ones, and employing them in preference. Bastardy was encouraged by fixing a regular tariff of allowance for each illegitimate child, till unchastity became a comfortable income, and sometimes actually a dower. The whole labouring classes were fast becoming pauperised ; corruption, indolence, and dependence were sapping the energies and virtues of our peasantry ; and the rates swelled till they seriously menaced the value of landed property.

At last the Government and the county magnates became alarmed ; political economists, and here and there enlightened philanthropists and clergymen, denounced the mischief; and in 1833 a Royal Commission was issued to examine the whole question. The revelations contained in the Report of that Commission were something astounding, and startled and shocked the country. The New Poor Law was passed—not, unfortunately, in the complete and scientific form in which it was first drafted by its authors, but still in a reasonably comprehensive spirit. Sound doctrines were laid down ; stringent rules were established ; and, above all, the root of the whole mischief was recognised to lie in the uncontrolled management of amateur, fluctuating, and untrained functionaries. A central and supervising authority was introduced to advise, direct, and check, the local boards of guardians ;—

originally the " Three Kings " of Somerset House, afterwards the existing Poor-Law Board, with a seat in Parliament for its President. Some proceedings were made obligatory ; others were declared illegal, and absolutely prohibited. The immediate effect of the return to something like correct principles and skilled administration, though vehemently thwarted by ignorance and prejudice, was astonishing and encouraging. In three years the average rates fell from 9s. 9d. to 5s. 5d. in the pound; the total expenditure from nearly seven millions to barely over four ; while nearly half-a-million of recipients were knocked off the pauper-roll. Wages rose, agriculture improved, industry and enterprise revived, and decency returned. But, unfortunately, the work of reform had not been thorough enough ; some of the old abuses—notably that of lax out-door relief —crept in again by degrees ; the authority of the Central Board was too novel and too opposed to the local prejudices and the vestry propensities of Englishmen to be popular ; it was vehemently assailed, and its powers—never quite adequate— were crippled by its unpopularity. Guardians and relieving officers were occasionally lax and habitually harsh ; the sick and infirm were often treated with neglect and brutality, while the able-bodied, voluntary, and hereditary pauper was allowed to bully and impose * The local officials thought more of keep-

* " It is well for the guardians of St Pancras that Englishmen are the most patient of mankind, and Londoners the most patient of Englishmen. While they have been maintaining their right to do as they like against their legal supervisor, Mr Goschen, their infirmary has been allowed to get into a state in which the poor who enter it are poisoned as if they had gone down a shaft full

ing down rates than of discouraging or repressing
pauperism, and did not know how to secure either
aim.   The Poor-Law Board, representing scientific
and trained administration, got into a chronic state

of foul air.   Death after death has occurred in one ward, and in
many cases is attributed directly to their condition.   It was
proved in evidence before the coroner, on the testimony of men
like Dr S. Solly, Vice-President of the College of Surgeons, that
in the female medical ward the air was poisonous with human
exhalations and the smell from the closets, till it " would produce
death in persons with a tendency to serous apoplexy," and his
statement was confirmed by Mr Brudenell Carter.   Two women
died from this cause only,—suffocated, in fact, through the guardians' neglect.   In the men's ward air is equally foul, while the
sick have to fight the rats which come up from the closets.   But
why sicken the public to no purpose?   If all the people were
stifled together, the last guardian left alive would declare for local
self-government, and the last member of Parliament would be
afraid of him.   A single decent official on £500 a year would
superintend a union better than any elected board can do, and
save a third of the rates besides ; but then that would be centralisation, and centralisation is un-English, except when letters
have to be delivered.   Consequently relapsing fever, a prevent-
able form of typhus, is so increasing in London—beginning in
St Pancras—that temporary fever hospitals will have to be opened
in many parishes.   .   .   .   Just look at the system?   The St
Pancras Guardians have been quarrelling with each other, the
Board, and themselves, to the neglect of every duty, for months,
till the old famine fever has revisited the parish.   The elected
Minister of the department, elected by the whole nation to keep
such people in order, has warned them, lectured them, censured
them, sent *ex officio* guardians to their meetings to teach them
decency, and, at last, has been driven to the desperate alternative
of annexing the parish to the Central London Sick Asylum district.   If self-government must go on, surely we might allow him
in extreme cases to suspend it—say for seven years, so as to give
the parish a respite from mismanagement.   If he used his power
on inadequate grounds, Parliament could punish him most effectually."—*Spectator*, Nov. 13.

of warfare with the Parish and Union Boards,—
embodying the old vestry spirit of amateur unskilful-
ness and ignorance,—and was not always conqueror
in the strife.   The result is, that pauperism is again
an encroaching and alarming tide, just as it was five
and thirty years ago; the recipients of parochial
relief have again reached the old million; and the
total rates in 1867 were £6,959,841, or higher than
they stood in 1833; in spite of free-trade, no corn-
laws, four hundred millions spent or spending in railways, and a commerce more than double what it was.

Naturally, the nation is becoming once more uneasy and indignant, and, as before, dimly perceives
the direction in which a remedy is to be sought, but,
as usual, is only prepared to apply that remedy timidly
and tentatively.   Mr Gathorne Hardy's bill of the
session before last practically recognised, without
articulately affirming, the correct principle of action,
when it equalised rates for certain purposes in the
metropolitan parishes, and claimed for the Government the right of appointing a certain number of *ex
officio* guardians.*   A further step in the same direction has since been suggested, and will, we hope, be

---

* Mr Goschen, in his recent speech on the Metropolitan Poor-
Law Amendment Bill, mentioned one little fact indicative of the
sort of petty motives and narrow views which often govern boards
of guardians. Speaking of the amalgamation of unions, he said
—"In this matter there was rather delicate ground for him to
touch upon, but he felt it his duty to do so. In the City of
London there were three unions—the City of London proper,
with rateable property valued at £1.800,000; and the West
London and the East London, each of which had rateable property valued at £200,000. In the first-named of these unions
the rate was only 7d. in the pound; in each of the two others it
was 3s. The Poor-Law Board had asked the guardians of the

soon brought forward for Parliamentary discussion. Two points are becoming clear to the public mind—the first, that taxes for the relief of the poor ought no longer to be levied exclusively upon one description of property or income ; the second, that the central control over pauper management must be rendered more peremptory and direct.   To meet both objects, it is proposed that the District Poor-Law Inspector shall be *ex officio* a member—perhaps even the Chairman—of the Board of Guardians ; and that, in consideration of the influence which this position would give him in enforcing the application of sound principles of administration, a certain proportionate contribution to the rates should be granted out of the Consolidated Fund, on the same plan now adopted in the case of the county police expenditure.   We merely throw out this suggestion by the way, our purpose in this article being to signalise a pervading evil, not to expose our position or complicate our argument by wandering off into the hazardous, and at present foreign, ground of practical proposals.

Two sets of facts have lately been brought prominently before public attention, which afford apt and

---

two latter unions whether they would consent to their own dissolution in order that they might be united to the rich union, the City of London proper ; whereby these rates would be reduced from 3s. to 11d. or one shilling.   He had not received an answer to that question ; but from the proceedings of the West London Union he perceived that the guardians were much dissatisfied with the proposal.   Indeed, it would appear from their debate that there was no chance of their consenting to it.   He had imagined that the union of the City of London proper might be opposed to his proposal ; but he had not supposed that the poorer unions would object to a scheme which would reduce their rate so considerably."

striking illustrations of our thesis of the inefficiency of amateur administration. The history of the severe and prolonged distress among the population at the East End of London, is at once instructive and disheartening to the last degree. The residents there consist almost entirely of working men, and of those who supply their daily wants ; and as the employment of those men is exclusively connected more or less directly with the commerce of the country, it is naturally fluctuating and precarious. The dockyard labourers are perpetually being thrown out of work for a week or two at a time, by a change of wind or a lull in mercantile activity. Ship-building, too, which employs hundreds of thousands, varies greatly with the variations of commercial enterprise. For a long period the trade of the Port of London had been singularly brisk ; our docks were always full, and our warehouses were incessantly being emptied and replenished. From the same cause, all the ship-building yards were unusually busy, and, from the two causes combined, the population of the district had been abnormally comfortable, and had been greatly augmented by influx from other quarters. Then came the crisis of three years ago, the sudden and general collapse and contraction of trade, and the discharge and destitution of those who had been maintained and drawn together by its previous inflation. Thousands of families found themselves at once, and for a prolonged period, absolutely without the means of earning their bread, and, for the most part, with nothing laid by out of the proceeds of their late prosperity. Under these circumstances, the unfailing sympathy and liberality

of the wealthier classes came promptly forward ; very
large sums were subscribed, committees of distribution were organised, and zeal and benevolence
rushed eagerly to the rescue.   During two deplorable winters amateur and ill-organised charity did
its utmost to relieve the accidental destitution, while
the parochial authorities dealt as they could with the
mass of ordinary pauperism.   It is useless to dwell
on the sickening details of the disastrous failure.   It
is enough to say that, by the nearly universal
admission of those most active in the work, and
most qualified by their opportunities of observation
to form a judgment, the distress was rather aggravated than relieved ; the whole district was gradually demoralised ;* genuine and struggling sufferers
were, in too many cases, scarcely reached at all
by the charitable funds, while impostors and idlers
fattened on the spoil ; vagrants flocked in from all
quarters to profit by the liberal harvest, till rents are
said (and we believe truly) to have actually risen
during the scarcity.   It was nearly impossible to
have spent a quarter of a million of money in doing
so little good and so much harm.   It is true that a
very different account would have to be given of a
somewhat similar and still more gigantic effort of
benevolence during the cotton famine in Lancashire
and Cheshire.   There destitution was really kept in
check and starvation effectually staved off during
three terrible years, and the population was not
materially or permanently pauperised.   But, in that
case, the unusual success is rather confirmatory of

---

* See " East London Pauperism," by Rev. Brooke Lambert, p. 9.

the proposition we are seeking to illustrate ; for the gentlemen who undertook the distribution of the large sums subscribed were, for the most part, manufacturers, whose whole life and occupation had been a training to the work of organisation and administration, and who, owing to the enforced suspension of their own business, were able to give their time and energies to the task before them.   They were volunteers, it is true, but volunteers already qualified by longer discipline and wider experience than most officials.

A few months ago, Dr Hawkesley startled the public by a statement, carefully made out and verified, of the aggregate income of " The Charities of London." It appears pretty conclusively that the entire amount thus annually available for the supply of the various wants, bodily, mental, and social, of the poor of the metropolis, including contributions given through the clergy, but excluding street alms, cannot be less than £5,000,000. If we add the parochial and State expenditure, the total eleemosynary expenditure reaches upwards of £7,000,000 according to Dr Hawkesley, and not less than £8,000,000 according to Dr Stallard.   How much of this is wasted by the way, how much is spent in administration, and how much ultimately reaches its original destination, it is impossible to ascertain with accuracy.   But allowing a million for management (or mismanagement), and assuming the smaller of the two figures as the more correct ; and calculating that of the three millions who inhabit the metropolis, one-sixth, or 500,000, are in a position to depend more or less on charity (surely a most liberal and most discreditable estimate), the amount would give £12 a head, or £60 a family, for the whole poor of London—enough certainly to preclude starvation, to render destitution and want impossible, almost to gild poverty with comfort. Yet what is the fact? In spite of this lavish provision—possibly in consequence of it—indigence and distress surround us on every side, fill our streets, haunt our walks, sadden our existence, menace our national well-being, cast gloom and doubt over our national future. Pauperism increases yet faster than either charity or wealth. In 1858 it included *three* per cent. of the population of the metropolis. In 1868 it accounted for *five* per cent. Is it not clear that, through want of sense and want of science, our £7,000,000 is spent, not in curing destitution, but in fostering it?

The inveterate old British prejudice in favour of private enterprise, as inherently and unquestionably superior to Government action, alike in promptitude, in efficiency, in economy, and, above all, in purity, has never received so great a shock as from the whole history of *railway undertakings.* From the outset, the nation, with curious unanimity, fell into the fatal error of failing to perceive that as railways were intrinsically, and must always become and remain, virtual monopolies, the State could not, without an entire abnegation of its special functions, hand them over either to individuals or associated bodies. They were in consequence, both in their inception and administration, left to competition, to the hope of gain, to the spirit of speculation and adventure. The Government seem scarcely to have entertained the idea of direction or control; it gave

s

its sanction under certain conditions when applied
to, but it attempted nothing more.   It neither
undertook the work itself for the benefit of the
community, as in Belgium ; nor secured, by its participation, the ultimate reversion of a vast and
lucrative property, as in France ; nor sketched out
and enforced a well-devised system of lines, as in
India.   The melancholy, and disastrous, and discreditable result we have all seen, and are now
beginning tardily to realise and to regret.   Considerable districts of country are left without railways,
though much needing them, because there they
would not pay as a commercial speculation.   Other
districts have been overrun with needless railways,
because rival companies desired to share in the
rich spoils of busy and wealthy neighbourhoods.
Out of four hundred millions spent, it is admitted
that, at least, one hundred have been absolutely
thrown away.   Thousands of shareholders have
been ruined—scores of thousands have been im-
poverished for life.   Money that ought to have
paid ten per cent. does not now pay three.   The
public, too, is ill served and heavily mulcted.   First
of all, we are inconvenienced by the hostility of
competing and connected lines, and then we are
fleeced by their amalgamations.   Every unremu-
nerative branch, every outlay incurred in Parliamentary contests, every loss brought about by
insane and ruinous rivalry, has ultimately to be
made good by increased fares for passengers and
higher rates for goods traffic.   One great company
is in Chancery ; many others are in difficulties ; all
are in debt.   In sheer despair the entire network of

Irish railways is entreating to be bought by Government; and sober economists and statesmen are beginning to consider whether it would not be wise to purchase the English ones as well. But this, bad as it is, is not all, nor perhaps the worst. The recent financial revelations of the affairs of embarrassed companies and bankrupt engineering contractors have laid bare a gigantic and wide-spread system of reckless expenditure, wild borrowing, shameless jobbery, cruel swindling and sharping, which it is safe to say that the most unscrupulous, selfish, and corrupt Government, in this country at least and in our times, could never have approached.

It may be thought that I have already brought a sufficiently broad and severe indictment against the amateur system of administration in public affairs. But if we wish to form a wholly adequate conception of its perils and its consequences, we must study its operation in a country where it is yet more universal and unmodified than with us— where it penetrates deeper, reaches higher, is pushed farther, and is even more fully ingrained into the mental habits of the people, than in England. America is, *par excellence*, the land of amateur administration. Everything there—public undertakings, local rule, central government, distribution of justice and law, to a great extent even war itself —is managed by vestries, committees, associations, by untrained and improvised volunteers, in short. In the United States, as we all know, any man may become anything; and most men in the course of their lives are many things. Judges, generals, sheriffs, municipal *employés* of all kinds, presidents, surveyors of taxes, revenue officers, are selected and created *pro re natâ*, with an utter disregard of preparatory instruction or professional requirements. No qualification appears to be needed, and no antecedents appear to be considered a disqualification. We in Great Britain go far enough in this direction; but our Civil Service, at least, is in a great degree an exception. Its members are permanent, belong to a sort of hierarchy, are trained by long practice to their work, have a decided, and on the whole a very salutary, *esprit de corps*, and now by degrees are becoming picked men. In America, every civil servant of the State holds office at the precarious hazard of party victory; he gets and gives up his appointment at every change of Government; he can count at most upon only a very few years of official life. The entire administrative staff thus consists, and in the main must consist, of "'prentice hands."* Few can remain in place long enough

---

* The following extracts give the American view of the facts of the case in far stronger language than I should have presumed to use :—

"The revenue department of this Government has been most shamefully maltreated, and by all political parties, as they have successively come into power. Its various institutions, instead of subserving the public interests, as they should, have been converted into hospitals, alms-houses, political fortresses, and places of refuge (if not refuse). Instead of capable officers, honest, respectable and faithful—brawling politicians, broken-down hacks, and imbecile persons, have filled the places, through favouritism, nepotism, or corruption of some kind. The Government has lavished its funds, and for the purpose of having its business faithfully transacted, it has appropriated an ample amount for

either to learn their work or to love their work, or
to have any professional pride in doing it well and
honourably.

that object; but intrigue and favouritism have almost neutralised
its legitimate and intended effects in several ways.　Incompetent
and inefficient men are foisted in; they constitute the corps of
loafers, whose time hangs idle on their hands, and who are con-
tinually hovering about the industrious, and are serious obstacles
to these.　By means of personal influence, and plenty of time to
wield it, they generally secure the fullest salaries, especially at a
season when salaries are raised.　Dishonest persons are another
corps, embezzlers, peculators, corrupt or venal; these insinuate
themselves into all branches as furtively as Ulysses managed to
elude the searching hands of Polyphemus.　Intemperate people
also use the public fund, not for their families, but to distress and
tantalise them.　Partisans, steeped in the elixir of ignorance, disgrace the public books with their scrawling chirography, their
blundering arithmetic, their dislocated orthography, and their down-
right assassination of grammar.　The services of such seem to be
venerated, and, therefore, they are very apt to sit in the highest
places, and to be most richly remunerated for their actual impo-
sitions upon their great almoner, their direct employer.　Nor is
this all; they are generally the most strongly fortified in their
positions, while the well-qualified, quiet, faithful, unobtrusive incumbent is often the first to be removed—for what?　To make
room for a green hand, of course inexperienced, and perhaps
unable to make good the vacancy at any time or by any discipline of training.　This makes the official business limp, and perhaps inflicts serious damage upon it.　Nor has the industrious,
competent, faithful victim been removed from an easy and lucrative, but from a decidedly laborious and meagrely-paid station;
and if it be too difficult for his inexperienced successor, the business will be diminished, or he will be provided with an assistant,
or another will be appointed his substitute, while he is transferred
to an easier, and very likely more lucrative post.

　　"Suffice it to say, that the Government appropriates enough
money to pay for the *aggregate* services rendered to it, but the
appropriation is so unequally and unjustly distributed that they
who do the most work, and the best qualified, get scanty salaries,
while the sinecure, semi-sinecure, and ill-qualified drones realise

America is a crucial example of self-government
—or government by amateurs. New York is a
crucial specimen even in America. Two or three

large and altogether disproportionate compensation. It is so—
truly so, incontrovertibly so, lamentably so. Very few do the
work, and are poorly paid; they work in and out of hours closely
and incessantly; salaries small. Others have most of the day
for yawning, gadding, spinning yarns to the annoyance of others,
snapping beans or corn, and reading newspapers, or writing for
them, to while away the official interval. Soon as the hour of
three arrives they are off quick as a flock of ducks at the discharge of a gun. They reap largely at the month's end, while
the workers who have been employed during their neighbours'
ennui, or who have been left behind, still plod on their drudgery,
and at the end of the month receive but an unjust, a shameful
pittance. Talk about injustice to factory operatives; the custom-
house clerk who does the work of others that really receive the
pay, is as unjustly treated as the operative. There are two
iniquities: the work is unequally distributed, and the pay is
unequally distributed.

" From President Jackson's time to the present, nearly forty
years, the partisan obligations of the candidate for office have
been held to be of more consequence than his qualifications for
the place for which he is a candidate, and every administrative
department of the Government has been 'used as an instrument of political or party patronage,' the discontinuance of
which system was one of the objects in view in the appointment
of this committee. The evil effects of this custom of discharging well-trained officers, and of appointing unskilled persons in
their places, has been well described by the present head of the
Treasury Department.

" Secretary M'Culloch says—' The importance of *retaining
tried and experienced clerks* can hardly be overrated, and the estimation in which such are held by business men is too often
exemplified by their withdrawal from the department under the
inducement of salaries offered them much greater than existing
laws permit them to receive from the Government. There have
been 531 resignations since January 1866, many of them by persons competent and of considerable experience in their respective
duties. Could ample salaries be paid and permanence of em-

years ago we were presented in the pages of the *North American Review* with a startling picture of the municipal government of that city, drawn by the hand of a countryman who had studied it for the sake of describing it, and, if possible, of rescuing his State from the deep disgrace and danger of such un-examined incapacity and corruption. Every man there seems to be an elector. There are in the city 77,000 foreign-born voters and 52,000 native ones. The "grog shop" interest alone can send to the poll 25,000 votes. The great bulk of the city property is in the hands of about 15,000 men, who are thus at the mercy of the 129,000; who for the most part have no property and pay no taxes. Seven elec-tioneerers or wire-pullers, it is affirmed, manage all elections, all appointments, and, directly or indi-rectly, all jobs. The members of the Town Council are for the most part young, vulgar, uneducated men, loafers or tradesmen of the inferior sort, ready to do any dirty work, and highly paid for the work they do.

"There is a certain air (says the native authority from which we draw our facts) about most of these young Councilmen which, in the eyes of a New-Yorker, stamps them as belonging to what has been styled of late years 'our ruling class'—butcher-boys who have got into politics, bar-keepers who have taken a leading part in primary ward-meetings, young fellows who hang about engine-houses and billiard-rooms."

---

ployment assured, independent of political questions, there could be no difficulty in organising the department on a basis greatly superior in point of efficiency than any private establishment. *A single experienced clerk can often perform with ease duties that could be but indifferently discharged by several inexperienced persons.*"— *Report of Select Committee of Congress.*

The government of the city appears to be in a condition of chaotic confusion.

"The Board of Aldermen, seventeen in number, the Board of twenty-four Councilmen, the twelve Supervisors, the twenty-one members of the Board of Education, are so many independent legislative bodies, elected by the people. The police are governed by four Commissioners, appointed by the Governor for eight years. The charitable and reformatory institutions of the city are in charge of four Commissioners, whom the City Comptroller appoints for five years. The Commissioners of the central park, eight in number, are appointed by the Governor for five years. Four Commissioners, appointed by the Governor for eight years, manage the Fire Department. There are also five Commissioners of Pilots, two appointed by the Board of Underwriters and three by the Chamber of Commerce. The finances of the city are in charge of the Comptroller, whom the *people* elect for four years. The street department has at its head one Commissioner, who is appointed by the Mayor for four years. Three Commissioners, appointed by the Mayor, manage the Croton Aqueduct department. The law-officer of the city, called the Corporation Counsel, is elected by the *people* for three years! Six Commissioners, appointed by the Governor for six years, attend to the immigration from foreign countries. To these has been recently added a Board of Health, the members of which are appointed by the Governor. Was there ever such a hodge-podge of a government before in the world?"—*North American Review*, Oct. 1866.

It will surprise no one, then, to learn that, under such a system, things are ill-done, done extravagantly, paid for, but not done at all, and that corruption and jobbery (of which detailed and well-authenticated specimens are given) have reached a pitch of shamelessness, lavishness, and method, never, we believe, yet recorded of any other land. The net result is, that in thirty-six years the taxation of the county and city of New York (identical areas) has increased from 2½ dollars per inhabitant to 40 dollars.

In 1830 the municipal government cost half a-million of dollars, in 1865 it cost more than forty millions. Yet in spite of this enormous expenditure, in spite of a permanent *democratic* majority of 30,000, which might be expected to look after the interests of the masses, many of the public institutions, and much of the poorer portion of the city, are in a condition at once perilous and disgraceful.

The same respectable authority which we have already quoted returns to the charge in a subsequent number, and writes thus :—

" The disgraceful character of the municipal government of New York is notorious. The absolute exclusion of all honest men from any practical control of affairs in that city, and the supremacy in the Common Council of pickpockets, prize-fighters, emigrants, runners, pimps, and the lowest class of liquor-dealers, are facts which admit of no question. But many respectable citizens of New York have been accustomed to console themselves with the belief that at least one department of the local government remained incorrupt ; that the judiciary could still be depended upon ; and that, whatever might be the fate of the public at the hands of aldermen, justice was yet impartially administered between man and man."—*North American Review,* July 1867.

The writer goes on to show, by a quantity of disreputable histories, traced through many years, how far this comfortable supposition is wide of the truth. There are several distinct courts in New York having separate jurisdictions ; and in all the judges are elected. They have considerable irregular patronage, and several among them abuse it shamefully ; the incompetence of some of them is notorious, and the partiality of others equally so ; they are almost invariably and manifestly very inferior, both in capacity and knowledge of law, to the barristers who plead before them ; and it is a recognised fact that to succeed in your cause before particular judges you must employ particular counsel.   Direct bribery—to judges as well as to judicial officers—has been not unknown in some cases, and is believed in many more : and though, no doubt, the majority of judges are trustworthy, and the majority of decisions pure and equitable, still the occurrence, and the easy possibility, of the abuses mentioned, must taint the whole administration of justice.

" To come down to the present time (continues our authority), it is indisputable that most of the judges in charge of criminal business in New York are coarse, uneducated men, knowing nothing of law except what they have picked up in their experience on the bench.   One of the best of them was a butcher till he became a police-justice ; another was formerly a bar-keeper. As a rule, they are excessively conceited and overbearing, and in some cases positively brutal in their demeanour.   The officers in attendance naturally take their tone from their superiors, and treat every one who enters the court-room with a roughness which makes attendance on such places ineffably disgusting."

The Annual Report of the Police Commissioners for 1865, an official document, and therefore naturally guarded and moderate in its language, sums up its account of matters in New York thus :—

" In no other city does the machinery of criminal justice so signally fail to restrain or punish serious and capital offences. . . . Property is fearfully menaced by fire and robberies, and persons are in startling peril from criminal violence.   This lamentable state of things is due, in a great measure, to a tardy and inefficient administration of justice. . . . As our laws and institutions are administered, they do not afford adequate protection to persons or property.   Some remedy must be found and applied, or life in the metropolis will drift rapidly towards the condition of barbarism."

We have heard lately that some of the better and bolder class of citizens, roused to action by the increasing impunity with which crimes and outrages of the worst description are committed, have adopted the usual American remedy in such extreme cases, and have organised themselves into a " Vigilance Committee " to enforce the execution of the law, and, if need be, to take it into their own hands. Some relief, it is said, has already been obtained from the dread of this new *imperium in imperio;* but the state of affairs is bad enough still, if the following picture, from a source usually disposed to look with favour and sympathy, rather than with severity, on American institutions and character in general, can be trusted :—

" The state of affairs in this city (New York) is such that nothing any one man can do will effect much improvement, and the poison is extending through the State. The present sheriff, O'Brien by name, has served six months in the penitentiary, and was a notorious rowdy, and is the personal friend of a very large proportion of the roughs who find their way into gaol. His deputies, who are all Irishmen, are mostly pugilists, or ruffians of the lowest type. One of his old friends, a man named Real, and a member of a notorious gang of criminals known as the ' Nineteenth-street Gang,' is now in gaol under sentence of death for the cowardly murder of a policeman in cold blood, and the day was fixed for his execution, and all the arrangements made, when proceedings were stayed under a writ of error; but the sheriff's personal relations with the prisoner were such that he could not be present at the execution, and had committed the superintendence of it to other hands. There is hardly an office of any value in the city government now which is not held by Irishmen of a very low class, and I believe it is the opinion of leading democratic politicians here of American birth that no more native Americans can be elected hereafter. The three leading managers, however, who distribute the nominations, are natives, but men of the worst character. Strangely enough, in the one remaining court in which

people have confidence, and in which the judges are men of high
character and of learning—the Common Pleas—the three judges
are Irishmen.   It is probably owing to this fact that the court
has escaped defilement so long ; but I have heard within a day or
two, on good authority, that it has been determined that no further
indulgence shall be extended to it, and that the youngest of the
three shall be turned out to make room for a young scamp
recently admitted to the bar, and the son of one of the most
notorious plunderers of the municipal treasury.   As I have frequently told you, more than one judge of the Supreme Court is
purchasable by the highest bidder, and one of them has now
grown so bold in his sale of himself, and is making such an open
trade of his decisions, that capital is at last getting alarmed.
Several of the great railroad companies are transferring their
offices to Boston, so as to get their assets and stock out of his
reach or that of his satellites.   In fact, the state of things has
grown so bad that many leading men talk of quitting the bar."—
Daily News' Correspondent, May 4, 1869.

Of railroad management in America we need not
speak in any detail.   It is not better than ours ; it
can scarcely be worse.   It appears to present
nearly the same features—waste, swindling, "fin-
ancing," "stock-watering," ruinous Parliamentary
conflicts—on a still more gigantic scale; adding
another which we as yet have not, namely, Parliamentary corruption.   It is no secret that bribery to
a startling extent, and shameless in form, is habitually
practised by the several "rings," as they are called,
or banded cliques, on the members of the State
Legislatures.   Mr Charles Adams, in a paper now
lying before us, affirms that last year a bribe of this
sort, to the value of 150,000 dollars, was paid to
a single member of the New York Assembly.*

* In 1868, the Senate of New York appointed a committee to
investigate the charges then openly circulated of the bribery of
senators by railroad promoters and companies.   The committee

There are in America 37,000 miles of railways, which have cost about £300,000,000 sterling. Their working expenses usually reach seventy per cent. of their gross receipts :—in England the proportion is generally under fifty per cent. Notwithstanding this, they appear to pay far better dividends—habitually, it is said, more than ten per cent. on their *bonâ fide* capital. Accidents are, however, far more frequent there than here, in spite of a much lower average of speed ; twenty-one passengers yearly being killed in New York and Massachusetts (for instance) against five in Great Britain. We will content ourselves with a single quotation from an elaborate (American) account of " railroad inflation" in that country :—

" The operations in the Erie line have long since degenerated into barefaced, gigantic swindling.* . . . The Credit Mobilier is understood to be building the Pacific Railroad, . . . but who constitute this Credit Mobilier ? It is but another name for the Pacific Railroad ' ring.' The members of it are in Congress; they are trustees for the bondholders, they are directors, they are stockholders, they are contractors ; in Washington they vote the subsidies ; in New York they receive them ; upon the Plains they

reported that " large sums of money were expended for corrupt purposes by parties interested in railway legislation ; that lobbyists were thus enriched, and in some cases received money on the false pretence that the votes of the senators were to be thereby influenced ; but that there was no proof of the actual bribery of any *senator*." They go on, however, to point out that, as the law stands, it is next to impossible to prove bribery; and conclude, " that some legislation is necessary to prevent the deposit of large sums of money with members of the lobby *for the purpose of corruption*."

* A really frightful picture of the frauds perpetrated by the Erie Railway directors appeared in *Fraser's Magazine* for May 1869.

expend them; in the Credit Mobilier they divide them. Ever-shifting characters, they are ever ubiquitous—now engineering a bill, and now a bridge—they receive money into one hand as a corporation, and pay it into the other as a contractor. Humanly speaking, the whole thing seems to be a species of thimble-rig, with this difference from the ordinary arrangement, that whereas commonly the 'little joker' is never found under the thimble which may be turned up, in this case he is sure to be found, turn up which thimble we may. Under one name or another a ring of some seventy persons is struck, at whatever point the Union Pacific is approached. As stockholders they own the road, as mortgagees they have a lien upon it, as directors they contract for its construction, and as members of the Credit Mobilier they build it. . . . Here is every vicious element of railroad construction and management—costly construction, entailing future taxation on trade; tens of millions of fictitious capital; a road built on the sale of its bonds, and with the aid of subsidies : here is every element of cost recklessly exaggerated, and the whole at some future day is to make itself felt as a burden on the trade which it is to create; and will surely hereafter constitute a source of corruption in the politics of the land, and a resistless power in its legislature. . . . Figures, in the skilful hands of railroad officials, seem made, like language in the mouth of a diplomatist, not to express truth, but to conceal it. One who has puzzled over them long and patiently writes, in language not too strong :—' The reports of the companies are not always to be had, and even when attainable, are so ingeniously devised to deceive, that only severe labour enables one to discover where the legerdemain is accomplished. The system is bad enough, but its administration is a perfect pest-house of corruption ; the dishonesty is almost incredible, and is practised without need or profit, frequently from mere habit.' "—*North American Review*, January 1869.

The evils arising from the system on which the Civil Service of the Federal Government is conducted are so notorious, and are so strongly felt, that a great effort was made last year to pass Mr Jenckes' Bill, with the double object of securing capacity by a competitive examination for all nominees, and honesty and zeal by some more permanent tenure of office. At present, as is well known—we rely merely on American authorities—the Government officials, almost from the highest to the lowest, change with each change of President or party in power.   They are by universal consent ill-paid, and usually ill-qualified, with little or no independence, little motive for exertion, little opportunity for distinction, but unfortunately much opportunity for illicit gain.   They are very numerous, but usually very inefficient.   It is openly stated, and not denied, that of the vast sums collected both by the Customs and Inland Revenue officers, a considerable proportion never reaches the coffers of the State.*   The *New York Imperialist* avers that—

" Not one of all the despotisms of the Old World employs such a locust swarm of officials, and not one has its various business so infamously ill-done."

And again—

" In France, under an Imperial Government, the full amount of every tax is collected and paid into the Treasury.   In America, under a Democratic Government, the Treasury loses fifty millions every year of the tax justly due on the single article of whisky, and fifty millions more in other departments of the revenue service; to say nothing of the uncounted sums abstracted from the State, municipal, and county taxes throughout the country."

---

* According to Mr Wells' Report, the average cost of collecting the revenue is not extravagant, however.   It amounted in 1868 to nearly 5 per cent. on the nett receipts for the internal revenue, and rather more than $4\frac{1}{2}$ for the customs.   This is lower than the cost in France, and somewhat higher than that in England.   " It has been demonstrated again and again," says an American writer, " that our tax and tariff laws call for 400,000,000 dollars of revenue annually, and that but 300,000,000 dollars reach the Treasury.   That this missing hundred million dollars is lost by the incompetency and rascality of some branches of the Civil Service has also been proved."—*Hunt's Merchants' Magazine*, May 1869.   New York.

The *Springfield Republican* says that—

" Lincoln's Secretary of the Interior used to declare that, if he dared, he could run his department with half its force of clerks, and for half its cost. M'Culloch might have put it even stronger as regards his office.   General Walker (in another branch) wished to reduce twelve clerks, but Congressmen came rushing to the rescue, and prevented the retrenchment."

The *San Francisco Times*, in the course of a long and bold denunciation of the general corruption, says :—

" It has come at last almost to this, that the mass of the public expect venality from public officials, and are agreeably disappointed when they find an honest man.   The accursed system of rotation in office has sapped the honesty of the people, and thousands have descended so far in the scale of morality that they are prepared to wink at the sins of officials, because they look forward to the time when they themselves will feed and fatten at the public crib."

It is in no spirit of ungenerous Pharisaism that I have referred to the errors and defects in the administrative economy of a nation, so many of whose characteristics are but reflections and exaggerations of our own ; but because ideas and principles can often be best judged when studied in their most extreme manifestations.   The tendency we are signalising is precisely the same in both countries ; in both it has its healthy and admirable side ; in both it is closely connected with that individual energy and self-reliance, that faculty of voluntary organisation and combined action, that readiness of resource, and that zealous love of personal liberty, which are among the finest qualities of the Anglo-Saxon race alike in England and America.   Our wish has merely been to point out that this salutary disposition has been carried too far and continued too long, and that now, in our advanced and complicated society, it is important to consider whether the interests of the community do not require its modification and control. It has been true, it is true to a great extent still, that we neither choose our rulers with care, nor subject them to very long or special training for the work they have to do, and so far our habitual mistrust alike of the capacity and disinterestedness of Government is not unreasonable. But then it is equally true that neither have we been accustomed to train *ourselves* for administrative functions, nor to select the fittest among ourselves for their discharge. We ought, therefore, to feel at least equal misgivings as to our own amateur attempts at government. For, after all, Cabinet Ministers are more likely than vestrymen to make honest and able officials, when both are alike inexperienced and selected on an equally unsound system. It is true again, that formerly, and to some extent hitherto, our rulers have been chosen by and from certain favoured classes mainly, if not exclusively, and some degree of jealousy might not unnaturally be felt lest they should fail in conscientious and scrupulous regard to the interests of the community at large. It must be admitted, therefore, that the sentiments which have usually led us, half-instinctively, both to limit the power of Government, and still more to confine its field of operation, are not without ample justification. But now, when the people, as a whole, choose their own representatives, and through those representatives the men who are to govern them; when the power of control is as direct and efficient as the power of choice; when

T

we can *insist* on good and honest work; when we can afford to pay trained men, and when the work of administration has become so complex and so vast as to need men of the most consummate training; and when we have already made so remarkable a progress towards obtaining an organised Civil Service of educated and tested men—is it not time to think of enlarging the functions of the central Government, and throwing more work upon it,—of forgetting our old mistrust, and teaching ourselves a new-born confidence? We have seen that incorporated companies, voluntary associations, vestries, and municipalities, habitually manage public enterprises abominably, are often signally incompetent, and sometimes flagrantly dishonest. We have seen that the Government manage their one monopoly at least, the Post-Office—a task they dare not neglect or bungle, and have no motive to abuse—with admirable efficiency and economy. Ought not these joint experiences to induce us to try sailing on a new tack? Under our new circumstances there can surely be no danger in enlarging the administrative functions of Government, in throwing more work upon it, in trusting it more fully, and endowing it with ampler powers. Surely, too, this is a line of reform in which both Conservatives and Liberals can consistently combine,—Conservatives, because their principle has always been to increase the strength and authority of Government; Liberals, because, now that the Government truly represents the people, it is obviously the people's best instrument for doing the people's work, and because, now that they choose their rulers, they ought certainly to be able to confide in them.

XII.

DIRECT *VERSUS* INDIRECT TAXATION.

ONE of the very first questions that is likely to occupy public attention with much vividness under the new *régime*, and the only one, so far as we can foresee, which threatens to be distinctively a class question, and to separate the *prolétairism* of the nation from the holders of property, whether land or personalty, concerns our system of taxation, in reference both to its principles and its incidence. It is a subject, moreover, on which the Liberal party more especially, and the local still more than the Parliamentary politicians, are prone to dwell in old ideas, to repeat exploded fallacies, to argue from obsolete or altered facts, to assume positions from which the foundation has been altogether cut away, and (in election times more particularly) to amuse themselves by airing old banners, the war-cries embroidered on which have long since ceased to be appropriate or true. It is a subject, too, so practical and immediate in its bearings on the material interests of the whole community and of nearly every individual, lending itself so easily to misrepresentations which miscellaneous and uninstructed audiences are unable to detect, and erroneous views regarding which, if once ingrained in the popular mind, are so fraught with danger, as likely, under

the new *régime*, to lead to embittered conflicts and
to unjust and impolitic legislation, that better service
can in no way be rendered at this moment than by
pointing out, in the most succinct form possible, a
few clear guiding principles bearing on the question,
and exposing a few of the fallacies which still
retain their hold on hustings manifestoes, and on
the impressions of the mass of the people. Happily
this can be done in a lucid shape and in a brief
space enough; for I shall state simply ascertained
results, leaving the detailed calculations by which
those results are ascertained to be verified by
means of the references I will give;* while the
principles which should decide our preference of
direct or indirect taxation, or our present blending
of the two systems, are far from recondite, but need
nothing but an equitable temper and a mind of
ordinary clearness to appreciate.

I. The ordinary *idea* is, that we are much more
heavily burdened by State taxation than our fathers
were. The *fact* is, that, large as are the additional
duties placed upon the Government—many of
these, as for education, police and the administration
of justice, mainly for the benefit of the poorer classes

---

* The entire materials and mode of working by which these
results were arrived at may be seen in an article on British taxation, published in the *Edinburgh Review* for January 1860. In
compiling that argument and those estimates, I had every advantage which access to all official information and enlightenment
could give me, in addition to the criticism and corrections of the
late Sir George Cornewall Lewis; and though there may be many
minor errors of detail, I have every reason to believe the main
conclusions may be relied upon. I would also refer the reader
to Mr R. Baxter's valuable pamphlets on *National Income* and
Taxation.

—the burden of taxation (properly calculated) *per head* has diminished rather than increased. Thus it was—

1807,	. . .	43s.	per head.
1815,	. . .	76s.	,,
1821,	. . .	52s. 6d.	,,
1851,	. . .	39s.	,,
1858,	. . .	41s. 2d.	,,
1868,*	. . .	40s. 3d.	,,

II. The *burden* of State taxation—*i.e.*, the taxes as compared with the wealth of the community—has, contrary to a common allegation, been progressively alleviated. Thus the percentage of the property of the country contributed to the revenue was—

1803, .	2.07 per cent.	1845, .	1.18 per cent.
1814, .	2.49 do.	1858, .	1.034 do.

And it is probably now *under one per cent.*

III. The current *impression* is, that Great Britain is in every point of view the most heavily-taxed country in the world, certainly far more so than France is now, or than America was before the Civil War. The *fact* is as follows :—The revenue of the two countries, as given in 1860 (and if the proportion has varied since, it has varied in favour of England), was 44s. 2d. per head in England, and

---

* These results will *at first sight* not appear always to be borne out by the figures given in official returns and ordinarily used, because, for purposes of fair comparison, certain preliminary rectifications are necessary. One of these relates to the cost of collecting the revenue, which used to be deducted from the payments into the Exchequer, but is so no longer, and which is generally put down at about £4,500,000. Another concerns the Post-office revenue, which many writers still persist in considering a *tax.*

39s. 5d. in France, including the charge for the interest of the debt.   But, leaving that item aside, the actual *State expenditure*, or cost of government, was 27s. 5d. in France, and only 24s. 3d. in England. Comparing the relative wealth of the two countries, Mr Norman (about the best authority we have) estimates that the taxation of the Frenchman, in proportion to his income, is *double* that of the Englishman.   Including all the elements for a fair comparison, the Englishman used to be more *heavily* taxed than the American *per head*, in the ratio of 54 to 28, more *lightly* in proportion to *his means*, in the ratio of 14 to 16.   *Now*, of course, the citizen of the United States is the most heavily-burdened mortal in the world.

IV. It is habitually but very loosely asserted that the cost of collecting the revenue in England is excessive, especially as regards the indirect taxes,— *i.e.*, the Customs and Excise.   The truth is, that our revenue is collected, on the whole, far more cheaply than in either France or the United States, and, as far as the indirect taxation is concerned, at less than one-half the cost.   The cost of collecting our revenue, moreover, has been steadily diminishing; is in some branches little more than one-half what it once was, and less than one-half of what is frequently affirmed. Practically and fairly, even on the face of the figures, it is now only $4\frac{1}{2}$ per cent.   And the real true nett cost of collecting the Customs revenue, the most incriminated branch of all, was 5 per cent. twenty years ago, and is only $3\frac{3}{4}$ per cent. now.

* See a very exhaustive and careful examination of the whole

V. The next erroneous popular impression is, that indirect taxes, Customs duties more especially, are a very wasteful and costly source of revenue, inasmuch as they take out of the pockets of the people a far larger amount than they pour into the coffers of the Exchequer. This, though theoretically true, is in actual fact as great a fallacy as the preceding ones, only it is a fallacy of exaggeration.

Taxes levied from the importer or manufacturer on articles of consumption no doubt involve to the ultimate consumer, not only an enhancement of price equivalent to the duty, but to the duty augmented by the profit chargeable on that portion of the merchant's and tradesman's capital which is employed in advancing the duty. That is to say, if an article is worth £100, and is charged with a duty of 10 per cent., the merchant, who in the first instance pays that duty, must recover his profit out of the consumer, not on £100, but on £110; and all tradesmen through whose hands the article subsequently passes must do the same. The extent of the indirect burden thus laid upon the capital of the country is variously estimated by different writers, and is enormously and ludicrously overstated by most. Sismondi, by a most transparent blunder (exposed in my *Essays on Political and Social Science*, i. 280), puts a case in which this burden *might* reach 70 per cent. (!) Ricardo appears to have estimated it at 10 per cent. I have estimated it to

question in a pamphlet (the authorship of which there is no reason why I should not avow), published in 1863, entitled *Real Cost of Collecting the Revenue, with reference to. Sir Morton Peto's Strictures.*

vary from 1¼ to 5 per cent. One of the tracts issued by the Liverpool Financial Reformers calls it roundly 25 per cent.; while the *People's Blue Book* puts it down at the sum of £10,211,483 a year. These widely divergent estimates suffice to show how little reliance can be placed on any which claim to be precise. But in truth this argument against Customs duties, valid to a great extent once, has lost nearly all its weight under the combined operation of railways and the bonding system. Not only are the stocks held by tradesmen far smaller than formerly, when communications and means of supply were so much less rapid and less easy, but importers now scarcely ever pay duty till they have secured a customer for their goods : nay more, they constantly sell their goods *in bond*, and the retail dealer who purchases from them only liberates the goods a day or two before he actually needs them to supply the wants of the ultimate consumer. This is especially the case with high-duty goods, such as tea, which often pays duty one chest at a time, as the grocer happens to want it ; so that, in a vast proportion of cases, the duty is only paid by the proprietor a few days before he *re-coups* himself from the consumer ; and the *ten per cent.* per annum which he is supposed to charge as profit upon the capital advanced, is chargeable only for these few days, and becomes, therefore, almost an infinitesimal amount.

VI. It is common to assert—still commoner to assume—that direct taxes can be and are levied at a considerably less expense than indirect ones. It

may almost be affirmed with confidence that the
precise reverse would be the truth, provided only
the direct taxes were equitably apportioned, rigidly
levied, and distributed over the whole population.
Of course, a revenue derived *solely* from a tax on
real and personal property, or imposed exclusively
on the incomes of the upper and middle classes,
might be collected at a comparatively low rate
(say 2 per cent.) if statesmen could be found dishonest or impolitic enough to propose, and a Legislature self-denying and short-sighted enough to
sanction, such a fiscal system. But that a direct
tax, of any sort whatever, of which the mass of the
people—the *wage-class*—should pay their proportionate share, could be collected for double that
amount, or, indeed, could be collected at all, I
think no competent person can be found to maintain. Our materials for arriving at a very accurate
estimate of the probable relative cost of the two
systems are, it must be confessed, somewhat meagre ;
but we must make the most of the few we possess,
and they will be found not inconclusive. First, we
find that the cost of collecting the direct taxes in
France, where the fact of the great majority of the
people being proprietors, renders the task peculiarly
easy, is 3¾ per cent,—*precisely the same rate as that of
our own Customs duties.* Next, it is obvious that,
cæteris paribus, the cost of levying any direct impost
will vary inversely according to the number of
persons on whom it is levied, and the largeness of
the sums in which it is levied. In other words, it
will be much cheaper to levy twenty millions from
one million of tax-payers than from thirty millions—

if it can be done at all.   Now, we do not know the
numbers who pay the direct taxes in Great Britain
(land-tax, assessed taxes, and income-tax), but we
do know that, in reference to the total population,
they are comparatively few.   The cost of collection
ought, therefore, *for a case of direct taxation*, to be
unusually low.   In the year ending March 1858, a
sum of £14,923,022 was levied at a cost of 3.23 per
cent. ; and in the following year £9,975,294 was
levied at a cost of 4.1 per cent ; the average being
about that which we have seen to be the real
expense of collecting the Customs duties.   If we
confine our attention to the income-tax alone, we
find that the rate per cent. at which it was collected
during the Napoleonic wars varied from 2 to
3 per cent., averaging *two and a half.*   Since
its reimposition by Sir Robert Peel, the rate has
ranged from £1, 16s. 11d. up to £3, 3s. 5d. per cent.
If, on the other hand, we inquire into the cost of
collecting the direct taxes before the income-tax
was imposed, we shall find that from 1839 to 1841
inclusive it averaged £4, 11s. 10d., or about 4.6 per
cent.   These results certainly would not encourage
us to hope that a system of direct taxation, levied
equitably on the entire population, whatever form
it might take, would be a very cheap fiscal device.*

* Some advocates of direct taxation, *soi-disant* friends of the
poor, have proposed a poll-tax of a pound a head on all persons above fourteen years of age, by way of making the working-
classes contribute their fair share to the revenue.   Now, we will
not enter upon a description of the intolerable irritation and the
constant pressure which the visits of the tax-gatherer—to demand
his three or four pounds per annum—would cause to the poor
man, who can with difficulty pay his rent, and who never has

VII. Strong objections have been urged against Customs and Excise duties on an independent ground, —viz., the irresistible temptations and opportunities

money in his purse. We will simply ask our readers to picture to themselves the difficulty and expense of collecting such an impost strictly and fairly. On an average, the family of the labourer will comprise three members above the statutable age—frequently more. The larger his family, the more pressing will be his needs, and *the heavier his taxation.* If the tax be demanded from him all at once, payment will be usually impossible. He must run into debt, or he must go to prison. If, on the other hand, in order to mitigate the pressure, it be demanded from him in small sums—at the rate of eighteenpence a week, or six shillings a month—not only will the annoyance be incessant, and the sore kept always raw, but, what more concerns our present argument, the expense entailed by these perpetual visits of the tax-gatherer will soon amount to a sum which will throw Customs and Excise collections into the shade. If contrivances be adopted to secure the payment of the tax by attaching his wages, or levying it through his employer—which in all probability would be found necessary—the complication of arrangements and accounts involved by such contrivances would soon multiply expenses far beyond the sum to be recovered. If the poor man did not or could not pay when required, legal processes must be resorted to ; imprisonment must often follow, and the defaulter must be maintained at the public expense while in prison. For, be it remembered, no arrears could be allowed, no exemptions sanctioned, no pleas of incapacity listened to for a moment—or the tax might as well be given up at once. In the case of the existing income-tax on incomes between £100 and £150 a year, it is often found necessary to excuse defaulters, and to wipe out arrears, simply because it would prove costly and perhaps impossible (without distraint or prison) to enforce payment. But in the case of a capitation-tax, no considerations of this sort could be permitted to intervene. If allowed in a single instance, they would be pleaded in five cases out of six. To all these causes of difficulty and expense must be added the necessity of a searching investigation into any secret deposits in savings-banks or any subscription to friendly societies belonging to the defaulter, and capable of being made available to the baffled tax-gatherer. Now, when which, it is alleged, they offer to fraud and evasion. The impeachment must be admitted :—as long as these duties exist there will be attempts, and successful attempts, at smuggling and illicit distillation. In the case of the Customs, however, this mischief has been enormously diminished of late years by reduction of duties and the liberation of some hundreds of dutiable articles.   But the objection applies with equal force to all species of taxation. Payments to the revenue, however levied, will always be evaded by some persons so long as evasion is possible; and fraud, lying, and concealment, with all their demoralising consequences, will result.   Even now, the dishonest practices stimulated by Schedule D. and by the legacy and probate duties, are formidable items of comparison to set against the violations of Excise and Customs laws ; and the frightful extent to which the former would be multiplied, were direct taxation levied on the masses, instead of, as now, only on the few, no man can foresee.   Moreover, there is one fertile source of temptation and of fraud appertaining to direct taxation, from which indirect is wholly free, namely, *exemptions.* Every magistrate is more or less cognisant of the deplorable amount of equivocation and false swearing once employed to prove, for example, that a house is only worth £19, 19s., and is, there-

these considerations are placed in array before us, and duly weighed, we ask with confidence, Is there any man of sense or experience in such matters who believes that such a poll-tax could be collected for less than *seven* or *ten* per cent.—or could be collected at all for two years running—or could be collected for a single quarter without causing the poor man to curse the day when his Financial Reform friends took a fancy to protect him, and to quarrel with Customs duties on his behalf ?

fore, exempt from the house-tax ;—that the effects of
a deceased person were under £20 in value, and that
therefore letters of administration need not be taken
out ;—that the income of the appellant is less than
£100, and that therefore he is exempt from the income-tax ;—that his carriage, or his horse, or his
dog, or his gun, or his under-gardener is exempt
from duty, on this or that assignable plea. When
all things are taken into consideration, it becomes
impossible to decide between the relative degrees of
demoralising temptation assignable to the two fiscal
systems ; and we must, therefore, leave this class of
considerations out of the question on both sides.

VIII. A very common fallacy, again, is to represent Customs duties on imported articles, from
which more than half our indirect revenue is
derived, as infractions of the principles of free-
trade. They are so in no sense whatever. Free-
trade prohibits *protective*, not honestly *fiscal* import
dues. It condemns taxes levied *for the pecuniary
benefit of a class*, not taxes to the national revenue,
imposed for revenue purposes alone. Sound commercial policy, no doubt, discourages all specially
onerous import duties, such as cripple industry and
limit trade ; but no candid person will probably be
found to urge that any fairly chargeable with a
character or practical operation of this sort now
disgrace our statute-book ;—spirits and tobacco, the
only apparent exceptions, have always been considered as legitimate sources of the largest revenue
they can be made to yield. That our trade *has not*,
as a fact, been crippled or discouraged by Customs

dues since the introduction of a wise fiscal system, is proved by the most irrefragable figures. Our aggregate tonnage inwards and outwards, which was 5,000,000 in 1821, and 10,000,000 in 1841, had risen to 26,000,000 in 1861;—and the total value of our import and export trade, which was £302,000,000 in 1856, had reached £534,000,000 ten years later.

IX. One more prevailing fallacy upon the subject remains to be noticed before we come to the last and greatest, and perhaps the most mischievous of all. The advocates of a system of direct imposts fix their exclusive attention on *one* attribute of taxation, and neglect other and more important attributes. In their estimates the cheapest impost is the best :—*Cæteris paribus,*—that is, the pressure on the various classes of the community being equal,—that form of taxation which takes least out of the pocket of the tax-payer in proportion to the amount paid into the Exchequer, carries its own paramount recommendation with it, and is to be preferred to all others. Now this we hold to be an unquestionable fallacy. Why is a costly tax an objectionable one ? Because it robs the tax-payer needlessly, and therefore does him an injury and an injustice. But a man may be injured otherwise than in his purse, and may be injured much more seriously than by any mere pecuniary mulct. He may be injured in his convenience; he may be injured in his feelings ; he may be injured in his temper. The State wants £20 from him. " This," say the financial reformers, " it can obtain, by a

direct levy, by taking from him £20, 10s. ; whereas,
if you get it by indirect taxation, you must take
from him £21 or £22, — clearly, therefore, the
former is the only right mode." (The proportions,
as I have shown, are not as here alleged ; but
never mind that ; we are concerned here with the
abstract argument.) But what if he is called upon
to pay the £20, 10s. at a very inconvenient time, in
a very peremptory manner, in a large sum, in an
undisguised and offensively ostensible form,—while
the £21 or £22 he pays just when he pleases, in as
small sums as he pleases, and, what is still more to
the purpose, without being aware that he is paying
tax at all ? What if, instead of being irritated
beyond endurance by the quarterly visits of the
tax-gatherer—always sure to be as ill-timed as possible, or to appear so—he never sees the face of
that obnoxious functionary from the cradle to the
grave ? What if, instead of being goaded into fury
by discussions, and proofs, and affidavits, and references to parish registers as to the age—taxable or
exempt—of his children, his most annoying dispute
is with his grocer,—whether he shall pay 4d. or 4½d.
a pound for his sugar ? What if, being something
of a practical philosopher, as nearly all of us are, he
should be of opinion that in no way could the extra
15s. or 30s. a year be so well laid out, that in no
way could it be made to produce so much comfort
or spare him so much pain, as by substituting indirect for direct taxation ? What if he naturally
prefers insensible perspiration to forcible extraction ?
What, in fine, if he should prefer *paying* not only
£22 but £25 in the one way, to having £20 *torn*

from him in the other ?—as every man of common sense, every man who is neither a pedant nor a *doctrinaire*, unquestionably will. Clearly, money is valuable only inasmuch as it can purchase the good things of life; clearly, freedom from periodical irritation is one of the best of these good things; clearly, therefore, if it is worth while to pay £20 a year to Government for protection, security, and justice, it is worth while to pay 20s. more for peace, a calm temper, and an unblaspheming tongue. Taxation must of necessity be a painful operation; it is simple cruelty and folly not to perform it, where you can, under the influence of chloroform. To me it seems too obvious to need argument that, if only our fiscal burdens are equitably apportioned and so contrived as neither to fetter industry nor to repress enterprise, that mode of levying them must be the best which is—not the cheapest, but—the least unpleasant and the least felt. Now there can be no doubt that indirect taxes are the least unpleasant; and, as we have endeavoured to show, there is every reason to believe they are really the cheapest also. As has been well said : " To obtain a large revenue you must levy it *from* the many : to obtain it cheaply, you must levy it *through* the few." Customs and Excise duties fulfil both these requirements.

Direct taxes, like any other taxes, are sure to be popular with those who do not pay them. But if the choice were fairly placed before the people, between indirect taxation as it now exists, and direct taxation of *which they must bear their fair share*,—between a tax on income, which they could not escape, and a tax on luxuries, which it was optional with them to pay,—who can doubt what would be their instantaneous and unanimous decision? Hitherto, the people have been systematically blinded as to the real question at issue, both by their own misleaders, and by a misjudging Legislature. How could they form a just estimate of the relative merits of direct and indirect taxation, when they knew the former only as an income-tax which spared *their* incomes, and a house-tax which spared *their* houses, and the latter as a burden which poisoned every pipe they smoked, soured every glass of beer they drank, and embittered every cup of tea they sweetened? But when the question is honestly propounded to them : *Not*—" Which do you prefer—a tax which the rich pay and you escape, or one which you pay in common with them ? " *but*, " Which do you prefer—a tax which you pay only *when* you like, *if* you like, and *to the extent* you like ; or one which, though perhaps smaller in amount, is yet taken from you periodically, inexorably, and however ill you can afford it?" —we are satisfied that the advocates of direct taxation will find few supporters.

In what I have written hitherto I have not designed to defend our existing system of taxation as either positively light, or ideally cheap, or practically faultless. I have only been concerned to show that those who affirm that the pressure of taxation is increasing, that it is heavier than in France or America, that it is collected at a great expense, and at a far greater cost than a directer system which might be substituted for it, and that it is inherently and incurably objectionable, are making assertions which we

U

can prove to be either enormously exaggerated or wholly false. It now only remains to show that the same character must be assigned to the assertion habitually put forward by the same parties, and with equal confidence,—that the actual incidence of taxa-tion in England is grievously burdensome and grossly unjust to the working classes—that, in fact, we levy our revenue mainly from the poor instead of from the rich.

And at the outset we must remind our readers that the taxation of the poor man is *entirely volun-tary*. He assesses himself, and he need not con-tribute one farthing to the revenue unless he pleases. No actual *necessary* of life is taxed. Bread and meat pay no Customs duties and no Excise. Tea, coffee, sugar, spirits, tobacco, and beer—though now by habit become almost indispensable—are in no fair and intelligible sense *necessaries:* a man may live, as all men used to do, and as numbers do even now, in perfect health, strength, and comfort, without touching one of them ;—nay, he will improve his health by abstaining from at least two out of the number. They are all, with the exception of beer, *recent* articles. The ancients were unacquainted with spirits :—distillation was not invented till the Middle Ages. Tea and coffee were introduced into Europe at the end of the seventeenth century ; and tea is still little consumed in any western country except England. Sugar was first imported into Europe in the twelfth or thirteenth century, and tobacco dates only from the discovery of America. They are all luxuries and superfluities ;—it is very right that the working man should have them, if he chooses; but why, any more than the rich man, he should have them without paying for them, it is impossible to see. If he can purchase them, it is because he has money to spend on superfluities, and the portion of his income that he can set aside for superfluities is surely a fair subject for taxation. If he pays any tax at all, it is because he has stepped voluntarily into the tax-paying class.

With this preliminary remark I will now proceed to ascertain in what proportion the existing taxes are divided among the upper and middle classes on the one side, and the working classes on the other, —the propertied classes and the *prolétaires.* * By the working classes I mean those who live by weekly wages or by handicraft, as distinguished from those who live on incomes derived from property, trades, and professions. The distinction is broad and intelligible, if not exact.

The following figures can of course only be given as approximations; but they were prepared after consulting the best-informed persons in each department, and I believe them to be correct in the main. The mode in which they were arrived at, and the returns and documents on which they were founded, are explained at length in the paper already referred to at the beginning of this chapter.

---

* It is interesting to compare the taxation paid by the working classes to *the State* with their *self-imposed taxation,* or voluntary expenditure on spirits, beer, and tobacco. The former, as we show, amounts to only £27,000,000 a year; the latter, as shown twenty years ago by Mr Porter, and again this year by Mr Smiles, reaches £65,000,000 at least.—*Companion to British Almanac,* p. 33.

TABLE showing the proportion of each tax that was paid in 1868–9, by the " Propertied Classes " and the " Wage-Class " respectively :—

Taxes for 1868–9.	Total.	Proportion paid by Propertied Classes.		Proportion paid by Working Classes.	
	£		£		£
LOCAL TAXATION, . .	20,000,000	all	20,000,000		
INCOME TAX and assessed TAXES, . .	12,250,000	all	12,250,000		
* STAMPS, Probate and Legacy Duties, &c., .	8,500,000		8,500,000		
EXCISE :—					
Malt Duty, &c., . .	6,700,000	20 pr. ct.	1,340,000	80 per ct.	5,360,000
Spirit Duty, &c., . .	11,000,000	10 ,,	1,100,000	90 ,,	9,900,000
Carriage and Railway Duty, ...	640,000	90 ,,	576,000	10 ,,	64,000
Licences, &c., . . .	2,740,000	33 ,,	913,000	67 ,,	1,827,000
† CUSTOMS :—					
Tobacco, ...	6,550,000	20 ,,	1,310,000	80 ,,	5,240,000
Sugar, ...	5,740,000	60 ,,	3,444,000	40 ,,	2,296,000
Tea, Coffee, Cocoa, &c.,	3,100,000	50 ,,	1,550,000	50 ,,	1,550,000
Spirits, ...	4,350,000	90 ,,	3,915,000	10 ,,	435,000
Wine, ...	1,500,000	100 ,,	1,500,000		...
Sundry Articles, . .	460,000	75 ,,	345,000	25 ,,	115,000
	83,530,000		56,743,000		26,787,000

That is, the *propertied classes*, 7,000,000 in number, with an aggregate income of £400,000,000, pay £57,000,000 taxes, or £8, 3s, per head, or 14 per cent. ; while the *prolétaire classes*, 23,000,000, with an income of £300,000,000, pay £27,000,000 taxes, or £1, 6s. per head, or 9 per cent.‡   Thus

* Fire insurance duty deducted, being repealed.

† Corn duty omitted, being repealed.

‡ These ratios are slightly different from those given in the article referred to, and afterwards corrected for 1866.   In that year the estimate was 16 per cent. for the upper, and 10 per cent. for the working classes.   The proportion must vary according to the severity of the income-tax in special years.   To show that the

it would appear that *taxation is now so equitably divided among the rich and the poor, that the former pay more than* six *times as much as the latter in proportion to their numbers, and nearly half as much again in proportion to their means.*

These popular misconceptions disposed of, the ground is now clear for the two practical conclusions it is desired to draw :—*first*, that a system of mingled direct and indirect taxation, into which duties levied on articles of general consumption must enter in a large and probably a preponderating measure, offers the easiest, kindest, fairest means by which, in this country at least, the great body of the nation, whom we usually describe as the working classes, can be made to pay their fit contribution to the national revenue ;—and *secondly*, that the clearest policy and

above calculation cannot be very wide of the mark, I annex two analogous estimates by very well qualified statisticians, who used somewhat different data, and proceeded by different methods, yet arrived at very similar results. Mr Levi's estimate of the earnings of the working classes, however, is unquestionably excessive, and that of the upper classes is certainly inadequate.

MR BAXTER'S ESTIMATE.

Propertied classes, estimated at seven millions, with an income of four hundred and ninety millions, pay fifty-two millions, or 10½ per cent., or £7 a head.

Working classes, twenty-three millions, with an income of three hundred and twenty-five millions, pay twenty-two millions six hundred thousand, or 7 per cent., or £1, 8s. 3d. a head.

MR L. LEVI'S ESTIMATE.

Propertied classes, estimated at eight millions, with an income of three hundred and forty-nine millions, pay fifty millions of taxes, or £6, 5s. a head, or 14 per ent.

Working classes, estimated at twenty-two millions, with an income of four hundred and eighteen millions, pay twenty-four millions, or £1, 2s. a head, or 5½ per cent.

the simplest justice alike imperatively demand that
from this fit contribution, whatever it may be, they
should on no pretext be exempted.   What their fair
proportion of the burdens of the State may be, or
how it ought to be determined, are questions of
great complication, both in principle and detail, and
I have no intention of entering upon the discussion
of them here.   But that no class needs the protection of Government so urgently as the poor, or,
under an equitable rule, profits by it more ;—that ·
by far the greatest proportion of the taxes levied
is expended in the supply of their wants or in the
purchase of their labour ;—and that participation in
the power and privileges of the State logically involves and righteously entails participation in its
obligations likewise,—are propositions which admit
of no dispute.   We have conferred full political
privileges upon the mass of the people—nay, even
preponderating political power in the last resort ;—
every householder has now an equal vote, and the
poorer householders largely outnumber the rich ;—
in the choice of legislators and rulers, proletairism
has, directly and before the law, as potent a voice
as property.   And most assuredly a country in
which the poor voted the taxes and directed their
expenditure while the rich paid them, would be
taking a short cut to extravagance, demoralisation,
and ruin.

XIII.

THE NEW *RÉGIME*, AND HOW TO MEET IT.

THAT a new political *régime* will be inaugurated by the Reform Act of 1867, it
is, I think, impossible to doubt. The change
may be less sudden and complete than many
persons fancy; it may come upon us more
gradually; its advent may be mitigated or de-
layed by influences not at present taken into calculation; and when it reaches us, its consequences
may be less wide and less disastrous than alarmists
fear; but that it is commenced, and will in time be
consummated, is as certain as anything future and
contingent can be. That political supremacy—the
means of outvoting all other classes at the poll, of
deciding the election of the representatives, who,
in their turn, decide the policy of the country—has
been placed within the reach of the labouring
classes, has been legally and theoretically extended
to them, has been potentially conferred upon them,
seems undeniable. According to the most trustworthy calculation, they will (leaving out the metropolitan constituencies) form 64 per cent. of the
borough electors, while the borough members will
form 62 per cent. of the House of Commons. This
looks like assured or attainable predominance at
least. That any class of any community should

have political supremacy offered to them, and yet
be too indifferent, or too modest, or too disinterested,
to take it up—especially when that class has many
wants, many disadvantages, and, as some fancy,
many wrongs—has never yet been seen in the
world's history. That, even if they were thus apa-
thetic themselves, their advisers, their *exploiteurs*
(to coin a much-needed foreign word), those who
wish to guide them, or who hope to use them,
would allow them to remain thus inactive and self-
abnegating, is not to be expected. Therefore we
must anticipate that sooner or later, probably
before very long, the suffrages of the lowest and
most numerous class in the constituencies, those
who live by wages, those who labour with their
hands, will elect the House of Commons—so far at
least as the borough members are concerned. As
regards the counties we do not yet feel competent
to speak ; but as a general rule, we may assume
that whom the working classes prefer (if they pull
together), those the boroughs will return, and that
what the borough members desire (if they pull
together), that the House of Commons will enact.
This is the great new fundamental fact we have to
face. It is a new *régime*, no doubt, and one of
grave import ; but we do not know that it may
not be regarded with more of hope than fear, if
only the upper and middle classes will distinctly
recognise that it is a new *régime*, and will act
accordingly.

If those who have borne sway hitherto wish to
bear sway still, they must recognise the fact that this
must be secured by different means to those which

have hitherto been found sufficing. If the higher and more educated ranks have any title to such sway, it is not by virtue of their superior social position, but solely by virtue of their superior political fitness. It belongs to them, if they deserve it; it may be assured to them, if they will assert it. Only, henceforth it must be asserted, justified, their title to it made good; it will not devolve upon them as heretofore—far less, at least, than heretofore—by the Constitution, by habit, by right of birth, by mere social circumstances. The leadership, the direction, the supremacy, which of yore came to them, in future they must seek, and strive in order to secure. I have little doubt that they may secure it if they will, and if they set about the task in the right way. The only danger is lest they should not distinctly and fully recognise and accept the indispensable conditions of the new *régime*, should not be deeply enough impressed at once with its obligations and its opportunities. There are two fatal mistakes they may commit; and there are indications abroad that they are not unlikely to commit both. They will fall into a fatal error if they allow either despair or a sort of contemptuous despite to take possession of them; if, perceiving that they can be outvoted, they therefore conclude that they will be powerless; if they shrink or abstain from the electoral conflict from disgust at being left in a possible and perhaps a hopeless minority; if they think the battle is lost because they cannot win it altogether and in both wings, or that it ought not to be fought because it is certain to be lost; if, in a word, they act as the correspond-

ing classes are said to have acted in America, and
think to indemnify themselves in social life, where
they can reign supreme, for the mortifications of
political life, where they are worsted. Any such
abnegation of their duties and their functions in a
country like England would be certain to be visited
with heavy penalties : the experience of France
and of the United States might teach us wiser and
nobler lessons ; social pre-eminence would be soon
invaded when political pre-eminence had been
effectually transferred elsewhere. Moreover, such
desertion of the field of conflict would be as premature and needless as it would be poor-spirited and
base : rank, wealth, character, and education, are
sure to win with us if they fairly and courageously
enter the arena ; they start for the conflict with
irresistible advantages—advantages partly inherent
in their own qualifications, partly arising from that
ingrained reverence for every social superiority—
even if it be but half-genuine and half-noble—which
it will take many generations of misgovernment to
eradicate from the breasts of Englishmen. Our
aristocracy are the first in the world, both for intellect and character. In the universities and in
the House of Commons they are able to hold their
own against competitors from any rank. Ample
wealth and leisure must always give them superior
qualifications for the life of politics, and we believe
in the sound sense and clear instincts of the mass of
the English people discerning true wisdom and
integrity from shallow declamation and self-seeking
intrigue, when both stand side by side before them.
It will be hard, indeed, if political sagacity and noble

character in the upper ranks cannot both influence
the lower classes generally, and win over to enlightened and trusting obedience a sufficient number
of them to obtain, when added to their own people
and the educated middle classes who will go with
them, an absolute and pretty secure majority of the
constituencies. The victory is secure if it be not
thrown away by faithless and timid inertia before
the first blow is struck.

But the governing classes must not fall into the
second error we have indicated as lying in their path.
They must largely modify their mode of action.
They have to obtain and to keep the command of the
constituencies ; and they must do this by obtaining
command of the minds, and not merely of the votes,
of the electors. There is a dangerous, and in its
essence a corrupt, idea floating half-defined in the
fancies of many, and principally of Conservative,
politicians. They think that a large proportion of
the new and the poorer electors will be easily induced
to vote as their landlords or employers may direct—
will not, in fact, dream of voting in any other way.
They rely on their dependence, social or pecuniary,
not on their intelligence. They intend to content
themselves with securing the interest, and not to
trouble themselves about the cordial allegiance, of
the lower orders. They trust to the poverty and the
snobbishness, instead of to the free adherence and
cordial support, of those whom they have endowed
with the franchise. This policy may succeed partially, locally, and for a time ; but it is too superficial and intrinsically unworthy to secure a permanent hold on the people. It cannot fail both

to augment and to prolong the influence of demagogues; for it places them on the vantage-ground
of being defenders of the freedom as well as of the
interests of the poor. If the upper classes wish to
become the leaders of the people under the new
régime, they must mingle with them, they must
instruct them and enlighten them, they must teach
them political economy, they must no longer stand
aloof from them everywhere save at the hustings ;
they must descend not only to study their views, to
enter into their feelings, to ascertain their grievances
and their wants, but to discuss these points with
them, explain to them where they are wrong, admit
and adopt their notions when they are right, and
thus beat the democrat at his own weapons. They
must no longer leave even municipal matters and
officers to local agitators and vestrymen ; they must
assert the rights of superior intellect and station by
discharging all its duties; they must, at whatever
cost and with whatever labour, inoculate the constituencies with their own ideas, or accept the ideas
of the constituencies where these happen to be
sound. Above all, they must show—and they can
show only by sincerely feeling—a determination to
grapple at once, and in a practical, honest, energetic temper, with those questions which more
directly affect the masses, which help to render
their daily life comfortable or wretched, which
decide their elevation or their degradation—those
questions, in fine, which to the working man are
nearly everything, and which he will no longer
endure to see treated as if they were tedious or
insignificant. In fact, the governing classes must

henceforth do their proper duties, if they would
hold their proper place; they must act for the
people, as the people would act for themselves
if they were as sagacious as they are virtually
powerful; they must "achieve greatness" and
leadership—they will no longer inherit it or have
it "thrust upon them."

We believe, then, that no serious danger need be
apprehended from the preponderating electoral
weight which the Reform Bill has placed in the
hands of the newly-enfranchised working men, if
only the educated classes are true to themselves—
that is, awake to the real character of the change
and equal to the obligations it imposes upon them.
Nevertheless, there are perils before us against
which it is essential to be on our guard. If the
upper ranks held together and acted in unison, the
mere numerical preponderance of the lower ranks
on the electoral register would count for little in a
class conflict; since the purely natural, legitimate,
and indestructible influences which the combined
aristocracies of title, wealth, and education could
bring to bear upon those below them, would be
certain to bring over a sufficient number of auxiliaries to their side to turn the scale. It is almost
needless to remark, however, that class conflicts,
or anything resembling them, are above all things
to be avoided. In all our great constitutional
struggles hitherto, the division of the nation has
been vertical, not horizontal; the parties which have
been arrayed against one another have been each
composed in not very dissimilar proportions of men
of all ranks and grades in the social hierarchy;

the severing line has cut through every station of
the community—has set at nought, instead of corresponding to, class boundaries.   Whether the subject
of the contest has been religious, political, or economical, has mattered little ; Catholic emancipation,
the repeal of the Test Acts, Parliamentary Reform,
Municipal institutions, Free-trade—all these questions found nobles, country gentlemen, Churchmen,
Dissenters, merchants, bankers, tradesmen, artizans,
and labourers, mingled in the opposing ranks ; our
national controversies have never for a moment
assumed the form of a struggle between rich and
poor, between employers and employed, though our
local ones occasionally have done so.   This happy
immunity from the worst of dangers may, we think,
be still in a great measure continued to us, if we
are wise and generous in forestalling all class controversies, in conceding what is due without waiting
till it is demanded, in "seeking conciliation" (as
Mr MILL once said), "not by compromise, but by
justice,—by giving to every man, not the half of
what he asks, but the whole of what he ought to
have."

This rock ahead, however, is a rock above water,
and it is not against this that we wish to utter a
note of warning.   People tell us—and probably,
except as regards questions of taxation, it is true in
the main—that the working-classes are not likely to
act together as a body ; that they, in common with
every other class, have their divergencies of opinion
and of character ; that some are Conservatives, if
many are Radicals ; that some will be warlike and
some pacific ; that, in fact, on most political ques-

tions some will take one side and some another. No doubt this will often be so ; but, on the other hand, it must not be forgotten that those classes to whom we look to counterbalance and control the new electoral element will have their divisions likewise. The danger that we desire to signalise is that which may arise from carrying unchanged our old system of party warfare and government by party into the new *régime.* So long as only two parties existed, each representing an essential and influential element of national life, and dividing the national strength and numbers pretty equally between them, the system worked well enough ; in all our Ministerial changes there was only a transfer of power—scarcely even that, but rather only a transfer of office—from party to party, not from class to class. Now, however, we may not disguise from ourselves that a notable modification has been introduced into the practical working of our Constitution. For the first time the labouring class has been endowed with the electoral franchise in such numbers as to render it a distinct and very appreciable, if not actually a preponderating, weight in the political scale. Politicians will, in consequence, be found to constitute themselves its leaders, to devote themselves to the task of organising it into a separate power in Parliament, to *chaperon* its interests and ideas—-to insist upon trying how every party contest can best be turned to its advantage—to form, in a word, a second " Brass Band," more numerous, more powerful, more intelligent, and far more unmanageable, because more incorrupt, than the Irish one, which in days gone by wrought us so much mischief.

Now, it is obvious that if party conflicts, the struggles for place and power between Liberals and Conservatives, are to be carried on henceforth with as keen a competition and as lax a patriotism as we have lately witnessed—if office is to be more valued by our senators and statesmen than either traditional principles or actual convictions—the new band we speak of will become indisputably masters of the situation. They will not, indeed, be able to secure office for themselves, nor therefore to undergo those moderating and enlarging influences which the insights and responsibilities of office bring to bear with such effect upon all but the shallow and the reckless ; the mischief will be all the greater on this account. But they will hold the balance between the rival candidates for power ; they, though not able to rule themselves, will be able to decide who shall rule ; their support will be indispensable to victory, and they will be in a position to dictate the conditions by which that support must be purchased. It will be held forth as a prize to the highest bidder ; and we know too well the price that can be extorted—especially in the crisis of conflict—from eager and passionate competitors for an assistance that is indispensable to the attainment of an object which neither party has the personal dignity nor the public virtue to forego. In this manner a compact body in the House of Commons, though perhaps a small minority both there and in the country, will be able to exercise all the deciding influence of an assured majority ; its aid cannot be dispensed with, and will be accorded only on its own terms. Those terms may be such as both the bidders deem exorbitant, dangerous, and immoral; but nevertheless they will be agreed to, sooner or later, unless the whole tone and standard of political morality in England can be raised; and a wholesale lowering of the suffrage does not seem the surest or most direct way to raise it. The terms *may* be a perpetual series of concessions to democratic pressure; an increasing tendency to submit to menace and to yield before mob encroachments; possibly even legislation in the direction of Trades Unionism. The terms almost certainly *will* be a continuous and gradual substitution of direct for indirect taxation, a pervading disinclination to put the law in force against the illegalities and outrages of organised associations capable of operating on elections, and a steady direction of petty legislative measures towards the removal of the few constitutional obstacles that remain to the supremacy of numbers—perhaps even concession to desires for a maximum of leisure and a minimum of wages. It is in the system of government for selfish party objects, the loose morality which the engrossing pursuit of those objects entails, and the encouragement which is thus offered to democratic pressure, that links the chief danger that besets our future—a danger which it is easy enough to foresee and denounce, but against which it is far from easy to devise a safeguard. The creation of a party formed out of the wiser and nobler elements of existing combinations, liberal in its ends, but scrupulously constitutional in its mode of action, strong enough in its integrity, independence, and breadth of view, to

x

dispense with adventitious aid and to defy both the ochlocracy and the plutocracy, is probably too complete a Utopia to be looked for just at present.

It is impossible, moreover, not to recognise that Mr Disraeli, during his recent tenure of office, did as much as a man could do to render the formation of such a party impracticable or at least remote. We see something of the real operation of his policy even now. We must wait probably several years before it can be fully realised or adequately measured. It is true that he stormed the Treasury benches for his followers. He led them into Downing Street when perhaps no other leader could have done so. He certainly kept them there longer than any other leader could have done. He distributed among them a vast amount of miscellaneous patronage. He nearly remodelled the judicial bench by the number of his appointments. But he did this at a cost which would have been a dear price to pay for twenty years of the sweets and emoluments of office; acting, in a word, as if office were an end and not a means—itself the aim of a great party's political ambition, instead of a step to enable that party to assert its principles and to carry out its purposes. He sacrificed the end to the means, because he simply mistook them for each other, or rather because he himself valued the one and did not care for the other; and he never understood how large a proportion of his followers looked at the matter in a very different light. In order to reach and to retain office, he surrendered the power for the sake of which alone office is desirable. He was guilty not only of the signal error, but the *sum-mum nefas*—

Animam preferre pudori,
Et propter vitam vivendi perdere causas.

By acting thus he brought about two results, both fatal to the permanent influence of the body which chose him for its chief. In the first place, he split up the Conservative party. Those who preferred place to principle, and those whom his subtleties were able to beguile into the delusion that they were not really deserting their principles, but only pursuing them by a tortuous or hitherto undiscovered route, followed wherever he led. Those whose convictions were too strong, whose heads were too clear, and whose faith was too dear to them to be thus hoodwinked, left him, and left him with scorn and open denunciation. Henceforward, the forces, once so compact, are divided by a wide gulf of separation. Nor does it seem as if the breach could be healed at any early day. While Mr Disraeli's political life lasts, it is not probable that the Parliamentary Conservatives can have any other leader; and as long as he leads it is not possible that the more honest and sturdy branch of the party—either the old Tories or the conscientious and philosophical Conservatives of whom Lord Salisbury and Lord Carnarvon may be taken as the representatives—can rejoin the ranks. Mr Disraeli has effectually disintegrated his party, because, while concurring in their immediate desires and playing on their more vehement prejudices, he neither shared their convictions nor sympathised in their sentiments, nor gave credit to the sincerity or firmness of their creeds.

But this is by no means the only or the worst mischief he has wrought. He has removed the old landmarks, bewildered the old faith, sapped the old enthusiasm, shaken the old confidence. The real weakness of the Conservative party in Parliament now is, *that the Conservatism of the country can no longer trust it.* The old Tory squires and clergymen and farmers no longer know what they may be working for, or whither they may be led. Why should men of the old creed and the old cause toil, and fight, and spend, and sacrifice themselves, in order to enthrone inscrutable Ministers who may surrender what they hold most dear and scoff at what they hold most sacred? What to them is a party victory at St Stephen's, if it is only a preliminary to seeing the measures of their enemies adopted and carried by their own friends? They understand struggle, but they don't understand strategy. They can be beaten in a fair fight, and yet lose neither heart themselves nor reliance on their leaders. But *volte-face* to avoid a battle—still more, abnegation of the old doctrines and degradation of the old colours—begets in them utter bewilderment and mistrust ; and there is no demoralisation for an army half so fatal as loss of faith in its generals. The Conservatism of the country is still wonderfully strong—its dread of democratic innovations, its attachment (often unreasoning, but all the tougher because of its unreason) to hereditary institutions and ideas, its clinging associations with the past, its undefined misgivings as to the future

But the Conservative opposition in the House of Commons no longer represents this sentiment, and is not trusted by it; it is not in harmony with it, and therefore it does not wield the strength which it might give.

But there is yet another view of the case which it is all-important to comprehend. It is a strange mistake to fancy that all the Conservatism of the country is to be found in the Tory ranks. That marked respect for rank and wealth, that keen appreciation of what is termed " the due influence of property," that instinctive desire to maintain the ancestral and established, the rooted conviction "that those who think must govern those who toil," and that the claims of education and intelligence ought to be paramount to the claims of mere numbers—which go to make up the sum of mingled thought and feeling which we call " Conservatism " —belong in not very dissimilar proportions to the upper classes in both political parties, especially where those classes are connected with the land or with the learned professions or the defensive services. Whig and Tory squires, and Whig and Tory officers and clergymen and lawyers, are much alike in hating democratic doctrines, and deprecating democratic rule, and in dreading rash and rapid progress, particularly in untried directions; and would usually be found side by side in combating these things if party zeal did not so often counteract natural affinities, and if Conservatism had chiefs whom both parties could trust. Liberal landlords and Liberal men of thought, wealth, and refinement, would willingly join moderate Tories of sense and

benevolence in all controversies involving either
national honour and security, or a clear invasion of
the just rights of property, or a distinctly unfair
division of the burdens of the State, or even an
obvious and practical transfer of rule to the hands
of the poorer classes; and if they did so the union
would be simply irresistible. But in order to encourage such a junction of the Conservative forces
of the country, to render it effectual or even safe,
to secure the purpose which alone would be held to
warrant such a severance of party ties, there must
be a leader who can be trusted to stand to his
guns, never to lower the adopted standard or surrender and betray the common object; and this
leader, it is obvious enough after what has passed,
cannot be Mr Disraeli. Take the very first question that is likely to come up, distinctly involving
the conflicting ideas and interests of classes, on
which property and proletarianism, statesmen and
democrats, are sure to take opposite sides—namely,
the substitution of direct for indirect taxation.
Any decided steps in this direction would be, we
cannot doubt, as shown in the previous chapter, a
grave economic error, and a fatal political blunder.
But it is quite upon the cards that some of the
Liberal leaders may propose to take dangerous,
indefensible, irretraceable steps in that direction.
It is certain that a large number of their followers,
and a few individuals of considerable name among
them, will eagerly urge them to do so. If the more
thoughtful and forecasting among the party, those
least disposed to tamper with clear convictions and
sound principles in deference to popular pressure,

make up their minds to sever themselves on this question from the majority of their usual associates, and so to render that majority powerless, what security could they feel as long as the Conservatives are governed by their present leader, that, after incurring all the unpopularity and obloquy which wait on renegades, and all the pain which inevitably attends the rupture of party ties and official friendships, they may not be thrown over, and find the cause for which they had sacrificed all this ignobly surrendered by a politician who could never comprehend either the strength or the sacredness of a principle, and who (if we remember aright) once so strangely falsified history as to describe Charles I. as " the holocaust of direct taxation ?"

There is obviously but one line of action through which the Conservatism of Britain can recover confidence and strength, or recruit its ranks by those accessions from other quarters which are fundamentally in sympathy with it, and which, once secured and embodied, would give it back something of its old ascendancy—its ascendancy, we mean, as a National party, not as a Parliamentary faction ;—and that is, to reorganise itself under a leader who will truly and at heart represent the Conservative feeling of the community, in whatever classes or sections it may linger or lie latent ; who can run a patient race and play a waiting game ; who can be relied upon to mind no temporary defeats, and to apostatise for the sake of no momentary triumph or apparent victory ; to lay deep in the respect and confidence of the country the foundations of *ultimate* command, and never, under any temptation, to sap them for the sake of immediate office.*   Then—and not till then—the Liberal Conservatism which now sits behind Mr Gladstone, and is found in every village and city in the land, may cordially and confidently join them, when critical conjunctures shall make it necessary.

The Liberal party appear to be in danger of committing a serious mistake, in their anxiety to meet the requirements and to place themselves in harmony with the feelings of the New *Régime*. They value mere economy too highly, and erroneously fancy that the new electoral body value it as highly as themselves. The error is a natural one, but it is one which, unless rectified in time, may lead them very far astray.

We may accept as proved—and, indeed, as too probable to need much proof—that Liberal Governments, as a rule, have aimed principally at economy, and Conservative Governments at efficiency, in the various departments of administration.   The respective virtues or claims belong to the traditions of the respective parties, and are inwoven in their several ideas and programmes.   The Whigs have always made their appeal to that element of the English mind which hates taxes, and has a keen suspicion of waste, sinecures, and jobs.   The Tories have preferred appealing to that other and perhaps stronger and more deep-rooted sentiment which is

* Though it is, of course, very gratifying to find my views in harmony with those of real Statesman-like intellects elsewhere, yet I do not wish to incur the possible reproach of unacknowledged plagiarism.   I may therefore be excused for mentioning that these remarks were written, and indeed printed, sometime before the appearance of "The Past and Future of the Conservative Policy," in the *Quarterly Review* of last October.

proud of Britain's power and preponderance, and desires that the country should always be mighty enough and prepared enough to do whatever it wishes and to forbid whatever it dislikes. We know that retrenchment was always a war-cry of the Whigs, and that some thirty years ago they un- deniably did cut down the public expenditure and the national defences below the point that was either economical or prudent. We know that in old times the Tories were recklessly extravagant, and not invariably very wise or very pure in their expenditure. It is undeniable, moreover, and is a fair ground for vigilance, that at present Conserva- tive Administrations, being in a minority, and con- sequently neither strong nor long-lived, find vigorous retrenchment more difficult than their antagonists. Rigid economy, cutting down establishments, dis- missing workmen, and the like, make many enemies, and rarely any friends, among political partisans ; and only really powerful and popular Governments can afford to give great immediate offence for the sake of slowly earning a high character in distant years, while parties in power only for a couple of years at a time and at long intervals have naturally many hungry adherents to feed, and can scarcely be expected very ruthlessly to diminish the number of loaves and fishes which are to feed them. There may, on the other hand, be some validity in the plea that the swelling estimates which have usually accompanied the Conservative advent to office are to be explained and justified by the inadequate expenditure of their predecessors, and the conse- quently incomplete, if not inefficient, state of the

protective services.   Lord Henry Lennox and
General Peel stand upon unassailable ground when
they urge that it is absolutely imperative upon us
to keep pace with all the newest inventions both for
attack and defence, whatever they may cost; and
when Mr Stansfeld charges them in reply with
spending large sums on obsolete and practically
worthless armaments and vessels, the retort is probably equally merited and unanswerable.   Lastly,
every one knows that Mr Gladstone, as Chancellor
of the Exchequer, was perhaps the most vigilant
and resolute guardian of the public purse that ever
filled that post; and all men conversant with such
subjects will recognise the weight of his argument,
that such plausible reasons can be adduced by every
separate department for every special proposal of
increased expenditure, that estimates can only be
kept in bounds by a dogged refusal to spend more
than a certain sum, to be adhered to in defiance of
all reasons whatever.

   But, we are satisfied, the interest felt by the
country at large in these controversies is far fainter
than that of the controversialists themselves; and, we
may add, its instinctive sentiments are far sounder.
" Retrenchment," whatever Liberal statesmen may
fancy, is no longer a magic word of power to con-
jure with, as it was in the old days when taxes were
oppressive in their nature and inequitable in their
incidence, and, moreover, were lavished on sinecures
and pensions.   The imposts which the nation pays,
large as is their aggregate amount, are now fairly
apportioned between property and population, as
every fresh inquiry and incrimination makes more

and more clear. Growing as they have done, they have not yet grown as fast as the wealth of the nation on which they are levied; they no longer fetter trade, or discourage enterprise, or injuriously check consumption; and what proportion of them the mass of the people contribute, it is not too much to say, they contribute unconsciously and, in a manner, voluntarily. The total margin between the strictest parsimony which a responsible Liberal Government would think it safe to urge, and the boldest expenditure which a responsible Conservative Government would venture to propose, would not make a difference of four shillings a head throughout the nation, nor certainly a penny a week to each poor man's family. Saving two or three millions out of a total expenditure of seventy has ceased to be a matter of practical and *felt* importance to the great body of the nation.

But besides this, the people, as a whole, think much more of efficiency than of economy; and they are right. They wish to be well served rather than to be cheaply served. They are less anxious to save their money than to get their money's worth. They know perfectly that England can well afford to pay whatever may be necessary for its safety, its tranquillity, its honour, and its good internal administration; and that these must be secured at the cost of any number of millions within the bounds of reason. They hate waste, but they hate stinginess still more. They scorn, instead of respecting, a Minister of Public Works who announces that his conception of public duty is not to do things well or nobly, but to do them cheaply, or to prevent them

from being done at all.   What they cannot endure is
to pay largely, and then to be told that they have
not got what they paid for.   Now, this temper of the
public mind is seldom clearly enough recognised or
duly respected by Liberal politicians, and especially
by official Liberals ; and half the ammunition which
they expend in party warfare, particularly on the
hustings, is in consequence wasted, and annoys and
wearies more than it excites or convinces their supporters.   They ought to lay themselves out for
proving, not that they spend less than their rivals,
but that they spend it better.   They ought to show,
not that the Tories cost the country more than the
Whigs, but that the Tories waste the revenue on inefficient or clumsy armaments.   They should charge
them, not with extravagance, but with incapacity.

We believe that large bodies of our countrymen
are of opinion that in certain departments we are
even unwisely and suicidally parsimonious, and
grudge moneys that ought to be liberally granted.
It is probable, too, that this sentiment will prevail
even more generally among the new constituencies
than among the old ones.   Mr Gladstone and
Mr Childers have both intimated that, in their
judgment, the Civil Service estimates, as well as
those for the Army and the Navy, have been
suffered to creep up unduly and unnecessarily.
We doubt whether this is an opinion which the
nation as a whole will be ready to re-echo.   For
instance, there is no question that the outlay on the
Miscellaneous Civil Services has steadily increased
for the last thirty or forty years.   But it is quite
arguable, even from an economic and certainly from

a social point of view, not only that this increase is perfectly defensible, but that the public might derive benefit from an even larger expenditure. The average annual outlay under these heads has been as follows :—

From 1830 to 1840, ...	£2,327,624
„ 1840 to 1850, ...	3,611,301
„ 1850 to 1860, ...	6,687,715
Since 1860, ...	8,054,634

Showing, no doubt, a startling enough augmentation in the aggregate. But of this increase a very large proportion has been incurred under three heads, which few considerate persons will desire to see cut down. Thus :—

	Salaries and Expenses of Public Departments.	Law and Justice.	Education.
	£	£	£
From 1830 to 1840, . . .	608,512	521,460	133,502
From 1840 to 1850, . . .	841,204	896,490	289,203
From 1850 to 1860, . . .	1,260,585	1,858,250	777,480
Since 1860, ...	1,554,403	2,900,034	1,413,406

Now, we must remember that during this period the public business in every department of administration has been enormously augmented, that new branches have been found indispensable, and that the vast majority of Government *employés* are probably not too liberally paid, and, compared with the enhanced cost of living, are certainly less well paid than formerly ; that county courts have been established, and their jurisdiction year by year extended ; that, even now, law and justice are not brought home to every man's door half cheaply or half promptly enough ; that assize business falls into arrear, and *remanets* abound and accumulate, to the great injury of suitors and the public, simply because the superior judges are quite inadequate in number to the work assigned them ; that much of the outlay under the second column is due to the establishment of a respectable and much-needed, but still wholly insufficient, police force through the kingdom ; and, finally, that the education vote, though increased *tenfold*, is still, in the opinion of many, deplorably scanty. And when we have given due weight to all these considerations, we shall probably be less inclined than the Premier to regret the annual augmentation in these estimates, and not greatly indisposed to suffer them to swell still further.

If we compare the expenditure of 1852-3 with that of 1867-8, we find that the Poor-law administration and supervision (independent, of course, of local management) has risen from £221,000 to £312,000; and few would wish to starve that service, though many wish to strengthen it. Then mines and factories have been brought under far more extensive inspection, and the cost of that inspection has risen from £15,000 to £39,000 ; but this is just what public interest and public feeling called for. Nearly all of us wish for a more energetic and omniscient police, and ought therefore to rejoice that Government, which paid nothing under this head in 1852, paid £289,000 in 1868. The establishment of county courts has been one of the most signal improvements of our day, and a general blessing. There was no provision for these in the estimates at the earlier date, but £144,000 at the latter, besides

£92,000 for the salaries of the judges charged on
the Consolidated Fund. Last year the entire provision in the estimates under this head, several new
things having been included, reached £493,000. In
Ireland, Government law charges and criminal pro-
secutions only figured in 1852 for £57,000, and
nothing was paid for the constabulary at all. In
1868, these two services received nearly £1,000,000,
of which the constabulary force received £850,000,
an amount which most assuredly was well spent.
On our prison and convict services we now lay out
£809,000, and it is not a shilling too much ; while
the education vote for the kingdom has risen nearly
fourfold, or from £468,000 in 1852 to £1,618,000
in 1868-9. These few items alone will account for
nearly two millions and a quarter of the increase
observable.

It is a mistake, we believe, to expect that the
working-class among the constituencies will ever
be much propitiated by the most lavish promises
of public economy,—if indeed they are not alienated
by them. Working-men do not object to a large
Government expenditure, unless it involves an
actual and felt increase of taxation to themselves
—which it scarcely ever does. They are shrewder—
perhaps more narrowly and short-sightedly shrewd
—on this matter than we fancy. They know that
the utmost amount of retrenchment that could be
carried would not relieve *their* taxation or reduce
their expenditure more than a penny or two a week,
while the increase of Government activity and outlay would increase the wages of hundreds of
thousands of them some shillings a week. They

know the local suffering and privation caused among
their class when administrative economy is the
order of the day, and when workmen are dismissed
from the dockyards of Portsmouth and Woolwich
and Chatham, when no more Admiralty contracts
are given out to the great shipbuilding establishments on the Thames and the Clyde, and no more
large orders for clothing are issued to the factories
of Lancashire and Yorkshire. They know, too, the
reverse of the picture,—namely, the stimulus given
to trade and the advance caused in wages in nearly
all districts by a lavish Government demand. They
know well enough—what the hustings advocates of
economy seem always to forget, and what some of
its most zealous preachers deliberately keep out of
view—that three-fourths at least of the expenditure
on the army and navy* goes directly or indirectly

---

* As a commentary on this point, we may mention that an
analysis of the army and navy estimates for 1867-68 shows the
following results :—

NAVY.—For effective services (minus miscellaneous, £168,000), . .	£8,950,000	
Of this was expended in pay, clothing, provisions, &c., for men and warrant officers (omitting commissioned officers), ... £4,800,000		
In naval stores, artificers' wages, and shipbuilding by contract, . . . 2,590,000		
		7,390,000
ARMY.—Effective services, ...	£13,000,000	
Of this was spent in pay, food, clothing, housing, and medical attendance for men and non-commissioned officers (about) £8,000,000		
For stores, and building, and manufacture of arms, ... 2,000,000		
		10,000,000

into the pockets of their class ; in the pay and keep
of soldiers and sailors, in wages to artificers, in naval
and military stores which they manufacture, in gun-
powder which they fabricate, and the materials for
which they procure, in arms which employ the
factories at Birmingham and Enfield and the iron-
works in Staffordshire and Lanarkshire. They
believe, in short (and they are about right), that of
every additional four millions laid out on the national
defences, in reference to which the Tories are said
to be so wasteful, three millions are *paid* by the
middle and upper classes, and are *spent* in the wages
of labour. Why, then, should they be in love with
economical administrations ?

The spirit in which to meet the new *régime*, and
the line of action to be adopted in order to fulfil its
obligations and to obviate its dangers, are not difficult of discernment. We must apply our energies
without delay to the urgent social requirements of
the time, and we must bring to the discussion and
solution of all the practical questions they involve
the same interest, the same eagerness, the same
concentration of purpose and vehement resolve,
which we have hitherto reserved, almost exclusively, for great party struggles, or for those controversies on the border-land of politics and religion
which elicit the passions peculiar to both. We

Thus 82 per cent. of the naval expenditure and 78 of the army
expenditure went into the pockets of the working-classes either
directly or indirectly, either as pay and maintenance of soldiers
and sailors, or in the wages of artificers, or in the purchase of
articles procured or fabricated by the labour of the working
class. Four-fifths of such Government expenditure goes in the
employment of labour, and of *poor* labour.

Y

must learn to debate questions between capital and labour as earnestly and thoroughly as hitherto we have only debated questions of the franchise or of foreign policy. We must be as serious, as resolute, and, perhaps, as angry, over the shameful condition of the agricultural labourer, as we were over the menacing terrors of the cattle-plague. We must be as willing to give up a whole session to the treatment of paupers and the cure of pauperism, as to the incomparably less vital question of the Irish Church,—and to whip up the whole strength of the party to each debate just as relentlessly. And, if possible, we must endeavour to deal with these subjects in the spirit of statesmanship, and not in the spirit of faction, and to avoid the criminal and fatal blunder of making these also the battle-fields of party. We must try, if we can, to work at them, instead of fighting over them.

In a word, we must begin to be interested, paramountly and sincerely, in the questions which most interest the great body of the people, and which must always most interest them, because they most concern them. As soon as we do this in an earnest and enlightened temper, we shall discern, somewhat perhaps to our surprise, that the same questions concern us also, in their reflex action, quite as deeply. We must throw our hearts and energies into social, instead of, as heretofore, into political reforms. We must go into them with the conviction—which it is a wonder and a reproach did not dawn upon us years ago—that these questions, as involving the condition, character, sentiments, and hopes of the masses, of the majority, of the broad basis of the

great social pyramid, of the bulk and substratum of
the nation in short, are of immeasurably deeper and
more urgent importance than any over which for
nearly a generation, session after session, Parliament
after Parliament, we have been lashing up our passions, wasting our strength, and damaging our
character. Now, what are the matters which most
especially interest and concern the new electors,
the working classes, those below them, and those
immediately above them ?—Not, assuredly, the
Irish Church, not the Irish land, not even (pri-
marily) the ballot, or the extension of the franchise;
—but education, cheap, appropriate, good, and acceptable to all;—protection for the rights of labour,
alike against grasping capitalists, oppressive unions,
and mistaken or inequitable laws;—some mode of
dealing with the requirements of the agricultural
peasantry, which shall render them once more
"their country's pride," in place of being, as now
too often, their country's shame;—such a searching
reform of the whole system of poor-law administration, that it shall cease to be, at the same time,
harsh to paupers and fostering to pauperism,—at
once an outrage on our humanity and a disgrace to
our sagacity;—such an organisation of charity as
shall re-transform that vice into a virtue, and make
it a double blessing, instead of being a double curse;
—some masterly and comprehensive provision for
the dwellings of the poor in great cities, so that they
may be housed like Christians and within reach of
their daily work;—and lastly (if that be indeed within
the power of national wisdom or administrative
functions), some superior control which shall pre-

serve us against those local and temporary, half-insane exacerbations of enterprise which seem to be inevitably followed by corresponding congestion and reaction—not always, alas! either local or temporary—such as have now for the last two or three years been desolating the East End of the Metropolis, and paralysing trade throughout the empire.

What we look for from the new *régime*,—from the vast accession of electoral influence which the lower classes have obtained,—is not so much aid or guidance as *impulse;* not wisdom in helping us to solve these problems, but power and resolution to *insist* that the wisdom of the nation shall at once apply all its resources to their solution ; and strength of volition to bid back or beat down all selfish interests and narrow prejudices that would interfere with the great work.

THE END.

PRINTED BY BALLANTYNE AND COMPANY
EDINBURGH AND LONDON

www.ingramcontent.com/pod-product-compliance
Lightning Source LLC
Chambersburg PA
CBHW021115270326
41929CB00009B/886